Sophocles: Antigone

COMPANIONS TO GREEK AND ROMAN TRAGEDY

Series Editor: Thomas Harrison

Sophocles: Antigone

Douglas Cairns

Bloomsbury Academic
An imprint of Bloomsbury Publishing Plc

B L O O M S B U R Y
LONDON · OXFORD · NEW YORK · NEW DELHI · SYDNEY

Bloomsbury Academic

An imprint of Bloomsbury Publishing Plc

50 Bedford Square
London
WC1B 3DP
UK

1385 Broadway
New York
NY 10018
USA

www.bloomsbury.com

**BLOOMSBURY and the Diana logo are trademarks of Bloomsbury
Publishing Plc**

First published 2016
Reprinted 2016, 2017

British Library Cataloguing-in-Publication Data
A catalogue record for this book is available from the British Library.

ISBN: HB: 978-1-47251-433-2
PB: 978-1-47250-509-5
ePDF: 978-1-47251-344-1
ePub: 978-1-47251-214-7

Library of Congress Cataloging-in-Publication Data
A catalog record for this book is available from the Library of Congress.

Series: Companions to Greek and Roman Tragedy

Cover image © Antigone from 'Antigone' by Sophocles (oil on canvas),
Marie Spartali Stillman (1844–1927), Simon Carter Gallery,
Woodbridge, Suffolk, UK / Bridgeman Images

Typeset by RefineCatch Limited, Bungay, Suffolk
Printed and bound in Great Britain

Contents

Acknowledgements

This book has been a long time in the making, but my work on it really got going while I was teaching at Florida State University in 2012. The students in my graduate class on *Antigone* at FSU stimulated and challenged my interpretations, but also demonstrated their own acumen as scholars in their splendid research presentations on some of the landmarks in the play's reception history. For the impetus that their work gave to my own I thank Ana Belinskaya, Sophie Crawford-Brown, Daniel Culbert, Ann Glennie, Buddy Hedrick, Stephen Kiepke, Travis King (my stalwart research assistant), Cliff Parkinson, Tommy Redmon, Allison Smith, and Evan Waters. Classics at FSU was a great environment to work in, thanks to the hospitality and helpfulness of my hosts, especially Patrick Byrne, Francis and Sandra Cairns, Laurel Fulkerson, Trevor Luke, John Marincola, Daniel Pullen, Allen Romano, Svetla and Don Slaveva-Griffin, and Tim Stover. Lunches with Kenneth Reckford, in which we discussed *Antigone* and a great deal more, were a joy.

For generously sharing their knowledge and their work I thank Bill Allan, Efi Athanasopoulou, Felix Budelmann, Alison Burke, John Cairns, Mirko Canevaro, Willy Cingano, Federico Condello, Elizabeth Craik, Cecilia Criado, Pat Easterling, Patrick Finglass, Bob Fowler, Mark Heerink, Alessandro Iannucci, Paddy Lyons, Agis Marinis, Andrea Rodighiero, Yoshinori Sano, and Olga Taxidou. Bill Dominik kindly shared not only an elusive copy of Osofisan's *Tegonni* but also a film of the play in performance. An invitation from Seth Schein to a marvellous Sophoclean colloquium at UC Davis gave me the chance to see a fine staging of *The Island*. In the summer of 2013 I had the opportunity to present several papers on *Antigone* in Japan and to make use of the library of the Classics department at the University of Bologna. Makoto Anzai, Martin Ciesko, Kiichiro Itsumi, Tetsuo Nakatsukasa, and Yoshinori Sano were excellent hosts and interlocutors in Tokyo and

Kyoto; Alessandro Iannucci arranged the Bologna visit, and Francesco Citti and his colleagues made me most welcome. António Caeiro invited me to speak at a very stimulating, philosophically oriented workshop on *Antigone* in Lisbon in July 2015, just as I was completing this volume. Visits to the Fondation Hardt, Vandoeuvres, made it easy to write in peace, but also in very convivial company. The staff of the Joint Library of the Hellenic and Roman Societies in London have been unfailingly helpful.

In preparing a book that I hope may be of interest to a wide audience I was often reminded of those to whom I owe my own love of Greek literature. I first encountered Sophocles at school in Shettleston, where I read *Ajax* in Greek with Alan Jones, after being introduced to the language by Alex Livingstone and Allan Murray. I wouldn't have written this book without them – or without Alex Garvie or Douglas MacDowell, first inspiring lecturers, then my PhD supervisors at Glasgow University. I don't think I ever write a word that does not somehow reflect their influence.

Equally, working on one of the most influential works of Greek culture has brought back many conversations with friends who have shared and stimulated my interests over the years. Some are thanked above for help with this specific project. It might be invidious to single out others. But I've never forgotten the sincerity and passion that Robin Hankey, Doug Little, and Agathe Thornton brought to our many discussions of Greek literature and thought in Dunedin between 1988 and 1992.

One does not need to read Sophocles to know that the Greeks were right about the mutability of fortune (and, let's face it, about *atê* and *hamartia* too). In the period before I finished this book I was lucky to be able to count on Steve Archibald, Donald Bloxham, David Carruthers, David Cartwright, Martin Chick, Frank Cogliano, Yvonne McEwen, Jim Pope, and Jill Stephenson, and on my family, Betty and Jim Aitken, Alan Best, and Owen Cairns.

Finally, I need to thank the publishers: they were Duckworth when I started, but are now Bloomsbury. I know I've tried the patience of three commissioning editors, and of the series editor, Tom Harrison, since I first promised to deliver this short book; I thank them very much for waiting.

DLC
Edinburgh, October 2015

Abbreviations

Ant.	Sophocles, *Antigone*
FGrHist	F. Jacoby (ed.), *Die Fragmente der griechischen Historiker* (Leiden: Brill, 1923–58).
Fowler	R. L. Fowler (2000) in bibliography.
LIMC	H. C. Ackermann and J. R. Gisler (eds), *Lexicon Iconographicum Mythologiae Classicae* (Zurich: Artemis, 1981–2009).
K-A	R. Kassel and C. A. Austin (eds), *Poetae Comici Graeci* (Berlin: De Gruyter, 1983–).
Maehler	H. G. T. Maehler (ed.), *Pindari Carmina cum Fragmentis* ii (Leipzig: Teubner, 1989).
M-W	R. Merkelbach and M. L. West (eds), *Fragmenta Hesiodea* (Oxford: Oxford University Press, 1967).
PMG	D. L. Page (ed.), *Poetae Melici Graeci* (Oxford: Oxford University Press, 1974).
PMGF	M. Davies (ed.), *Poetarum Melicorum Graecorum Fragmenta* i (Oxford: Oxford University Press, 1991).
Poltera	O. Poltera (ed.), *Simonides Lyricus, Testimonia und Fragmente* (Basel: Schwabe, 2008).
Radt	S. L. Radt (ed.), *Tragicorum Graecorum Fragmenta* iii (Aeschylus), iv (Sophocles) (Göttingen: Vandenhoeck and Ruprecht, 1985, 1977).
West	M. L. West (ed.), *Iambi et Elegi Graeci ante Alexandrum Cantati* (second edition, Oxford: Oxford University Press, 1989–92).

From Myth to Plot

The myth and its background

Many Greek tragedies treat mythological subjects that had been dealt with at least once, and often several times before, in earlier Greek literature. It is often the case that, even where earlier versions do not survive in their entirety, we can reconstruct with some confidence the relationship that exists between surviving tragedies and previous versions of the myths that they dramatize. This is a more difficult task with Sophocles' *Antigone*. Though the Theban cycle of myth to which the story belongs is clearly older than Greek literature itself (since it is presupposed in the *Iliad*), Antigone's own role in the saga is not securely attested before the fifth century BC, when her name begins to crop up not just in Sophocles, but in other contemporary sources. This raises a question – one that we may never be able to answer with any certainty: how much might the members of Sophocles' audience have known about Antigone when the play was first performed? And that question prompts another – when *was* the play first performed?

The 'arguments' (*hypotheseis*) that are reproduced in the mediaeval manuscripts in which the texts of Greek tragedy are preserved often contain documentary information, deriving ultimately from Athenian records, regarding the plays' dates of first production. No such record survives for the *Antigone,* but an anecdote preserved in the first of its three *hypotheseis* claims that the success of the play was a factor in Sophocles' election as general (*stratêgos*) in a year in which Athens was involved in a campaign against the Samians. In the year 441/440 BC the Athenians deposed the oligarchic government of Samos and installed a democracy, imprisoning a number of oligarchic hostages on Lemnos.[1] Sophocles' involvement in these events as *stratêgos* has good independent support.[2] On the grounds that a link between Sophocles' generalship and the *Antigone* (as opposed to some other successful production) would not have been made unless someone had known (rather than merely surmised) that the play's first production closely preceded his election, *Antigone* is often dated to 442 or 441 BC. If one accepts this logic, then 442 is likelier than 441:[3] the implication is that *Antigone* was part of a prize-winning production, but we have evidence that Euripides was the victorious tragedian at the Dionysia of 441;[4] and in any case the probability is that the election of generals for 441/440 will have taken place before the Dionysia of 441,[5] so that, if the election that *Antigone* allegedly influenced was in 441, the play must have been produced in 442. R. G. Lewis, however, has argued that since, as epigraphic evidence shows, Sophocles held the position of *Hellenotamias* (treasurer of the Delian League) in 443/442 (T 18 Radt), he will scarcely have had the leisure to compose, rehearse, and produce a set of four plays for the Dionysia of 442. Using the evidence of the ancient *Life* of Sophocles (§9, T 1. 35–6 Radt) that Sophocles was general 'seven years before the Peloponnesian War' (in what seems to have been a sort of mopping-up campaign following the Samian War), Lewis suggests a date of 438 for the play and 437/436 (seven years, by inclusive reckoning, before the Peloponnesian War) for the *stratêgia* that was the consequence of its success.[6]

A date of either 442 or 438, however, assumes that the linking of the success of *Antigone* with Sophocles' election as general is based on factual knowledge of their dates rather than mere conjecture. The security of that assumption has been challenged by Scott Scullion,[7] who suggests that *Antigone* was offered as the influential play purely because of the sentiments of Creon's speech at 175–90, later cited as a paradigm of orthodox civic virtue by Demosthenes (*On the False Embassy*, 19. 246–8). The same hypothesis that preserves the anecdote about Sophocles' generalship also tells us that the *Antigone* is counted as the thirty-second in the chronological list of Sophocles' plays. Sophocles is said to have been victorious (over Aeschylus) with his first production at the Dionysia of 468 and to have written over 120 plays in total, in a career spanning some six decades.[8] On the assumption that Sophocles' plays were more or less equally spaced throughout his career, and on the basis of stylistic considerations, Scullion suggests that this evidence supports a date for *Antigone* of around 450 BC. But if Sophocles had been (like Euripides) a little less prolific in the earlier part of his career than later, it would also fit well enough with the suggestion that the play was produced in the 440s,[9] and so the story of its influence on his election as general may just rest on knowledge of its actual date after all.

However that may be, the *Antigone* was certainly composed and first performed in a period by which the various stages of the Theban saga had been told and retold in a number of different versions.[10] In considering its relation to the mythopoetic tradition, two questions arise: first, how much knowledge of the general Theban saga does the *Antigone* presume in its audience, and of which particular versions? Second, how much, if anything, does the average member of the original audience know about Antigone and her exploit? According to the speaker of a fragment from Antiphanes' comedy *Poetry* (fr. 189. 5–8 K-A), in the fourth century, at least, one had merely to say 'Oedipus' and the audience would recall everything about him and his family. But this reflects a time *after* the success of our play, and is in any case not specifically about Antigone; in the 440s, and especially with regard to the role of Antigone herself, things may well have been different.

Sophocles' text is quick to situate the play's action against its immediate mythological background: Antigone identifies Ismene (by name) as her sister in line 1, and refers to the ills of their father, Oedipus, in line 2. The contrasting treatment proposed for their two brothers, Eteocles (23) and Polynices (26) by Creon (named in 21, already referred to as 'the general' in 8, and identified in his own words as the four siblings' nearest male relative at 174), is the burden of the news that she has to impart (7–10, 21–36). Ismene fills in some further details: Oedipus is dead, having blinded himself on discovery of his crimes (49–52, cf. 900–3); his wife and mother, who is never named in the play, hanged herself (53–4, cf. 911); and the brothers whom Creon proposes to treat so differently died at each other's hands (56–7), during the battle between Theban and Argive forces that ended with the rout of the latter, during the night that is only now coming to an end (15–16). The entrance song of the Chorus gives further details of the city's deliverance: Polynices (whose name, 'man of much dispute', is etymologized at 110–11), appears to be regarded as the instigator of the conflict;[11] the attack pitted seven Argive captains against seven Thebans at the city's seven gates (141–2);[12] and the arrogance of the Argive aggressors is exemplified in Zeus's punishment of one of their number, struck with the thunderbolt as he reached the top of the city's ramparts (127–37).

The entrance song of the Chorus in particular indicates that a certain amount of knowledge is being taken for granted. The Argive captain punished by Zeus is not named, but is readily identified as Capaneus by anyone familiar with the Aeschylean trilogy that culminates in the extant *Seven against Thebes*, a play that is extensively evoked in the Chorus's initial song. The *Seven* was produced in 467 BC; the other plays in the tetralogy were *Laius*, *Oedipus*, and the satyr-play, *Sphinx*. The *Antigone* agrees with what we can glean of Aeschylus' tetralogy (largely through references and allusions in its only surviving member) in Oedipus' self-blinding (*Seven* 782–5), the death of his wife and mother, the mother of his children (*Seven* 752–7), long before the Argive attack (implicitly: she does not appear in *Seven*), the enmity of Eteocles and Polynices, the pairing of attackers and defenders at the city's seven gates, and the impiety and arrogance of (all but one of) the attackers (*Seven* 375–719). The influence of Aeschylus' treatment, and the familiarity of that play to at least some of Sophocles' original audience, can be taken as read.

The myths of Oedipus and the two expeditions against Thebes (the first involving Polynices and his Argive allies, the second mounted by the leaders of the next generation, the Epigonoi) are as old as Greek literature itself: Oedipus' parricide and incest appear in *Odyssey* 11. 272–4, and both expeditions against Thebes are referred to in *Iliad* 4. 372–99, 405–10. The Theban saga had also been a popular epic theme in its own right (in the lost *Thebais*, *Oedipodeia*, and *Epigonoi*),[13] and had featured in an extensive lyric version by Stesichorus (fr. 222(b) *PMGF*).[14] In earlier tragedy, as well as the tetralogy mentioned above, Aeschylus had produced another, containing, in an order that is uncertain, *Nemea*,

Argeioi or *Argeiai, Eleusinioi,* and *Epigonoi. Eleusinioi* will have centred
on the intervention of the Athenian hero, Theseus, to bury the bodies
of the Argive champions who led the campaign against Thebes.[15]
Numerous other pre-Sophoclean attestations point to the wide currency
of the Theban cycle.[16]

This tradition exhibits a core of regular features: Oedipus is always an
incestuous parricide and the enmity of his sons, Eteocles and Polynices,
together with the latter's Argive marriage, alliance, and expedition against
his native city, is a constant.[17] But there is also a wide range of variation,
including many details that are incompatible with the background
presupposed by Sophocles in the *Antigone*. In the *Odyssey*, for example,
Oedipus certainly marries his own mother (called, as we noted, Epicasta),
but it is not clear that there are any children of this union,[18] and Oedipus
continues to rule in Thebes, his sight perhaps unimpaired, after the
discovery and Epicasta's suicide.[19] In some versions prior to *Antigone*
Oedipus has more than one wife, and the one who is his mother is not
necessarily the mother of his children.[20] In the long lyric poem attributed
to Stesichorus (probably composed in the first half of the sixth century),
whose surviving lines treat the conflict between Eteocles and Polynices,
their mother appears as a character, interceding in an attempt to resolve
their hostility.[21] Either this is a version in which Oedipus' mother is
the mother of his sons, but does not kill herself after discovering her
husband's identity,[22] or this is a second wife, as in the *Oedipodeia* and
Pherecydes. As far as the burial of Polynices and his fellow attackers is
concerned, in Aeschylus' *Eleusinioi* the bodies were recovered (as a result
of the peaceful intercession of Theseus, according to Plutarch, *Theseus* 29.
4) and buried on Attic soil;[23] but in Pindar there seems to be no prohibition
against the burial of any of the attackers, and the Argives, together (one
assumes) with Polynices, are cremated at Thebes (*Olympian* 6. 15–16,
Nemean 9. 24).

In dealing with these events, then, Sophocles takes a definite line,
different in some ways from other versions with which some of his
audience may have been familiar, and provides the detail required for
an audience to construct the background from which the action of his

play springs. On some of the implications of these events, however, he is silent: what, for example, is to happen to the corpses of Polynices' fellow attackers, the Argive champions? Nothing is made of this, and lines that seem to raise the issue (1080–3) may be interpolated.[24] Why did Eteocles and Polynices quarrel and what was the sequence of events leading to their confrontation on the plain of Thebes? Again, nothing is said, either of their being cursed by their father or of the failure of any mechanisms designed to avoid fraternal conflict.[25]

Another sign that Sophocles wants us to focus mainly on the events that unfold in the play (and their immediate background) and less on specific details of the wider mythological tradition is the play's almost total silence regarding earlier stages of the Theban myth and the vagueness of the few references that do occur. An audience familiar at least with the tetralogy that contained Aeschylus' *Seven* will have known something about Oedipus' father, Laius, and the background to Oedipus' predestined parricide and incest,[26] but Laius is mentioned in *Antigone* only as Oedipus' predecessor as ruler of Thebes at 165–6. The play does contain two references to Laius' own father, Labdacus, as the founder of the dynasty (593, 862),[27] but these occur in passages whose point is the recurrent theme of the generational cycle of misfortune in Antigone's family (cf. 1–10, 49–50, 379–80, 471–2, 582–625, 857–71, 892–4). These passages hint at possible explanations for Antigone's character and misfortunes in the history of her family (see Chapter 3), but the only specific examples that are given of previous cases of the same pattern are those of her father, mother, and brothers. Though the second stasimon (582–625) in particular does encourage an audience to apply whatever background knowledge they may have about the history of transgression and suffering in Antigone's family, it is not clear that any specific version of any particular event or series of events is being alluded to, and all that the ode positively requires is a general sense that there have been generations of trouble in the house of Labdacus.

There is one exception to this general lack of allusiveness.[28] The confrontation between Creon and Tiresias contains two references, one at its beginning and another at the end, to Creon's reliance upon the salutary application of the seer's powers in some previous but unspecified emergency (993–5, 1058). Even if at this stage the audience do not think of a specific event as the target of these allusions, a tension is created between the impression given in this scene (that Creon has been involved in the political and military leadership of Thebes for some time) and the implication of his own opening speech that he is new to and untested in office (170–7).[29] Perhaps audience members simply assume (at least for the moment) some subordinate yet still significant role under Eteocles (Creon has, after all, been a 'general' in the recent conflict, 8; cf. 1162); or it may be that they activate their knowledge of a version in which Creon acted as regent during Oedipus' sons' minority.[30] But the initial obscurity of these references is resolved when we learn, in the play's final scene, that Creon's wife, Eurydice, committed suicide because she regarded him as responsible for the deaths of *both* of their sons, not only Haemon, but also Megareus (1303–5, 1312–13). Megareus has not been mentioned before, but this revelation that Eurydice had already lost one son before Haemon explains her own and the Messenger's observations (at 1191 and 1250) that she is experienced in coping with suffering. Megareus, son of Creon, appears in Aeschylus' *Seven* as one of the Theban champions who are allocated to their posts at the city's seven gates by Eteocles. A descendant of the Spartoi, the 'sown men' of Thebes' foundation myth,[31] Megareus would, according to Eteocles, either kill his Argive opponent or 'by dying repay in full his debt of nurture to the earth' (*Seven* 474–9). Eurydice's castigation of Creon for his role in Megareus' death perhaps suggests a version of the story, known from Euripides' *Phoenician Women* (930–1018), that a descendant of the Spartoi (i.e. Creon or a son of Creon) must die in order for Thebes to survive the Argive onslaught.[32] While it may seem unlikely that Creon should be grateful (as he is at *Ant.* 995) for a prophecy that entailed the death of his own son,[33] the belated introduction of the idea that he had previously regarded the death of a son as a price worth paying for the city's salvation (again see 1058) is entirely in keeping with the relative importance that he has placed on the interests of the family versus those of the city since his first appearance; with the death of his wife and surviving son he has no immediate family left, and so realizes, too late, the importance of the claims that he has neglected.

To an extent, Sophocles wants certain things both ways. He wants Creon to be a new and untried ruler whose statement that sound principles must be tested in office is ironically exemplified by his own downfall, but he also wants to prepare for the belated introduction of an episode from an earlier stage of the mythological story that compounds the element of 'poetic justice' in the suffering that Creon brings upon himself (at least partly) because of his rigid belief that the city always comes before family. In the latter case, the specific allusion to the necessary mythological background is withheld until it is needed, but prepared for by means of hints that take on their full significance only in retrospect. The audience are perhaps encouraged by these hints to activate their knowledge of the wider mythological background, but the point of the allusions is eventually made (more or less) explicit anyway. All necessary knowledge of the mythological background is explicitly activated in the text; where no such explicit activation occurs, it appears that no acquaintance with unmentioned elements of the tradition is necessary.

The *Antigone*, then, does not require extensive knowledge of mythological traditions and rehearses in the text itself all elements of the myth that are essential for the understanding of the play. Its main focus is on Creon's edict and its consequences, first in Antigone's defiance and then in Creon's own downfall. The background against which this action is to be understood is first of all the Argive attack on Thebes, in which both brothers perished, then the sufferings of the siblings' parents, especially their deaths and the shame of incest, and beyond that merely a general sense that this is a family in which misfortune has been the norm for generations. None of this is novel. Yet the dramatic action that is played out against this relatively sketchy background is, as far as we can tell, without parallel in earlier versions of the Theban myth.[34]

As we noted, the prohibition of burial following the Thebans' victory over their Argive foes is not a new motif; but in Aeschylus' version (in *Eleusinioi*) the prohibition extends to all the Argive commanders, not just Polynices, and this is the premise also of Euripides' later treatment in the

Suppliant Women (c. 424–416 BC).[35] At the end of Aeschylus' surviving *Seven against Thebes* (861ff.) Antigone does appear, arguing as she does in Sophocles for the burial of both her brothers, but the consensus is that the lines in which she does so are spurious, influenced not only by the *Antigone* itself, but also by Euripides' *Phoenician Women*.[36] If that is the case, then Sophocles' play is the first surviving work of literature to treat Antigone's action in defying Creon's prohibition in order to bury Polynices, and there must be a strong suspicion that this is because it was in fact the first work ever to do so. But this does not necessarily mean that Sophocles has simply invented his main character. It is possible, but not certain, that Antigone had already appeared in some guise in one of the early, epic versions of the Theban saga, the *Oedipodeia*. Pausanias justifies his view that the version of the Oedipus story presumed by the *Odyssey* did not presuppose that Oedipus had fathered children on his own mother with reference to the *Oedipodeia*'s version that his children were born of a second wife, Euryganeia. Pausanias' reference to *four* children may indicate that the children of that union in the *Oedipodeia* were the usual four, Eteocles, Polynices, Antigone, and Ismene; but it may be that Pausanias' memory of the details of the second marriage in the *Oedipodeia* has been affected by his knowledge of what had become the standard version; and in any case his report does not actually name the four offspring of Oedipus and Euryganeia.

The name of Antigone is not in fact attested before the fifth century, and (if the end of Aeschylus' *Seven against Thebes* is indeed not genuine) it seems that its first occurrence is in Sophocles' compatriot and older contemporary, the mythographer Pherecydes.[37] This is an eccentric version, very different from Sophocles', in which Oedipus is given no fewer than three wives, and the (usual) four children are attributed to his second one, Euryganeia. Assuming that the scholiast (on Euripides' *Phoenician Women* 53) who reports this information renders Pherecydes' account accurately, and given the likely dates of Pherecydes' activity as a writer,[38] this is likely to be our earliest reference to Antigone by name. In any case, the nature of Pherecydes' work very likely implies that there were traditions in which Antigone featured prior to his compilation, and it is clear that such traditions could differ considerably from the version offered by Sophocles. We see this, for example, in the statement that Sophocles' contemporary and (apparently) friend,[39] Ion of Chios, wrote a choral lyric poem in which both Antigone and Ismene are burned to death in the Theban temple of Hera by Eteocles' son, Laodamas (Ion 740 *PMG*). This story seems to presuppose Antigone's burial of Polynices, and may be earlier than Sophocles' play.[40] Ismene and Haemon are also attested in earlier traditions, but not in the roles that Sophocles gives them: as well as falling victim, along with her sister, to Laodamas, son of Eteocles, in Ion, Ismene is also reported to have been killed during the first expedition of the Seven (by Tydeus, according to Mimnermus, fr. 21 West and Pherecydes fr. 95 Fowler).[41] Haemon, for his part, appeared in the *Oedipodeia* as a victim of the Sphinx.[42] Creon also features in previous versions of the Theban myth;[43] and Tiresias is an all-purpose seer who can, by virtue of his longevity, be deployed at several different junctures of the Theban saga.[44] It is therefore going too far to suggest that Sophocles has invented Antigone for the purposes of this play; she may even have been associated already with the burial of Polynices. Rather, it seems that Sophocles has enlisted a number of characters who had already appeared in different roles in earlier versions of Theban myths,[45] but has put them to work in a plot which had very likely not been narrated in precisely this way in any previous version.[46] In all probability, the play's original audience will have had little idea of what to expect as the action began; in some cases, indeed, Sophocles' innovative version will have required his audience to disregard things that they might have assumed about Creon, Ismene, and Haemon from their knowledge of earlier versions. This will have helped make *Antigone* a gripping and absorbing play.

The play in the theatre

The *Antigone* is a thoroughly 'classical' tragedy in its form and structure: an opening scene involving two-actor dialogue is followed by the entrance song of the Chorus, following which scenes of dialogue, involving a maximum of three actors together with the leader of the Chorus, alternate with choral song. Conventionally (after Aristotle), the opening scene is called the prologue or *prologos* and the final scene the *exodos*, with the main body of the play consisting of alternating *epeisodia* (mainly spoken dialogue) and *stasima* (choral songs). The *Antigone* has six *epeisodia* and five *stasima*. The fourth *epeisodion* and the final scene (*exodos*) both feature actor's song, either with spoken or chanted responses (in the final scene) or with both speech and song (in the fourth *epeisodion*). Such scenes are typically called *kommoi*.

Prologue, 1–99

The scene is set before a house, from whose central door two actors exit to begin the prologue in the typical Sophoclean manner, i.e. involving dialogue and dramatic action from the outset, as opposed to the expository prologues favoured especially by Euripides. Each speaker identifies the other immediately (Antigone addressing Ismene by name in line 1 and Ismene Antigone in line 11). Antigone names their father, Oedipus, in line 2, and describes their family history as one of suffering and disgrace (2–6). It is just about dawn (16, cf. the entrance song of the Chorus, especially 100–5), and the night that has just ended has seen the departure of the Argive army that threatened Thebes (15–16), the deaths of their two brothers (12–14, 55–7; they are named in 24 and 26), and Creon's proclamation that only Eteocles should receive burial (7–8, 21–36).

The house from which the girls (identified as such by their masks and costumes) have emerged is thus not just any house, but the house of Labdacus (593, 862), a house with a history, in which Oedipus lay with his mother (53, 863–5), in which both Oedipus and his wife seem to have died (49–54), and in which their incestuous children will have been born. The setting of the play at a point around dawn cues the Chorus's opening hymn of thanks for the sunrise that symbolizes Thebes' deliverance, but the connotations of hope that the sunrise brings have by then already been undercut by the prologue's affirmation that the troubles of the royal house have not yet ended, but will continue (9–10, 17, 49–60, 82, 92–7). The location of the dramatic action at dawn suggests that Sophocles might (as Aeschylus does in the *Agamemnon*) have exploited the coincidence between dawn in the dramatic world of the play and the rising of the sun in the real world of the audience, given that tragic performances began at dawn (but only if *Antigone* were the first play of the four to be performed that day).

The emergence of two girls from the central door of the house is motivated by Antigone's explanation that she brought her sister outside in order to discuss the latest misfortune to strike their family without being overheard (18–19). This is not only dramatically effective, in that right from beginning of the play everything should appear to happen for a good reason, but also culturally significant, in that it motivates the appearance of unmarried girls of good family outside their home.[47]

Two unmarried girls, then, cross the boundary of the private world of the household into the public sphere. These two are the female siblings (indeed the female counterparts) of the two brothers who killed each other in battle. Like their brothers, they are offspring of the House of Oedipus (in which ties of family love and loyalty have been subverted in multiple ways). In these few facts lie the issues of the opening scene. Antigone begins with expressions of affection and familial closeness for Ismene. There is emphasis in both their speeches on the number two (in particular using a Greek form, the dual number, reserved for pairs of people or things). They are two sisters of a pair of brothers (3, 13–14, 21, 55–62). With Antigone's report of divergent treatment of the two corpses (21–30), differences emerge between Antigone and Ismene too: Antigone proposes to defy Creon's proclamation, while Ismene maintains a normal feminine subservience to male authority. In this way the subversion of the categories of friend and enemy which was the legacy that Polynices and Eteocles received from their parents imposes itself in their sisters' case as well. This is reflected visually in the action. At 99 Antigone and Ismene go off simultaneously. Staggered, rather than simultaneous, exits are the norm in Greek tragedy, and so simultaneity can have a specific point. Here, the sisters depart in different directions, Ismene back into the house, and Antigone (by one of the side passageways that lead into and out of the *orchêstra*) for the battlefield where her brother's body has been left exposed. Their departure illustrates both the rupture of their relationship and their divergent responses to the challenge posed by Creon's edict: Antigone remains in the public sphere, in the world of men – indeed her departure confirms her decision to defy the will of the head of her own household and the ruler of her city. Ismene goes back into the private, unseen, domestic world of women.[48]

Entrance song of the Chorus (parodos), 100–61

Enter a Chorus of older male Thebans. Their song consists of two pairs of lyric stanzas, each followed by a passage of recitative in a metre that is typically used to accompany locomotion. The Chorus are figures of some authority in the city, summoned by Creon to hear his edict (159–61) on account of their loyalty to the city's previous rulers (164–74) and later addressed as 'lords of Thebes' by Tiresias (988). As befits their position as representatives of the city, their song is a hymn of thanksgiving for its recent deliverance, hailing the rising sun (100–5), which has, they hope, brought an end to the city's troubles. This stance, together with their age and especially their sex, marks them as more naturally inclined to side with Creon's view of events than with Antigone's. The *Antigone* is like the *Women of Trachis* in having two focal characters, a female and a male, but whereas Deianira in that play has the support of a female chorus, Antigone is, as Griffith observes, 'isolated ... to an unusual degree'.[49] In the remaining five extant Sophoclean plays, chorus and focal character are of the same sex.

In their final run of anapaests (155–61) the Chorus at once motivate their own arrival with reference to Creon's summons and at the same time announce the entrance of Creon himself that the audience has been expecting since it was foreshadowed by Antigone at 33–4.

First Act (first epeisodion), 162–331

Creon has already made his proclamation, presumably on the battlefield (as reported by Antigone at 26–32), but now repeats it before his internal audience, the Chorus, and before us, the external audience. We do not stop to ask ourselves why the proclamation is made twice: Antigone's statement that he wishes to bring it to the attention of those who did not hear it at first hand (33–4) is natural enough. But the iteration of the proclamation is only the first example of a pattern of 'doubling' that is repeated throughout a play in which 'twoness' is of immense importance.

In contrast to the expected entrance of Creon is the sudden appearance of the Guard (223). He must have been visible to the audience as he entered *via* one of the long side entrance passages (the same one, no doubt, by which Antigone had previously exited) during the exchange between Creon and the Chorus. In what may be a mildly metatheatrical touch, he draws attention to the lack of haste in his arrival, something that is uncharacteristic of tragic messenger figures (223–36).[50] The detailed characterization of this minor figure goes beyond what is necessary for the plot, but his prevarication and long-windedness serve to increase Creon's fury (with implications for Creon's characterization that we shall explore below). Creon no doubt exits into the palace at 326, the Guard's affirmation 'you'll never see me here again' (329) delivered once he has entered the stage-building. The Guard's relief and determination not to risk Creon's fury again serve to underline Creon's character (his anger encompasses both the guilty and the innocent – he is a dangerous man to work for), but it is also a case of false foreshadowing.

Choral song (first stasimon), 332–75

The Chorus sing a song, the famous 'Ode to Man', prompted by what they have seen and heard in the previous Act.

Second Act (second epeisodion), 376–581

Immediately after they have completed their song, the Chorus (in chanted anapaests, 376–83) announce the approach of the Guard and Antigone. The Guard has come back after all. With first the Guard, Antigone, and Creon, and then Antigone, Creon, and Ismene onstage at the same time, the present Act requires three speaking parts. According to Aristotle's *Poetics* (1449a18–19), the third actor was introduced by Sophocles himself; when Aeschylus' *Oresteia* was produced (in 458 BC) the use of a third actor may still have been a novelty; but by the time of the *Antigone*, it had no doubt become familiar. Yet full three-way dialogue always remained relatively rare in tragedy; masked, open-air performance before large audiences seems to have favoured one-to-one interactions rather than scenes in which all three speaking actors participate fully. This is an area in which tragic practice developed over time, from less to greater use of three-way interaction: *Antigone* makes more use of three-cornered dialogue than do *Ajax* or *Women of Trachis*, but the three speaking parts are less closely integrated than in two three-actor scenes in *Oedipus the King* (631–48, 1110–85) or in the three later plays (*Electra, Philoctetes, Oedipus at Colonus*).[51] In this play, all Acts except this one consist of two-actor scenes. This Second Act has three distinct scenes, the first and third of which require three speaking actors onstage, but still one-to-one interaction dominates: Antigone is silent in the first scene, in which Creon and the Guard speak, and the third scene involves two-person interaction first between Antigone and Ismene, and then between Creon and Ismene. Only at 531–9 do we have something like three-way interaction: Creon addresses Ismene, and she replies, only for Antigone to intervene; her confrontation with Ismene then postpones the resumption of the dialogue between Ismene and Creon until 561.

The Chorus address Antigone in their anapaests at 379–83, but she remains silent. The Guard instead answers the Chorus's questions (384–5). Creon entered the palace at the end of the previous Act, and now needs to be brought onstage. The Guard asks where he is (385), and both the Chorus-leader and Creon himself comment on the fact that his unmotivated entrance comes just at the right moment (386–7): a dramatist as good as Sophocles can motivate an entrance by drawing explicit attention to the absence of motivation. There follows a dialogue between the Guard and Creon, leading into the Guard's report of how Antigone was captured while attempting the burial of her brother's body (388–440).

This scene raises two issues of dramatic technique. The first is that of the 'two burials', the focus of many scholarly discussions:[52] someone (and the audience have no reason to assume that it was anyone but Antigone)[53] has already 'buried the body by sprinkling thirsty dust upon it and performing the necessary rites' (245–7); so (scholars ask) why does Antigone go back? What was wrong with the first burial? Is it that the first sprinkling of dust was a necessary preliminary, but not a sufficient burial;[54] or does Antigone want to be discovered, to compound her defiance? But there is not much point in any of this speculation; Antigone just does go back; she just does get caught. We should not make an issue of something when the text gives us no encouragement to do so. Nor is it in any way a fault to leave Antigone's motivation unclear. No one in the theatre would give it a second thought. Since no reason for Antigone's return to the corpse is provided in the play itself, no reason that we might supply could ever be definitive; and no particular reason is required. The two burials belong to a sequence of doubling that recurs at many points of the play:[55] already we have had two proclamations from Creon (one reported by Antigone and the second delivered onstage) and two scenes involving the Guard, the second contrasting with and reversing the expectation created by the first. This 'doubling' as an aspect of the plot reflects the recurrence of duality as a theme within the text. The two burials are clearly deliberate, and so is the opacity of Antigone's motivation; we need to concentrate upon what Sophocles does, not on what he does not do. And what he has chosen to do is amply justified by the effect of postponing the expected capture and reappearance of Antigone, reversing the expectation that the Guard would not return, motivating the irony of the first stasimon's concentration on the ingenuity of *men*, and in the effective juxtaposition of two reports of the uncanny circumstances surrounding each burial – the first in which the culprit appeared and disappeared without trace, and the second in which she is concealed by a sudden dust-storm that appears from nowhere and facilitates her access to the body.

The second scene between Creon and the Guard also raises a more substantive dramatic point. Antigone is present throughout Creon's interrogation and the Guard's report, but does not speak until 443. Creon's question at 441–2 ('You there, you, the one inclining your head towards the ground, do you admit or deny doing this deed?') not only effects the transition between the first scene of this Act, between Creon and the Guard, to its second and central scene, between Creon and Antigone (the Guard exits at 445), but also supplies a stage-direction for the previous scene – Antigone, silent since she was led in, has been 'inclining [her] head towards the ground' (441). Her posture has been a silent accompaniment to the Guard's tale of her deed; though unmentioned until 441, it must have attracted the audience's attention and encouraged them to speculate on the attitude that it expressed.[56] When Creon draws attention to it, we are encouraged further to speculate both about the meaning of Antigone's demeanour and about Creon's own understanding of it. There is a moment of uncertainty: is she afraid (the phrase used of her posture at 441 is used with reference to fear in the Guard's initial report at 269–70)? Avoiding eye-contact can also indicate shame or deference (especially the deference expected of women). But it immediately becomes apparent that Antigone's attitude is not one of shame or submissiveness – quite the opposite. Gaze-avoidance can also indicate lack of respect, the refusal to engage; and when Antigone does engage, her defiant lack of deference towards Creon is clear. Creon asks whether she knew that burial of the body had been forbidden (446–7). Her reply is terse (448): 'I knew; how could I not know it? It was well publicized.' Antigone's demeanour, and the way that Creon draws attention to it, are highly dramatic; latent in the initial opacity of her body language are a whole set of alternative possibilities, until it becomes clear that her gaze-avoidance betokens a gulf between her and Creon that will now never be bridged; her silence and avoidance of visual contact act as an effective foil for the defiant provocation of Creon's anger that ensues in the subsequent confrontation, first in two speeches of roughly equal length, and then in alternating line-by-line dialogue (*stichomythia*).[57]

This dramatic highpoint (a confrontation between two characters) is followed (as it was preceded) by another three-actor scene. Ismene is summoned by Creon at 491, and her entrance is announced in choral anapaests at 526–30. A dialogue between Creon and Ismene begins (531–7), but is immediately commandeered by Antigone in an intense exchange that rehearses the issues of the prologue and underlines the sisters' estrangement. First in *distichomythia* (two lines apiece) and then in *stichomythia* the confrontation between Antigone and Ismene mirrors the immediately preceding confrontation between Antigone and Creon, further underlining Antigone's isolation. Antigone dismisses Ismene's attempt to share responsibility for her deed: 'Save yourself; I don't begrudge your escape' (553). This is cruel, but will, as Antigone predicts, save Ismene's life. Ismene, for her part, tries to save Antigone's life, on a very different basis, of affection and devotion rather than Antigone's insistence on her own sole responsibility, and by doing what Antigone would never do, entreating Creon from a position of female inferiority. Ismene's introduction of a new piece of information, the betrothal of Antigone to Creon's son, Haemon (568ff.), prepares for the next phase of the play. Antigone and Ismene are then led off at 577–81. In contrast to their separate exits at the end of the prologue, this time they go off together, but only because they are both under arrest. They are led into the palace by attendants, but Creon remains onstage.

Choral song (second stasimon), 582–625

The Chorus now sing a song on the 'archaic' theme of the generations of disaster within a single family, clearly prompted by Antigone's situation, and especially by the way that her suffering implicates and replicates that of her whole family. But in its second half the song focuses on the power of Zeus's law and on human blindness, with concluding lines which will come to sum up the case of Creon. An application to Creon is already suggested by the simple fact of his presence while the song is sung.

Third Act (third epeisodion), 626–780

Again a choral song is followed by a passage of anapaestic recitative. Now the Chorus draw Creon's attention to the entrance of his son, Haemon, no doubt *via* the opposite passageway from that by which the Guard entered with Antigone at the beginning of the previous

Act.[58] Haemon already figures in the traditions of Theban mythology, but there is good reason to believe that this is the first version of the Theban story to make him the prospective husband of Antigone. His confrontation with Creon constitutes the play's major set-piece debate or *agôn*. It takes a typical form: after minimal preliminaries (631–8, i.e. four lines each), each party delivers an extended speech of (virtually or precisely) equal length,[59] followed by two lines of comment by the Chorus-leader (commending, as usual, the good sense of both sides), before the increased intensity of the scene is reflected in quick-fire exchanges of (initially) *distichomythia* (726–9), then *stichomythia* (730–55). Each character then delivers a four-line coda (758–65), Haemon storms off, and Creon is left to divulge the means by which he intends to put Antigone (but not Ismene) to death (766–80). As is typical in Sophoclean *agônes*, meaningful communication degenerates into invective; there is no meeting of minds.

In lines 760–1 Creon orders Antigone to be brought in, in order to have her killed before Haemon's eyes; but Haemon leaves before the problem that would be raised by the presentation of such a scene onstage has to be faced. Sophocles has observed the tragic convention against the onstage presentation of extreme acts of violence, but toys with the prospect of flouting it. Yet Antigone *is* brought in from the palace by attendants, at 806; did the attendants obey Creon's order, only to find that circumstances have changed when they appear, or is the order simply ignored because Haemon departs and Creon's threat can no longer be carried out? The former solution dispatches the extras needed to bring Antigone in at 806, but leaves the attendants' delay unexplained; the latter leaves us with an unmotivated reappearance.[60]

At 765, Haemon storms out, after saying that his father will never set eyes on him again (763–4). The Guard said something similar at 329, but that proved to be false preparation. This scene mirrors that one, at least in that detail, as the Guard's reappearance mirrored his first encounter with Creon. Without being specific, the Chorus-leader's comment ('My lord, the man has left in haste and in anger; the mind of

the young is bitter in its pain', 766–7) leads us to expect a negative
outcome. Creon will, as it turns out, set eyes on Haemon again; but in
circumstances that fully justify the Chorus-leader's foreboding (1226–
34). But the confrontation between Creon and Haemon also recalls
another scene, in which expressions of regard between blood-kin
similarly degenerate into open enmity as attempted persuasion fails.
The way in which the *agôn* between Creon and Haemon visually,
dramatically, and thematically recapitulates the opening confrontation
between Antigone and Ismene (itself 'doubled' in their second onstage
confrontation) suggests a parallel between Antigone and Creon and
thus constitutes an initial indication of a more pronounced parallelism
between their fates that emerges in the final stages of the play.[61] Here,
the breakdown in ties between blood relatives that is so prominent in
Antigone's family and that is dramatically presented onstage in her own
estrangement from Ismene is dramatized also in Creon's case.

The sequence at the end of this Act might suggest staggered exits:
Haemon leaves at 765, to be followed by Creon at 780.[62] But if that is the
case, then Creon has to reappear for no reason at 883 with an expression
of impatience at the length of Antigone's laments. His words there must
indicate that he has heard these laments; and if he does not enter at 883
there is no suitable point at which he might enter, unannounced and
with nothing immediately to do, before that. So Creon must remain
onstage throughout the choral song and ensuing exchange between
Antigone and the Chorus from 781–882, just as he remained onstage
during the previous choral ode. This helps to substantiate the impression
that Creon's orders (of 760–1) are acted upon and fulfilled: he sends for
Antigone and waits until she arrives.

Choral song (third stasimon), 781–800

The song that the Chorus sing at this point is formally a hymn, beginning
as hymns do with an invocation of the god and second-person catalogue
of his or her haunts, powers, and so on. Normally, this is followed by a
specific injunction or request, but not here. Hence all concentration is

on the power of Eros, the god of erotic love, the force that the Chorus detect behind Haemon's support for Antigone and his estrangement from his father (especially 793-4, 'You have also stirred up this kindred strife of men', with a pun on Haemon's name and the adjective translated 'kindred', *xynaimon*). Eros is 'unconquered in battle' (781); his mother, Aphrodite, is invincible (799); and Creon is present to hear.

Fourth Act (fourth epeisodion), 806-943

Once more, choral anapaests announce an incoming character (801-5), and Antigone enters under guard, lamenting her fate in lyric metre (806-82), answered by the Chorus in (at first) non-lyric anapaests (817-22, 834-8) and then (853-6, 872-5) in lyric iambics. This is a poetic and dramatic form generally referred to as a *kommos*. Musically and emotionally, this is the climax of Antigone's role, as her lyrics take the place of the lament that would normally accompany the deceased's passage from life to death, with all the pathos that this suggests (see especially 847, 876, 881-2).[63] But references to 'moving', 'going', and 'being led' in her lyrics and the spoken iambic verses that follow also evoke the bride's passage from her birth family to her new home with her husband (806-16, 867-8, 876-8, 891-3, 916-20, 939); if, as has been suggested, she has re-appeared in her wedding dress, this aspect of the scene's meaning will have been immediately and vividly apparent to the audience.[64] Creon intervenes at 883-90, whereupon Antigone goes over much of the same ground in spoken iambics (891-28). The difference of mode is a difference of perspective and of emotional colour and intensity; it is not just a matter of spoken dialogue recapitulating points that an audience may have missed in lyric delivery, or of lyric emotion versus iambic argument. Both her song and her speech outline the pathos and injustice of her plight.

At 885-8 Creon issues an impatient and peremptory order for Antigone to be removed; she is not, and Creon has to repeat the order, with a complaint at the slowness of the attendants, at 931-2. This is almost unparalleled; in tragedy orders issued to mute attendants are normally carried out forthwith.[65] Here Antigone has a speech of 38 lines after the order is issued. During this speech, according to David Bain, the action freezes: Antigone speaks, and Creon and his attendants are transfixed. The effect is to concentrate all attention on Antigone's last words (and in fact her very last words in this speech, at 925–8, are especially significant and ominous, virtually predicting the rest of the play). It is possible to naturalize this phenomenon – such is the force of Antigone's words, perhaps, that the attendants are stopped in their tracks; or perhaps they are reluctant to act anyway. Alternatively, one could see the freezing of the action as a non-realistic feature. But either way, the departure from the tragic norm and the emphasis that it throws on Antigone's speech are very powerful.

Antigone's anapaests at 929–43 accompany her final departure. But there is no sign that Creon also departs.[66] At the beginning of the next Act (988), the seer Tiresias enters. He addresses the Chorus first, but it is Creon who answers (991, 'What is your news, Tiresias?'), and his words do not suggest that he has just entered. It would be awkward to have him enter either with Tiresias or as Tiresias speaks, and there is no time for him to enter after Tiresias speaks. No doubt Tiresias addresses the Chorus first because he is blind, but in calling them 'lords of Thebes' he also suggests a role in leadership that implicitly diminishes that of Creon. If, then, Creon remains onstage throughout the choral song at 944–87, he has been onstage since 387, during each of the choral songs since that point. He will not leave the stage until 1114; this is a point to which we shall return.[67]

Choral song (fourth stasimon), 944–87

For the third time, the most significant element of the staging is that Creon is almost certainly onstage during the ode. Potential references to him in the language and content of the ode are physically underlined by his presence. On the surface, however, the point of this very difficult ode is the Chorus's continued search for parallels for Antigone's unusual and pitiable fate.

Fifth Act (fifth epeisodion), 988–1114

Each of the first four choral songs led into a passage of choral recitative announcing the entrance of a character. Recitative was also used in mid-Act at 526–30 to announce the arrival of Ismene. In fact all entrances until now, except that of the Guard at 223, have been announced. Even the Guard's entrance had been prepared for to some extent – we expect the consequences of Antigone's determination to defy the proclamation, as expressed in the opening scene, to be brought to Creon's attention somehow. But now there is surprise. Tiresias, led by his guide, enters unannounced, and there has been nothing about Tiresias in the play so far, nor has he been summoned (as he is in *Oedipus the King*).[68] This new arrival shifts the play into a higher gear and sets a new sequence of events in motion. As in the (later) *Oedipus the King*, things begin to happen very quickly in the final third of the play.

The appearance of Tiresias, like that of the Guard, upsets Creon's equilibrium. The subject of each report is the same (concerning the corpse of Polynices). Creon's reaction is the same: he blazes with anger, blames the Messenger for the message, and senses conspiracy driven by the desire for material gain. The Tiresias scene can also be compared to the Haemon scene: each begins cordially, but both degenerate into insult. Each successive stage of the dramatic action so far has centred on aggressive one-to-one interactions: Antigone and Ismene; Creon and the Guard; Creon and Antigone; Creon and Haemon; and now Creon and Tiresias; at the centre of that sequence is the fundamental confrontation between Antigone and Creon themselves. Tiresias' function in the play is also the same as Haemon's: each is a 'warner'. Tiresias' departure also mirrors Haemon's: he leaves in anger (1090), and the Chorus-leader's comment on his departure at 1091 begins with exactly the same words as does his comment on Haemon's exit at 766 ('My lord, the man has left …'). Both warnings are justified, both departures (as the Chorus-leader notes each time) ominous.

The similarities between the three scenes involving the Guard, Haemon, and Tiresias underline what they tell us about Creon. Now all the focus is on him. As Tiresias leaves, Creon is alone with the Chorus, and the stance that he has maintained since his first appearance now collapses: he hesitates (1095–7), then, on the Chorus-leader's advice, gives in (1099–1106), exiting at 1114 for the first time since he entered at 387. He has been a continuous presence for 700 lines, as the dramatic and thematic focus has narrowed ever more closely on him. The Tiresias scene mirrors the Haemon scene, but in the meantime Antigone has gone (for good); and to the imperative, 'save Antigone', Tiresias' warnings and prophecies add a second: 'save yourself'. The later scene's mirroring of the earlier one also extends to their outcomes, at least partially: in both cases, Creon gives ground, but only after his angry interlocutor has departed. Following Haemon's departure, Creon abandons his decision to kill Ismene as well as Antigone (769–71); following Tiresias', he accepts advice to reprieve Antigone and bury her brother. This looks like a major difference between the two scenes: but in the former his concession was too little; and in the latter it will turn out to be too late. Yet Creon's total change of heart in the second case creates an impression of hope, at least in his own mind. Some in the audience might share that hope, while others, a majority perhaps, encouraged by the dire and categorical prophecies of Tiresias (1064–86, including the loss of a son, 1066–7) will expect the appearance of hope to be illusory. But the possibility of an alternative outcome had been, albeit prior to his dire prophecies, a premise of Tiresias' arrival, and the play is constructed in such a way that there must be *some* element of suspense when Creon announces his determination to free Antigone (1108–15). This suggests that the tale of Antigone is not a familiar one; perhaps no one in the original audience had encountered it before, at least in anything like the form that Sophocles gives it; catastrophe may be awaited, but it is probable that the form that it would take remained unclear.

Choral song (fifth stasimon), 1115–52

The ode exploits the fact that the audience will have had no positive notion of exactly what to expect next, and, by invoking Dionysus to come and purify the city of its sickness (1140–5), compounds the illusion of hope. As in *Ajax, Women of Trachis,* and *Oedipus the King,* an optimistic song immediately before the catastrophe makes the latter feel worse by contrast. But what if the city *is* purified of its sickness, precisely through the devastation of Creon's family?

Final Act (Exodos), 1155–1353

The remaining section of the play falls into two parts: first a Messenger reports Creon's failure to save Antigone and the suicide of Haemon over her corpse (1155–1256); then the stage is momentarily empty, as choral anapaests announce the arrival of Creon at 1257–60. The play then ends with a second *kommos* (1261–1346) and a brief choral tag in anapaests (1347–53). The *kommos* in which Creon sings in lamentation is more than twice as long as the earlier one in which Antigone does so. This time the Chorus's response (like that of the Messenger) remains on the less emotional level of spoken iambics.

The final choral song (like the previous) ends without any entrance announcement to follow. Instead, in bursts a Messenger, his sudden appearance immediately undercutting the apparently positive tone of the song that has just finished. The arrival of a Messenger at this stage is conventional, as are his proverbial reflections on the mutability of fortune, but in this case the application of this pattern to Creon serves the important function of emphasizing, first, that whatever else the play may be, it is the tragedy of Creon, but second, that this tragedy arises directly from the tragedy of Antigone. (We shall say more about this in the chapters that follow.) Both the appearance of the Messenger and the content of his opening speech (at 1155–71) suggest summation and closure. The scene then continues in a conventional way, the Messenger's opening announcement leading to questions from his internal audience, the answers to which are preliminary to his full report (1172–9). But before that report can be delivered there is a wholly unexpected turn: a new character is introduced (announced and named as Creon's wife, Eurydice, by the Chorus-leader in spoken iambic trimeters at 1180–2). There have been no previous references to Creon's wife, and nothing to suggest that that she would feature in the play at all. Eurydice is certainly not a fixture of the Theban myth: Creon's wife is called Henioche at Hesiod, *Shield of Heracles* 83, and there is no previous mention of his wife's suicide in the extant mythical tradition. So the surprise appearance of Eurydice here is most likely a Sophoclean innovation. Hers is the second shortest speaking part in all tragedy (and she uses most of it, 1183–9, to motivate her appearance, as a respectable married woman, in public).[69] Her main function is to provide a silent presence during the Messenger speech, to act as an additional internal auditor with a much higher emotional investment in the report than a typical Chorus would have. Her role as an internal auditor thus colours the message as it passes to the external audience. Having heard the report, however, Eurydice will withdraw, and then act; her action will then require an additional report of a second catastrophe to redouble Creon's pain.

Eurydice's silence during the Messenger speech is as dramatic as that of Antigone during the Guard's report at 408–40; even as the audience focus on the words, they also focus on the potential reaction of the silent figure. Equally dramatic is Eurydice's silent exit at 1243, a technique that Sophocles also employs in the case of Deianira in *The Women of Trachis* and Jocasta in *Oedipus the King*; in all three cases the silent queen exits to kill herself. This is now the third exit on whose ominous character the Chorus-leader (together, in this case, with the Messenger, 1244–56) has had occasion to comment. The ominousness of all three exits spells disaster for Creon.

The second part of this last Act parallels the first in that it begins in an expected, conventional manner, only to be interrupted. The Chorus announce Creon (in anapaests at 1257–60), and that he is carrying his son's body in his arms. The body is most likely represented by a dummy, or conceivably by an extra; some deny that Creon actually carries the body and suggest that instead it is brought in on a bier.[70] It is true that the Greek of 1258 (cf. 1279, 1298, 1345) need not mean that he carries it, but only that he holds on to it. But it is dramatically more effective that the audience should focus at this stage only on Creon and the dead body of his son, rather than on Creon, the body, the bier, and the attendants who carry it. The fact that the body is still 'in his arms' at 1279, 1298, and 1345 is no obstacle to this: once he has entered, Creon presumably kneels and cradles the body in his arms.

Creon's lament over Haemon's body is interrupted by the sudden reappearance of the Messenger, who went into the palace at 1256, just before Creon returned, in order to find out what had happened to Eurydice. He now announces the Queen's death, and at 1293 her body is displayed to Creon and the audience either by the emergence of the low, wheeled platform called the *ekkyklêma*, used in tragedy for the display of interior scenes, or simply by being brought out of the central door by attendants.[71] To this visible presence of the bodies of the son and wife whose deaths Creon has caused is added a reference to the death of another son, for which Eurydice also regarded him as responsible, in the report of her suicide at 1302–5. The final images of the play present a broken man, mourning his son and his wife as a result of his attempt to negate ties of kinship by marriage and of blood. Creon's utter ruin is represented by this proud ruler's polite request to be escorted out (1339), and by the sight of him looking back and forth to the bodies that are no doubt removed as he is led into the stage-building (1341–2). Finally, the doors of an *oikos* which has now been devastated close on the man who caused his own and others' suffering. The Chorus file out through a side entrance, chanting the moral as they go (1347–53):

> Good sense is by far the first part of happiness (*eudaimonia*); one must not show any impiety towards the gods. Great words of the boastful are requited by great blows and thus teach wisdom in old age.

Concentration simply on the presentation of the action in the theatre, without much in the way of textual interpretation, reveals what an extraordinarily powerful play *Antigone* is. The use of parallel scenes for linkage, contrast, climax, and suspense is especially noteworthy. There are two scenes between Antigone and Ismene; two scenes involving the Guard, each focusing on one of the two burials; two 'warner' scenes; and two Messenger scenes, each reporting the death of one of the two members of Creon's family whose deaths result from his choices. Finally, two bodies are brought onstage, and so Creon effectively delivers two laments in a second *kommos* that duplicates the earlier one involving Antigone. The emphasis on duality that we noted in the prologue is not fortuitous. And, of course, in some sense, there are two tragedies here, that of Antigone and that of Creon. This is the general topic that we shall pursue in the next three chapters.

Tragedy and Sympathy

Whose tragedy is it anyway?

Much of the older scholarship on the *Antigone* is unduly concerned
with the issue of identifying the play's main character, a search that is
governed by an unwarranted assumption that there must be *one* main
character. The fact is that *Antigone* just does have two major characters.[1]
A related approach seeks to determine which of the two main characters
is the 'hero', defining that term with reference to a construct of the
'Sophoclean hero' as harsh, isolated, extreme, and uncompromising that
is developed by scholars such as Hans Diller and (above all) Bernard
Knox.[2] On this view Creon's yielding and abandonment of his resolve
following the prophecies of Tiresias mark him out as different from
Antigone: she, like a true 'Sophoclean hero', does not yield.[3] The
'Sophoclean hero' is an empirical construct, built up by good scholars
on the basis of the primary evidence of the plays themselves; but it
would be wrong to essentialize that construct as an *a priori* interpretative
template. All such generalizations need to be tested against the
specificity of the individual case. In any event, labelling either Antigone
or Creon as 'the Sophoclean hero' in this play would not settle the most
important questions we should like to ask of it.

Aristotle's theory of tragedy is closer in time to the classics of the
fifth-century theatre than any modern interpretative construct. But
while the *Poetics* commands our attention both as a contribution to
fourth-century debate on tragedy's place in Greek culture and as the
document of a great mind's engagement with Greek society's most
prestigious living art form, still its approach is a selective and prescriptive
one that does not by any means fit each and every surviving tragedy.[4]

Yet it is instructive to note that, for Aristotle, a good tragedy is the representation of an action (*praxis*), of which the stages unfold in a causal sequence of probability or necessity; it need not concentrate on the fortunes of a single agent.[5] This is an approach that does fit the *Antigone*: a single *praxis* begins with Creon's prohibition of burial and Antigone's resolve to defy it. Antigone's death follows from her defiance, and what happens to Creon follows first from his prohibition of burial, and then from his decision to condemn Antigone to death for her defiance of that prohibition. A crucial choice is made, and the sufferings of both Antigone and Creon follow as consequences (by probability or necessity) of that choice.

The plot of the *Antigone* dramatizes a single action involving two major figures. Malcolm Heath is right to stress this aspect of Aristotle's theory, and to show how closely it accounts for the practices of tragedians, even in plays in which modern critics have found lack of unity.[6] Heath also shows how the notion that tragedy dramatizes a single *praxis* can accommodate what he describes as mobility of focus. 'Focus' is his term for the presentation of a character in a major role as the object not just of audience attention but also of sympathy. The account of the *Antigone*'s scenic sequence in the previous chapter itself indicates that the play does involve a substantial shift from Antigone to Creon as the focus at least of audience attention, if not also of audience sympathy: Antigone, her problems, and her undertaking are introduced first, and her role culminates in the pathos of her final lament; but thereafter she fades from the audience's attention, which by the end of the play is exclusively focused on the utter ruin of Creon.[7] We need to discuss how this shift takes place and what it entails.

Not everyone would agree that, because we see her first and because our attention is initially on her predicament, Antigone is the focus of audience sympathy in the first part of the play.[8] Equally, it is not self-evident that an audience will be initially antipathetic to Creon simply because he is Antigone's adversary.[9] But it is at least undeniable that the play ends with attention focused largely or entirely on the sufferings of Creon; by then Creon is at least a potential (and most people think an actual) object of audience sympathy, and so – however we may feel about him on his first appearance and immediately thereafter – it is clear that his presentation in the play's final scenes differs markedly from that in the scenes with Antigone, Ismene, and Haemon, in which not even his most ardent apologist could maintain that he remains wholly sympathetic.[10]

Creon himself is the vector of the shift in attention from Antigone's predicament to his own. As we noted in Chapter 1, he is onstage continuously from 387–1114, a constant through the central scenes of the play, which feature his confrontations with Antigone (and Ismene), Haemon, and Tiresias. At the beginning of that sequence, the issue is Antigone's conduct and its consequences; at the end, the main issue is Creon and his family. Creon's continuous presence from 387–1114 means that he is onstage for three of the play's six choral odes. A marked feature of these odes in general is the way that they prepare for and promote the movement away from Antigone and towards Creon, often by means of latent reference to Creon's actions and their consequences. The first stasimon (332–75, the famous 'Ode to Man') immediately precedes the reappearance of both Creon and the Guard. Its ironies (which we shall discuss in more detail in the next chapter) set the scene for the odes which follow and for the shift from Antigone to Creon. The ode is apparently prompted by the bold act of whoever buried the body of Polynices, but also by Creon's claims for the primacy of civic obligation and the need for strong leadership in his opening speech. But burial is not really an example of the awesome or terrible (*deinos*, 332–3) potential of human skill and ingenuity.

A central irony is that, though the ode begins in gender-neutral terms ('Many are the *deinos* things, but nothing is more *deinos* than a human being [*anthrôpos*]', 332–3), it soon becomes gender-specific: hunting is the pursuit not of mankind (*anthrôpos*), but of man (*anêr*) at 348. Antigone is an *anthrôpos*, but she is not an *anêr*. In expressing themselves in this way, the Chorus recall Creon's assumption in line 248, that the person who buried the body of Polynices must be a *man* (*anêr*).[11] What the Chorus sing about man, therefore, is not about

Antigone; but it may apply to Creon. The general theme of the ode is man's attempt to master his environment through art, science, and skill;[12] but its final stanza (365–75) makes the point that skills are ambivalent: they bring bad as well as good (365–7); a man is 'high in the city' when he reveres the laws of the land (or the earth, *chthôn*) and the justice of the gods (368–7), but 'without a city' when he does not (370–5). Skills, moreover, are limited in what they can achieve. 'Man', the Chorus sing at 360–4, 'has a resource for everything; resourceless he proceeds towards nothing that is to come. Only from Death will he not devise a means of escape; but he has contrived remedies from incurable diseases.' The statement that man is resourceful in all respects is immediately contradicted by the reference to death; here is a domain that is beyond man's control. Creon has already emphasized that it is only through time that the quality of a man's judgement becomes apparent (175–7). In asserting his control of the city of Thebes in his opening speech (162ff.) Creon invites his audience to judge him by the results of his decisions;[13] the first stasimon makes it clear that the outcomes of men's attempts to control the world are uncertain and potentially ambivalent, that there are things beyond human control. Having already been invited to suspend judgement on Creon until the results of his actions become clear, and confronted by a song which emphasizes the fragility of (especially) men's attempts to impose their will on the natural, social, and supernatural environments, we wonder whether his skills are sufficient to respect the laws of the land (or the earth), to keep him 'high in the city', to secure benefit rather than harm, and to escape incurable diseases. The irony of the first stasimon puts the focus on Creon as man and as ruler.

For the next three odes. Creon is onstage, his presence a visual point of reference for the latent implications of the Chorus's words. The second stasimon (582–625) picks up on a theme of the previous Act (especially 471–2), that Antigone's actions and sufferings instantiate a recurrent pattern in her family, but its second pair of stanzas concerns the power of Zeus to withstand the transgressions of *men* (again the gender-specific term, *andres*, is used, 604–5), the deluded hope that leads *men's* minds astray (*andres* again, 616), and the phenomenon by which bad seems good to someone whom a god is leading towards ruin. In particular, the reference to the eternal law of Zeus's power, power that never sleeps nor is worn down by the passage of time (604–13), recalls the principles that Antigone enunciated in the previous Act at 450–7:

> Yes, for it was not Zeus who made that proclamation, nor did the Justice that dwells with the gods below define such laws among people; nor did I think that your proclamations had such force that you, a mortal, could override the unwritten and unfailing ordinances of the gods. For they live forever, not just for now and yesterday, and no one knows their origin.

The third stasimon (781–800) is a hymn to Eros, explicitly prompted by the preceding scene in which Haemon interceded on Antigone's behalf with his father. Love is another unconquerable divine force (781, 799–800), and if it is active in this play,[14] then it is Creon who has sought to overcome it.[15] The (very difficult) fourth stasimon (944–87) takes its starting point from Antigone's imprisonment, and offers two clear mythical examples (Danae and Lycurgus) of figures who were, like Antigone, walled up alive.[16] As presented here, both Danae and Lycurgus resemble Antigone; in the case of Lycurgus, however, the detail that he was imprisoned is found only in this version (957–8),[17] and may have been invented for the sake of the comparison. What Lycurgus is famous for is his *theomachia*, his resistance to the god, Dionysus (*Iliad* 6. 130–40). This is prominent in the Chorus's presentation here too; we note in particular the detail that Lycurgus 'tried to stop the god-inspired women' (963–4). Again an application to Creon, as someone who opposes the divine and seeks to restrain irresistible forces, is suggested.[18] All three mythological examples in this ode, in fact, emphasize that it is impossible to resist the gods or one's fate. The Danae story in particular makes this point at length: 'The power of fate is formidable (*deinos*); neither wealth nor war, not a tower, not black ships beaten by the sea can escape it' (951–4).[19] If Lycurgus is a discordant parallel for Antigone (because his conduct resembles Creon's more than it does hers), so too is this presentation of the Danae myth: for it was Danae's father, the one who imprisoned her, who tried to evade his fate (that he would be killed by his daughter's son),[20] not the imprisoned woman who serves as a parallel to Antigone. In this play, the analogue to Danae's father is not Antigone, but Creon. And it is Creon who stands before the audience as the Chorus sing their song.

The first stasimon, therefore, raises questions about man's power to control his environment, and names Hades as a power than man cannot master. The next three choral songs, which are sung with Creon onstage, have an underlying reference to Creon and to powers (Zeus, Love, and Fate) that human beings cannot control. Creon is the one who tried to make human law superior to the divine laws of the universe, and the cosmic disruption that this has precipitated is the focus of Tiresias' dire warnings in the scene that immediately follows the fourth stasimon.[21] Creon's presence throughout this sequence guides the choral odes' latent references to him, until the point of those references becomes explicit. These choral odes (from the first stasimon to the fourth) play a major role in setting up the climax of the play in the fate of Creon. *After* the fourth stasimon things begin to move very quickly. Whereas the message of the first Warner (Haemon) was 'save Antigone', the message that Creon takes from the second (Tiresias) is that he must act at once to save himself and his family;[22] this he then tries to do, leaving the stage at 1114 for the first time since 387. By the time he does so, our attention has shifted to his fate and that of his family.

And this concentration becomes total. The Messenger's speech at 1155–71 presents Creon as a paradigm of the mutability of fortune. His report of the scene in the cave that serves as Antigone's prison, tomb, and bridal chamber presents it from Creon's perspective, focusing primarily on his anxiety for Haemon.[23] As the Messenger describes the scene, Antigone's death has already occurred; it becomes an element in the final estrangement of Haemon and Creon and a circumstantial detail in the presentation of Haemon's death from Creon's point of view. As we noted, the Messenger's report of the scene is also coloured for the external audience by the presence of Creon's wife and Haemon's mother; her ominous and silent departure maintains the focus on the fate of Creon's family. Then in the final scene we see Creon himself lamenting over two bodies, both visible onstage. Antigone's body is left where it was; and despite the vividness of the Messenger's report, the visual effect of Creon's lamentations over the bodies of his son and his wife makes a greater impression upon an audience in the theatre than a report of an offstage scene. The last reference to Antigone in the play is at 1240-1, where she is described as the bride of Haemon in death. In the final scene (1257ff.), there is no mention of Antigone at all. The shift in the audience's focus from Antigone and her predicament, as presented in the prologue, to the downfall of Creon in the Exodos has been total; and whether we like it or not, the fate of Creon, a man, a head of household, and a ruler, has superseded that of the woman, Antigone, and forms the climax of the play.[24]

But the fact that the play culminates in the tragedy of Creon does not mean that the tragedy of Antigone is unimportant. On the contrary, her isolation as she leaves the scene, to be immured alive, is poignant and full of pathos. The song that she sings as she departs (806-82; cf. 891-943) takes the place of the wedding song that she will never hear and the funeral lament that should be sung by the deceased's female relatives, not by the individual herself before her death. The unity of the play's action is reflected in the perfect balance between the fates of Antigone and Creon. Antigone dies for family ties, ties which Creon thought subordinate to loyalty to the state and to its ruler (in his opening speech, especially 183-90, 209-10; cf. the much more 'tyrannical' version in the *agōn* with Haemon at 658-76). More than once, Creon affects a disdain for ties of kinship that borders on blasphemy: 'whether she [Antigone] is my sister's child or closer to me in blood than my whole circle of Zeus Herkeios, she and her sister will not evade the worst of deaths' (486-8); 'so let her sing her hymns to Kindred Zeus . . .' (658-9). In the scene with Haemon, it appears that he regards a son as virtually an extension of the father (639-46) and the city as the property of the ruler (734-9); both as a father (634) and as a ruler (666-7) he demands unconditional obedience, whether he is right or wrong. City comes before family, but self, it seems, comes before both. By the end of the play, however, Creon is forced to realize what family ties mean, especially through the death of Haemon, whose name is derived from the Greek word for 'blood' (*haima*), a root that recurs in those very passages in which Creon disparages the sanctity of blood relationships – 'closer in blood' at 486 is *homaimonestera*, 'sister' in 488 is literally 'blood-sharer', *xynaimos*, the same word as is applied to Zeus ('Kindred Zeus') at 659.[25] Creon subverted both blood ties (with reference to Polynices and Antigone) and marital ties (between Antigone and Haemon); as a result he loses a blood-relative, Haemon, and his spouse, Eurydice.

As Tiresias eventually presents the matter, Creon's fundamental error is to detain a corpse in the world of the living. The counterpart to this is his decision to entomb Antigone while she is still alive, in such a way that Antigone's position begins to resemble that of her brother – she too is between worlds. This is a theme in the play even before Antigone's imprisonment: 'you are alive, but my soul died long ago', she tells Ismene at 559–60. In her lamentations, after her sentence has been pronounced, she dwells on her anomalous status: Hades, who puts all to bed, is leading her (as a bridegroom would) to the shore of Acheron alive (810–13); she has no home either among the living or among the dead (850–2);[26] bereft of friends she goes to the caverns of the dead (920). Once she is gone, Tiresias draws attention to the complementarity of what Creon has done to Antigone and what he has done to Polynices (1068–71):

> You have cast below one of those who belong above, settling a living soul in a tomb without due honour, and you have kept here one of those who belong below, a corpse deprived of its due, unhallowed by funeral rites, unholy.

But the balancing and parallelism does not stop there. At the end of Antigone's last long speech before she is led to her death, she prays (927–8):

> But if it is these men [i.e. Creon] who are in error, may they suffer evils no greater than those that they are now inflicting, without justice, upon me.

And so it turns out: in presenting Creon as a paradigm of vicissitude, the Messenger observes, 'When a man loses his pleasures, I do not count him as alive, but a living corpse' (1165–7). Creon himself reacts to the news of Eurydice's death with the exclamation 'Aiai, you have killed a dead man a second time' (1288).[27] 'Lead me away,' he begs his attendants at 1320–5, 'I do not exist.' The anomalous, 'between worlds' condition that Creon inflicted upon Polynices and Antigone comes in the end to be his own. It is not just that the one *praxis* ruins both Antigone and Creon; there is a distinct balance and parallelism in the way that it does so.

Who is right?

Burial

It is important to approach the issue of the rights and wrongs of Creon's edict prohibiting the burial of Polynices' corpse not in the abstract, but with due regard for its presentation in the play.[28] Antigone is naturally aggrieved and outraged at the proposal: it is the latest in a catalogue of ills that bring disgrace and dishonour on her family (4–6); it distinguishes between the honoured and the dishonoured dead, leaving Polynices without his share of funeral honours, mere carrion for the birds (21–30). This is a slight that Antigone takes personally (31–2): 'Such is the noble Creon's proclamation for you, and for me – yes, me, I tell you.' To deprive Polynices of honour, of course, is precisely what Creon intends: he was a traitor who intended to destroy his native city and its temples, to taste the blood of his fellow citizens, and to reduce others to slavery; he deserves not an honourable burial, but to be left as food for birds and dogs, his mutilation a visible warning to all (198–206). Creon will not put his kinship with Polynices before his loyalty to the city (175–90).

Antigone is shocked and outraged by Creon's proclamation; but hers is precisely the kind of partisan reaction that Creon believes should be overcome by civic duty and loyalty. In all normal circumstances, burial is a duty, non-burial a horror, and failure to obtain burial for a member of one's own family is an unbearable disgrace.[29] In the literary tradition that begins with the *Iliad*, mutilation and non-burial of the dead are outrages that tempt the victor, a means of obliterating the honour of the vanquished opponent, but the ideal norm is that all are entitled to burial (it is the 'privilege of the dead', *Iliad* 16. 457, 675, 23. 9; cf. *Odyssey* 24. 190, 296), and it is this norm that is memorably and powerfully restored when Achilles abandons the fury that led him to drag Hector's body behind his chariot and instead, out of pity and a sense of the community of human suffering, restores his enemy's body to Priam in the poem's final book.[30] The Iliadic presentation of exposure and mutilation by dogs and birds as the ultimate horror is implicit in both Antigone's and Creon's presentation of the edict at 29–30 and 205–6 (respectively), their words clearly evoking lines 4–5 of the *Iliad* proem, '[the wrath, which] made the men themselves prey for dogs and a feast for birds'.[31] The desire to deny burial to one's enemies is presented negatively in tragedy too, notably in Sophocles' *Ajax*, where it is the tactic of the contemptible brothers, Menelaus and Agamemnon, and opposed by the humane arguments of Odysseus,[32] and in Euripides' *Suppliant Women*, which dramatizes a version of the same general story as the *Antigone*, and which extols Theseus' intervention to secure the burial of the Seven against Thebes in the face of Theban vindictiveness.[33] In both these plays, the right of the dead to burial is supported by appeal to universal values of justice and to Panhellenic custom derived ultimately from divine law (*Ajax* 1129–31, 1332–45, 1363–5; *Suppliant Women* 377–8, 524–37, 559, 561–3, 670–2).[34] These are arguments to which Antigone also has recourse (450–7). The poetic tradition, therefore, gives substantial evidence of the ideals that support Antigone's case; and if in the *Iliad* (and in Euripides' *Suppliant Women*) the focus of concern is the treatment of enemies in wartime, the issue in the *Ajax* is more nearly parallel to that in the *Antigone,* in that both concern the denial of burial, justified as a matter of civic order, towards a traitor who had turned against his own community. There can, moreover, be no doubt that Creon's prohibition of burial is ultimately shown to be wrong: it occasions a sacrificial crisis in which the gods no longer respond to human offerings, because the retention of a corpse in the upper world of the living (balanced by the consignment of a living person to a tomb) confounds the balance of the cosmos as a whole (as Tiresias authoritatively insists at 998–1022, 1068–73).

But this is not necessarily a conclusion that an audience would reach at the outset. The right to burial was not absolute in contemporary Athens.[35] Themistocles, the most prominent Athenian statesman of Sophocles' youth, was declared in his absence a traitor to Athens, and when he died (in 459 BC), in order to comply with his wish to be buried in Attica, his relatives had to bring back his bones and bury them in secret, since, as Thucydides explains (1. 138. 6), it was not permitted to bury someone exiled for treason in Attic soil.[36] A document that purports to be the decree outlawing Antiphon, the leader of the oligarchic coup of 411 BC (and his fellow oligarch Archeptolemus), prohibits burial in absolute terms.[37] Further evidence is provided by Plato's *Laws*, which envisage expulsion of the offender's corpse as a penalty for a number of serious offences. These are new laws for a fictitious Cretan city, but Plato was an Athenian, and his language in some respects reflects both Athenian law and Attic usage. The assumption that casting the body of a malefactor beyond the borders of the state is equivalent to leaving it unburied is therefore suggestive.[38] In the mind of the average Athenian, denial of burial and denial of burial within Attica may have come to very much the same thing, and it is entirely possible that many in the original audience will have failed to notice that Creon's stipulation that Polynices' corpse be left unburied *where it is* (on the plain of Thebes) represents a crucial difference between his proclamation and the Athenian treatment of traitors.[39] Members of the original Athenian audience will also no doubt have been familiar with the 'pit' (*barathron* or *orygma*), into which criminals (including traitors) were thrown, either to kill them or perhaps to leave them to rot after execution (scholars are divided on its function, and some think that it changed over time).[40] And we can tell from the bizarre anecdote of Leontius and his irrational desire to look at corpses in Plato's *Republic* (Book 4, 439e-440a) that it was possible to see such sights in classical Attica.[41] In these cases, too, one can argue that whatever was done with the malefactor's body did not amount to the simple exposure of the corpse where it lay, as demanded by Creon – the 'pit' may have been conceived as a (particularly ignominious) method of burial, a way of disposing of the body, at least in a ritually sufficient sense.[42] But again, these are refinements that may not have suggested themselves to an audience on first hearing Creon's proclamation.

There is a possibility, then, of a certain gulf between the ideals of epic and tragedy and the attitudes of ordinary Athenians, especially in so far as they are informed by Athenian penology.[43] The *Antigone* will turn out to endorse the ideals of 'literature' in this regard rather than the pragmatics and politics of 'life', but there may have been many in the original audience who at least initially saw Creon's original prohibition of burial as no more than they themselves would expect to see imposed on a traitor in their own city. The complications of this may well not have occurred to them, and so the issue in the mind of our hypothetical 'average Athenian' may initially have been a not easily resolvable one between the claims of family and religion, as stated by Antigone, and those of the state and its right to punish those who betray it, as represented by Creon. In some respects, indeed, this may be too sharp an antithesis. Creon is not only head of state, but also head of Antigone's household: the link he draws between a man's role as ruler of his household and his activity as a good citizen in his confrontation with Haemon at 659–62 is a conventional one with which, in the abstract, many in the original audience will have agreed. Equally, religion is a matter with which the *polis* is intimately concerned.[44] Creon upholds forms of inter-relatedness between *polis* and *oikos* and between *polis* and religion that will have appeared normal to the average fifth-century Athenian male. For any who thought along these lines, it *may* have taken the intervention of Tiresias, with his demonstration of the consequences of exposing a corpse at the heart of the *polis*'s territory, to underline the differences between what Creon has done and what might be done in contemporary Athens.

For all that, we must also reckon with the possibility of misgivings over Creon's edict, at least among some in the audience, from the outset. For one thing, there is the influence of the idealism of epic and tragedy with regard to burial of the dead and the treatment of enemies, even traitors. The stock of religious, ethical, and emotional norms and attitudes on which members of the audience could draw was not restricted to the pragmatics of contemporary politics and penology. It is also telling that it is not only Antigone who is horrified at what Creon proposes to do. Ismene is too, and though she feels unable to act, she nonetheless sees the force of the obligation that drives Antigone (65–6: she will beg Polynices' pardon, for her situation forces her to neglect her obligations; cf. 78–9); and though she pronounces Antigone 'mad', she also regards her as 'truly dear to her dear ones' (99). The Chorus, too, are elderly, cautious, and conventional, naturally inclined to side with Creon (and, later, to take a censorious view of Antigone), but even their leader suggests the dubiety of Creon's policy when he suspects that the initial covering of Polynices' body with dust may be the work of the gods (278–9). There is enough here to arouse the disquiet of at least some in the original audience. Those whose response took this form would find further support in Antigone's statement of the principles that drove her to act (450–60, 502–4, 511–23), and would not have been surprised by Tiresias' revelation of the consequences of Creon's prohibition. Finally, as a matter of general principle, we need to remember that evidence that a practice (such as non-burial of traitors) is widely regarded as acceptable in a society cannot in itself prove that an individual member of that society (such as a tragedian) cannot choose to problematize that practice. The assumption that Sophocles does not challenge the common beliefs of the democratic *polis* (if such these are) is an unsafe one.

Whether the recognition that Creon is wrong arises early or late in the minds of the audience, it arises as a recognition not just that it was a mistake not to cast the body of Polynices beyond the boundaries of the state, but that it was wrong to deny the proper burial that Antigone wanted. Though the negative consequences of exposure that Tiresias describes follow from the fact that the presence of the body is polluting the city's altars and corrupting its interactions with the gods (1016–22), this crisis is resolved, following Tiresias' pleas (1015–32), the Chorus-leader's advice (1101), and Creon's change of mind (1102–14), by the full and proper burial of Polynices' body within the boundaries of the *polis* (as the Messenger reports at 1196–1204). The way that this issue is resolved offers no encouragement for the view that full and proper burial is more than the situation required. Clearly, the audience are not expected to protest that Polynices was, after all, a traitor and should not have been buried within the confines of the state. If the Athenian treatment of traitors initially led some members of the audience to regard Creon's edict as warranted, the reversal of that position (demanded of anyone who is following the logic of the plot) requires the view not just that Creon was contingently wrong (in insisting that the body be left exposed in the wrong place), but absolutely wrong.[45]

Antigone's defiance

But if it becomes clear that Creon was wrong to prohibit Polynices' burial, does this mean that it was right for Antigone to defy Creon's order and to attempt to bury her brother? Burial of the dead was a familial duty, and a process in which the women of the family were heavily involved, e.g. in washing, laying out, and lamenting the corpse. This is a role that Antigone has already performed in the past (900–3), and one that she would normally be expected to perform for all members of her family.[46] But overall responsibility for arranging the funeral belonged to the deceased's nearest male relative. In Polynices' case, that person is Creon.[47] But if Creon would, in normal circumstances, bear the responsibility of arranging burial, this clearly cannot mean that he is justified in denying burial; it is one thing for a woman to rebel against the head of her household in normal circumstances or where that person acts as he should, but another to do so in abnormal circumstances in which the head of the household is demonstrably wrong.[48] Antigone's defiance is an issue, but it is an issue of her defiance of the political authority invested in the ruler, of Creon himself, and of Creon the man; it is not presented as a matter of a woman's trespassing upon the right of the nearest male relative to arrange or deny burial.

In classical Athens, women of citizen status were in effect regarded as perpetual minors, and remained for their entire lives under the legal guardianship of their nearest male relative (the father before marriage; the husband thereafter; and the next nearest relative in default of either of those).[49] After the deaths of her father and both of her brothers, Antigone, as an unmarried girl, is now under the guardianship of Creon. Yet she defies him, not only as the head of her household (an issue that Creon himself raises at 531–3 and 659–62) and as a man (484–5, 525, 678–80, 740–1, 746, 756), but also as the representative of the *polis*. This is the issue that is raised in her opening encounter with Ismene – not just that women must bow to men (61–2), but more specifically that Antigone is proposing political action against the will of the city (79): Ismene is unable to follow her in acting 'in violation of the citizens' will' (cf. 44, 47, 65–8). Many in the original audience may have found Antigone's subversion of the female role (on all these levels) more troubling than we do, especially when set beside the well-grounded acceptance of the normal constraints that is manifested by Ismene. The significance of the separate departures of the two sisters at the end of the prologue – Antigone beyond the city walls to defy the edict of the city's ruler and Ismene back into the house – will not have been lost on them. When Creon identifies Antigone (and, wrongly, Ismene) as 'unleashed', a 'woman on the loose' (578–9), he is pointing to her abandonment of the ordinary constraints under which an Athenian citizen would expect his womenfolk to live.

If the opening scene does create at least an ambivalent and possibly even a negative impression of Antigone, such an impression would be set against what is likely to be an initially positive impression of Creon. His opening speech is so orthodox an expression of the individual's duty to the state that Demosthenes (19. 247) quotes part of it (175–90) as a good example for all who seek power in the *polis*.[50] Creon has summoned the Chorus as honoured and loyal representatives of the city to hear his edict (164–74), and the Chorus never once acknowledge that Antigone is right; even where they sympathize with her plight they continue to rebuke her for her defiance and wild stubbornness. Accordingly, some scholars (especially Sourvinou-Inwood) argue that admiration for Antigone and her stance is anachronistic; an Athenian audience would not have admired her, they allege, but would have seen her action as threatening and subversive, and condemned it on that account.[51]

The argument from the position of women in contemporary Athens, like the one based on Athenian attitudes to treason discussed above, assumes a relation between tragic and everyday norms that is far too simplistic. First, these views essentialize and homogenize the values and attitudes of the fifth-century audience;[52] the multitude of points of view that are given voice in fifth-century tragedies themselves is just one piece of evidence among many of the plurality of political, social, and ethical views in contemporary Athenian society.[53] One can accept the general premise that tragedy must be understood in the light of the norms and values of the society that produced it and yet still reach conclusions that are both firmly based on ancient evidence and radically different from those of Sourvinou-Inwood.[54] Second, approaches of this sort exhibit a naïve and simplistic view of the relation between the products of artistic imagination, the culture from which they spring, and the audiences that receive them. True, tragedy *is*, in its ritual, festive, and poetic origins and in its role as an element in fifth-century Athenian civic and religious life, an art form that is deeply embedded in contemporary Athenian culture. An Athenian audience's experience of tragedy as a mass, popular, civic phenomenon is unlike that of the modern bourgeois theatre-goer. But this does not mean that tragedy's contribution to social, political, ethical, and religious debate is limited to the sort of thing that might arise if one were somehow, by questionnaire or focus-group, able to approximate the views of the average Athenian in the agora.[55]

The differences between the three surviving tragedians in these and in other matters are enough in themselves to demonstrate the importance of artistic creativity.[56] To respond sympathetically to other people, whether in literature or in life, requires imagination, the imagination that it takes to be able to see the other person and his or her situation as in some way relevantly similar to oneself and one's own situation. This power to imagine the lives and experiences of others is immeasurably enhanced by literature. Thus, while the responses of the Homeric Achilles, when faced with Priam's appeal for the return of Hector's body, or of the Sophoclean Odysseus, insisting that his enemy, Ajax, the man who tried to kill him, nonetheless deserves burial, are no doubt unlikely to have been normal in historical situations of war and conflict, they remain available as elements of the repertoire of fifth-century audiences for tragic, epic, and other poetry. One of the ways in which fictional genres, such as drama, extend our capacity for sympathy is precisely that there is no immediate call to put such sympathy into practice. The audience enjoy the luxury of sympathizing with the characters of fiction, broadly defined, with none of the costs that would be incurred by similar responses in 'real life'. Accordingly, considerations of how one might react in real life do not settle questions of how an audience react to drama.

Tragedy draws on fifth-century values and realities, but does not merely replicate them. In particular, its confrontation with heroic myth in a fictionalized setting allows the representation and exploration of many forms of behaviour that would not be open to fifth-century Athenian women. Prominent among such forms of behaviour is the female appropriation of assertive heroic values in times of stress. Female bravery, for example, of a sort that would be quite unthinkable in everyday life, is a recurrent phenomenon in Euripidean tragedy. In the *Children of Heracles* and *Iphigenia at Aulis*, as well as in the fragmentary *Erechtheus*, a central role in the plot is played by a maiden who voluntarily offers herself in sacrifice in order to secure an important good for her community.[57] These maidens are not exactly like Antigone. They are not 'martyrs' and do not manifest their courage in response to male persecution; they benefit the community rather than challenge its leaders and their pronouncements.[58] But they are not typical fifth-century girls next door either. The everyday norms of female behaviour are in fact rather prominent in tragedy, and the relation between such norms and the often larger-than-life female figures that the genre presents is a common topic. But there is no simple correlation between the degree to which a female character in tragedy abides by these norms and the extent to which an audience will support her case or sympathize with her. If Antigone is, according to Creon, a 'woman on the loose' (578–9), so too, according to Clytemnestra, is Electra (Sophocles, *Electra* 516–20; cf. Aegisthus at 1445–6); fifth-century norms regarding the conduct of unmarried women are invoked, but this does not by any means settle the matter of an audience's sympathies, whether moral or emotional. Electra's inability (as she represents it) to abide by such norms is a substantial theme in the play;[59] but her failure to be a good girl by the conventional standards that pertain in ordinary social circumstances in contemporary Athens does not by any means settle the question of whether the matricide that she so fervently supports is justified.

The broader argument regarding the extent to which the play supports a positive judgement of Antigone's actions requires more discussion. We have seen that Creon is proved wrong. For most interpreters, the fact that Creon is wrong is enough to suggest that Antigone is right. The audience are prepared for that eventual judgement, it might be argued, by means of the doubts about Creon's policy that are sown from the very beginning. When Creon justifies his prohibition of burial with reference to the paramount status of civic obligation, the response of his internal audience amounts to much less than an endorsement: the Chorus-leader does not say that Creon is right to proceed as he does, but only that he has the power to do what he wants (211–14).[60] When Creon then demands the Chorus's support (219), their leader indicates that they will side with Creon rather than with a hypothetical opponent for the simple reason that the penalty for doing the latter is death (220). The principle behind Antigone's defiance has been accepted by Ismene in the prologue, but Ismene feels unable to put those principles into practice; the Chorus-leader, for his part, says nothing in endorsement either of Creon's principles or of the wisdom of his proclamation as an embodiment of those principles. Like Ismene, the Chorus-leader merely wishes to remain safe. Neither Ismene nor the Chorus-leader would risk their lives for a principle; but we know already that Antigone will. The question raised by the Chorus-leader's remark at 220 is whether death really is the worst thing there is; whether it is nothing but folly to risk one's life in order to do the right thing. The issue is raised, but the answer is not yet clear.

Though Creon's civic ideals are unobjectionable, there is no word of support for his denial of burial. It soon becomes apparent, too, as he becomes more and more tyrannical in his dealings with the Guard, Antigone, Ismene, Haemon, and finally with Tiresias, that his motivation is much less civic duty than the egotism of a man who is insecure about his own power, even about his own manhood. As this impression of Creon grows, it must surely colour our impression of Antigone. If the positive aspect of his characterization is the soundness of the principles that he enunciates in his opening speech, his character will appear in a less positive light the more it seems that his motivation is personal and ignoble rather than political. The edict itself is never endorsed, and ultimately proves catastrophic. For many readers and spectators, the development of the plot, as it reveals not only that the body should not have been exposed, but also that the man who decreed its exposure is insecure, tyrannical, sadistic, pig-headed, and weak, justifies Antigone's defiance of such a man.

Logically, however, the fact that Creon is wrong does not itself prove that Antigone is right. Perhaps they are both wrong. Perhaps it is right that Polynices should be buried, but wrong for a girl like Antigone to defy familial and civic authority and bury him.[61] The logical possibility that an action may be right under one aspect and wrong under another is by no means an unfamiliar consideration in Greek tragedy. Much of the dialectic of right and wrong as it concerns the cycle of retaliation within the family in Aeschylus' *Oresteia* makes use of this possibility.[62] Just so, one might argue, it is right that Polynices should be buried, but wrong for Antigone to take it upon herself to attempt to bury him. The burial is achieved, and this is right,[63] but Antigone herself does not achieve it: 'The attempt to bury Polynices is a complete failure, as Ismene foresaw, and its *only* consequence is the death of three people.'[64] On this view, Antigone's action is not vindicated either by the demonstration that Creon was wrong or by the necessity of burial, but instead is both wrong (as an act of defiance) and misguided (as a means to the end that Antigone sought to achieve).

Creon and the Chorus condemn Antigone's act, and even Ismene thinks it is crazy. Ismene's argument, however, is not that defiance of Creon is illegitimate, but only that it is impossibly dangerous and inevitably disastrous in its consequences. Creon's condemnation is neither here nor there: we expect him, as Antigone's adversary, to condemn her, and the condemnation of someone whose actions are decisively proved wrong carries little weight. That of the Chorus is more substantial.[65] They are incredulous at Antigone's disobedience and see it as folly (381–3). They comment on the temper that she has inherited from her father and on her refusal to 'yield to misfortune' (471–2), and observe that she retains this defiant spirit to the last (929–30). These judgements focus on her lack of concern for her own safety and her defiant demeanour. But the Chorus also condemn her action as such. She 'advanced to the extreme of boldness' and 'stumbled against the high pedestal of Justice' (853–5; though she may also be paying the penalty for something that her father did, 856). Their final judgement on her conduct concedes her virtuous motives, but also emphasizes her transgression and her responsibility for her own sufferings (872–5):

> To show reverence is a form of piety, but power, in the eyes of one who cares about power, is in no way to be infringed. In your case, it is your self-willed temper that has destroyed you.

The expression, 'to show reverence (*sebein*) is a form of piety (*eusebeia*)', is difficult and paradoxical, but seems designed to make precisely the point raised above, that a single action can express a virtue in one sense, but fail to do so in another. The Greek verb, *sebein*, can be used of the gods and religious duties, but also of human superiors and human institutions. Antigone has shown reverence for her brother and for what she has described as the eternal laws of the gods that demand his burial. But she has shown none for Creon or the *polis*. The Chorus clearly disapprove of Antigone's demeanour; perhaps there is (here, and at 471–2 and 929–30) a suggestion in their minds that a less defiant and more consolatory attitude towards Creon might have led to a different outcome. The interesting aspect of their condemnation of her act of defiance, however, is that it is expressed not from their own perspective, but from that of someone 'who cares about power'. This person is obviously Creon. Creon is onstage,[66] as indeed he has been since Antigone was first led in by the Guard. The Chorus express no judgement on Antigone's action that is not potentially conditioned by the fact of Creon's presence.[67]

The Chorus's one positive judgement on Antigone's action is the somewhat grudging observation that 'to show reverence' is at least a *kind of* piety. But this judgement comes after the audience have heard a much more positive endorsement. The Chorus deprecate the quarrel between Haemon and his father, and they deprecate the sexual passion, the *erôs*, that they take (following Creon's lead at 746, 750, 756, 760–1) to be its cause (781–800); but in the *agôn* between Creon and Haemon itself the Chorus-leader does what Chorus-leaders typically do in *agônes* and commends what he sees as valuable in the arguments of both sides (681–2, 724–5). Haemon has sought to dissuade his father against carrying out his sentence on Antigone, and as part of that argument has given voice to what he says are the 'dark words' that express the city's mourning for her (693–700): she has performed 'the most famous of deeds' and 'deserves golden honour', because she did not leave her own brother unburied, to be devoured by dogs and birds.[68] The 'whole populace of Thebes' approves of her action, he says (733). These may be, as Sourvinou-Inwood observes, unsubstantiated assertions.[69] But even as unsubstantiated assertions they prove incontrovertibly that admiration for Antigone is a potential and authentic fifth-century reaction. The suggestion that it is a purely modern construct is thus simply not tenable. Haemon is not impartial.

None of the positive evaluations of Antigone's actions is – not Ismene's statement the Antigone is 'truly dear to her dear ones' (99), not Antigone's own that her burial of her brother will win her a glorious reputation (502–4), and not Haemon's either. At 504–7 Antigone claims that the Chorus share her own exalted view of her actions, but keep quiet out of fear of Creon. This is unlikely; but Creon *is* an intimidating character (for which we have the Guard's word at 223–36, 238–40, 327–31, and 388–91, as well as the evidence of Creon's own behaviour), and we have seen reason to believe that the Chorus may indeed modify their words as a result of his presence, though not quite in the way that Antigone alleges. For Creon, however, Antigone is wholly isolated – no one else in Thebes thinks like her (508); this in itself should make her ashamed (510). Haemon's claim, therefore, that Antigone does have popular support comes as an inconvenient challenge to Creon's certitude. And when it does come, Creon's reaction is revealing: to Haemon's claim that 'the whole populace of Thebes' approves of Antigone's action, Creon counters (734): 'And will the *polis* tell me what instructions I should give?' This is an attitude he maintains (736, 738): 'Am I to rule this land for anyone but myself? . . . Isn't the *polis* considered to belong to the ruler?' Creon no longer denies that Antigone has popular support; he merely declares an intention to ignore it, since the *polis* is his to treat as he pleases. This presentation does not seem calculated to suggest that there is no substance to Haemon's report; on the contrary, it suggests that Creon is dangerously out of touch.[70] There are ordinary fifth-century values behind what Creon says here; but they are anything but support for his position.[71] Haemon may be partial; but the citizens whose views he reports are not. And though this report is unsubstantiated, there is no encouragement in the scene itself to discount it, and some reason, in Creon's own tacit acceptance, to accept it. One might even suspect that Haemon's reference to an offstage collective judgement implicates the theatrical audience.

One must concede, however, that Haemon's report does not settle the matter: we need more evidence. Prior to Haemon's intervention, Antigone has both stated her principles and provoked Creon with her insolent defiance. Ismene has belatedly attempted to share the responsibility for Antigone's act, and thus provided an additional, though not unbiased, perspective on its rectitude. Creon, for his part, has declared a determination to put both sisters to death, a judgement that he himself soon comes to regard as an error (771), even before his position is undermined by Tiresias. Haemon then provides not only his own positive construction of Antigone's actions, but the reported views of the offstage majority. Support for Antigone in these two episodes is matched by the way that Creon's sound political arguments (which persist: 661–75) are undercut by tyrannical tendencies and personal insecurities. The next episode, in which Antigone laments her journey to her living death, emphasizes the pathos of Antigone's position, but also ends with a challenge that has a crucial bearing on the central issue of right and wrong and a major role in steering audience response to that issue in the scenes that follow. Antigone has a short anapaestic passage of complaint and protest as she is led away (937–43), but apart from that, these are her final words (921–8):

> In what way have I departed from divine justice? Why should I continue to look to the gods, wretched as I am? Who can I call on for support, when, in spite of my piety, I am charged with impiety? If this is right in the eyes of the gods, I shall learn by experience that I have erred. But if it is these men [i.e. Creon] who are in error, may they suffer evils no greater than those they are now inflicting, without justice, upon me.

The issue of Antigone's abandonment by the gods is explicitly raised. If she hopes for salvation, it will not be forthcoming. So perhaps she – and we – learn by experience that she has erred. If, on the other hand, error on her part or on Creon's are the only two possibilities (as she seems to suggest), then it matters that Creon is in fact proved wrong. His sufferings are indeed closely parallel to those he inflicted upon Antigone. Antigone encourages the audience to see the issue of right and wrong as a zero-sum game, and makes what happens to Creon the decisive factor in determining the winner. The obverse of Creon's error is Antigone's vindication.

With these words, Antigone initiates a decisive shift in the plot; from now on, all focus is on what happens to Creon and what this tells us. Tiresias proves conclusively that Creon is wrong: Antigone's term, *hamartanein* (to err, whether intellectually, pragmatically, or ethically), recurs in Tiresias' warning (twice at 1023–8) and in the final verdict on Creon's actions as delivered by the Chorus at 1259–60 and accepted by Creon himself in 1261.[72] That the terrible consequences of Creon's exposure of the body are revealed only after Antigone has been led away and persist despite her attempts at burial is not an indication that her defiance has been futile, but a function of the plot, which requires at this point a motive for Creon belatedly to change his mind. Nothing in the text suggests that the continuing danger of pollution, the cosmic imbalance represented by the still-unburied corpse, constitutes a failure on Antigone's part. Ismene is able to predict dire consequences, yet still to endorse the imperative to which Antigone responds; at a later stage, indeed, when Antigone is apprehended before completing the second burial, Ismene will seek to share the blame, despite Antigone's failure to complete the task. The evaluations of her conduct offered by Haemon (including the judgement of the citizens that he reports) concern the character of her acts themselves, not their consequences. Tiresias' condemnation makes use, for persuasive purposes, of the consequences of Creon's action, and he assumes that, once Creon appreciates those consequences, he will want to remedy his error if he can (1023–32); but his point is not merely that Creon has done something that happens to have turned out badly, but that these are the consequences of an action that was fundamentally wrong, both in violating the dead (1029–30) and in transgressing a universal order whose regulation is a matter for gods, not men (1068–76).

In condemning these actions, Tiresias echoes Antigone's challenge at 925–8: for her, Creon's suffering as she suffered would demonstrate that he, not she, was wrong. Tiresias, for his part, prophesies that Creon will be afflicted by the same evils as he inflicted upon Antigone and Polynices (1064–76, especially 1076: 'so that you are caught up in these same evils'). In reacting to this prophecy, Creon explains his change of mind with reference to his 'fear that it may be best to end one's life in preservation of the established laws' (1113-14). At an earlier stage, the 'laws' that Creon sought to uphold were his own, especially his edict concerning the corpse of Polynices (59-60, 213, 381-2, 449, 452, 481, 663-5, 847). Though there is a superficial, verbal resemblance between Creon's words at 1113-14 and the principles that he claimed to follow earlier in the play,[73] the kind of law that he refers to now is different: the *fiat* of a ruler does not make a law an 'established' one (in spite of his claim at 481);[74] Antigone's view of law, of the laws that are unwritten and unfailing, that live for ever, not just for today and yesterday, has prevailed. To end one's life in the attempt to preserve the established laws – Creon's present participle (σῴζοντα, 'preserving') in 1114 does not imply that the action is completed or successful – is precisely what Antigone has done; this is *ariston*, the best thing (1114). Creon's judgement is not consequentialist, but concerns the principles that he neglected and Antigone espoused. Haemon (710, 723) urges him to *learn* that he is perpetrating injustice (743) by trampling on the prerogatives of the gods (745); as the Chorus point out (1270), Haemon's death does finally enable him to learn where justice (*dikê*) lies; 'I have learned,' he says (1271), but it is too late. Creon's fate confirms Haemon's analysis, and his analysis was that Antigone was right. Close attention to the development of the action in scenic sequence and to the detail of the text makes the argument that Antigone is not vindicated quite untenable.[75] Antigone's 'test' for determining where right lies is fulfilled, and Creon himself is made to demonstrate that his error implies her vindication. But though Antigone is vindicated, she is not saved; this is a topic to which we shall return.

Many good scholars will disagree with the above analysis, and readers will of course reach their own conclusions. The interesting thing is that conclusions are difficult to draw: Antigone is very far from perfect, and although Creon is proved wrong, he is not just a stage tyrant, but rather a well-intentioned man tested in time of stress and found wanting. The *Antigone* is not a study in black and white.

Antigone's principles are vindicated. Creon's principles are not misguided, nor is his aim of keeping the city safe. His remarks on the primacy of the city's interests, remarks that Demosthenes was able to cite in support of a similar point a century later, remain valid in general and attractive to an Athenian audience in particular. We do not conclude from the outset that Creon is a villain. The Chorus's lukewarm response (211–14) is to his proposed treatment of the corpses of Eteocles and Polynices (in 192–206), not to the principles upon which he bases that proposal (175–91, 207–10). If there is anything that undercuts his initial statement of principle, it is not a matter of the content of his speech, the way in which he presents it, or even the fact that we already see him as Antigone's adversary,[76] but simply the emphasis that he himself places on his lack of experience as a leader (162–74: his assumption of power dates only to the deaths of Eteocles and Polynices on the previous day) and (immediately thereafter) on the need to see how a leader performs before pronouncing on his character or judgement (175–7):

> It is impossible thoroughly to learn any man's mind, thought, or judgement until he is tried and tested in office and laws.

Creon sets himself high standards, of putting the safety of the city before other considerations (184–90), and invites us to judge him, an untested ruler, by results. The aims that he enunciates remain valid, but he fails to achieve them. The decision that he justifies in his opening speech proves to have endangered the city – 'the city suffers this sickness as a result of your thinking', as Tiresias says at 1015. That decision, significantly enough, is presented as Creon's *phronêma* ('Such is my thinking', he says at 207, having explained his proclamation at 192–206); at 175–7 he said that it is impossible to discover a man's *phronêma* until he is tested in office. The test of Creon's way of thinking (*phronêma*, 176) is the failure of his policy with regard to the corpse of Polynices (*phronêma*, 207).[77] In a sense, the principles of both characters are validated; but Creon falls short both in the policy that his principles sustain and in the extent to which he puts his aims and his principles into practice. Yet there is much more to the play than principle.

Which side are you on?

To an extent, our sympathy or antipathy towards the characters can vary independently of the above considerations regarding the issues of right and wrong. As Malcolm Heath has pointed out, positive feelings towards a dramatic character can override and depart from moral judgement, provided that we can be induced to be well disposed for other reasons, just as arguments can be morally justified, yet the characters themselves unsympathetic; goodwill and antipathy are subject to various forms of bias, in drama and in life.[78] Perhaps the most remarkable thing in this regard in the *Antigone* is Sophocles' success in eliciting total sympathy for Creon by the end of the play. And there can be no doubt that this sympathy is meant to be total. The Messenger takes considerable care, before delivering his report of the scene in Antigone's tomb, to emphasize Creon's status as a paradigm of the mutability of fortune (1155–71). As we saw, Antigone is not mentioned again once he has delivered that speech. In the final scenes, the deaths of Haemon and Eurydice attract greater emphasis than that of Antigone. Their bodies are visible, and form the focus for the onstage performance of Creon's utter despair. The sympathy that this elicits is all the more remarkable because Creon had, prior to his change of mind, become a highly unsympathetic character. There are signs throughout that the Chorus are afraid of him, signs that are taken up by the semi-comic anxieties of the Guard. Such fears are justified by his anger at the Chorus-leader (280–1), his paranoia about conspiracies against his rule (289–303), and his threats to punish the (innocent) guards if the culprit is not found (304–26). His comments about breaking Antigone's will as if she were a slave or even an animal are repellent (473–9). He is insecure about his own masculinity (484, 525, 678–80), and about what he sees as a challenge to his status on the part of Haemon (726–7, 740, 746, 756). He sentences Ismene to death, despite her innocence (488–96, 530–81), and delivers what has been called 'perhaps the coarsest line in Greek tragedy' in his observation that there are other fields for Haemon to plough (569).[79] In the *agôn* with Haemon he descends into despotism

(667, 734–9, 744). His conspiracy theory resurfaces in response to Tiresias' warnings (1033–47), before he begins to hesitate (1095–7): it is a dreadful thing to change one's mind, but better that than risk ruin. Yet while all this is going on, there is a growing certainty that disaster awaits him, and when it strikes, no detail is allowed which would mitigate our sympathy.

As with Creon, so with Antigone, unalloyed sympathy becomes certain only as the catastrophe overtakes her. In the opening scene we have Ismene to guide our impression that Antigone is right to be horrified at the edict, but Ismene also, as an ordinary young woman, provides a pronounced contrast that reveals Antigone as an extraordinary, harsh, and extreme figure. Out of duty to one sibling, who is dead, she treats another (who is alive) as an enemy (69–77, 86–7, 93–4). She actively hopes that her defiance of Creon's edict is discovered and proclaimed (86–7) – she has 'a hot heart for cold deeds' (88) and is 'in love with the impossible' (90). She embraces the idea of death (72–6) and looks forward to lying beside her dear brother for ever (73, 76). We shall return in a subsequent chapter to her fixation with death and with her dead brother; but part of that fixation is certainly her deliberate provocation of Creon, her active pursuit of the death penalty that Creon has laid down (458–70, 497–500, 559–60).

And yet, in that same opening scene, there is stress on the history of suffering in Antigone's family (2–6, 11–14, 49–57), and it is clear that non-burial is a further painful indignity for both Antigone and Ismene. It is also clear that Antigone's resolve to bury the body is virtually certain to bring about her death (44, 47, 82, 84–5), and Ismene's emphasis on the difficulty of women defying the will of men (61–8, cf. 78–9, 90, 92) also stresses the extraordinary courage of Antigone's attempt. Eventually the pathos of all this is brought out, as Antigone re-emerges from the palace to sing a song that replaces both the funeral lament and the wedding song that she will never have. At this point, even the Chorus pity her (801–5), though they continue to criticize her defiance. The major theme in the ensuing scene before Antigone's departure (806–943) is the notion that, for her, death replaces marriage.

This idea features as a theme in epitaphs of girls who died young,[80] a sign of the pathos that was, to Greek eyes, inherent in a girl's failure to fulfil the purpose of a woman's existence in marriage and childbirth. Antigone's final scene is clearly meant to be deeply moving.

The play is therefore constructed in such a way that we are to sympathize, in the emotional sense at least, with both main characters, though neither is wholly sympathetic. These emotional sympathies will, at different points in the play, very probably run counter to an audience's, and perhaps especially an ancient audience's, evaluation of the rights and wrongs of the characters' actions.[81] Antigone's abandonment of the woman's role and defiance of political authority perhaps alienated some spectators, whereas Creon's initial stance may have appeared justified. Antigone's behaviour continues to be problematic in many respects, even as her actions are vindicated; while Creon rapidly becomes egotistical, cruel, and despotic, before his policy is unambiguously shown to be wrong. Yet the final appearances of both – the second *kommos* mirroring the first,[82] Creon's lamentation as extensive as that which he had earlier brusquely condemned on Antigone's part – present them as characteristic specimens of suffering humanity, and we sympathize.

Progress and Pessimism

The first stasimon

The play's first stasimon (332–75) is notable for its reflection of contemporary fifth-century debate on the origins of culture, the development of civilization, and the human potential for progress. Similar ideas surface in other fifth-century sources,[1] and were probably generally 'in the air' in the middle of the fifth century; but there is a strong similarity between these passages and the extended account of human progress offered by the prominent fifth-century thinker, Protagoras, in Plato's (fourth-century) dialogue of that name, and Protagoras – famously associated with the dictum that 'man is the measure of all things' – was no doubt the most prominent fifth-century exponent of such views.[2] The position that technological and cultural progress depends on the rational capacities which have allowed human beings to master their natural environment and establish civilized communities stands in sharp contrast to what might be regarded as the traditional 'archaic' view, as represented in Hesiod's *Works and Days*, of a decline from better to worse conditions of existence.[3]

As examples of human skill (*technê*) the Chorus offer seafaring (334–7); agriculture (337–41); hunting and fishing (342–8); the taming of animals (348–52); language, thought, and law (354–6); house-building (365–60); and medicine (361–3). But there are limits: medicine cannot protect us from death (361–2). And there are qualifications: skill has bad as well as good applications, good and bad outcomes (365–7). The limits and ambivalence of *technê* that are explicit in these lines are in fact implicit throughout the ode. There is ambivalence in the ode's striking opening phrase ('Wonders are many, and there is nothing more

wonderful than humanity'): the adjective *deinos* covers a wide range
from 'clever' to 'strange', but its etymological roots are in words denoting
fear. It means not only 'formidable', but also 'terrible'. The activity of
ploughing that is central to the development of agriculture involves
'wearing away the highest [i.e. the oldest, but also the most reverend] of
the gods, earth the unwaning, the unwearying' (337–9).[4] 'Thought'
(*phronêma*) is 'windy' (354), which suggests speed, but also lack of
substance. The word *phronêma* itself can also mean 'pride'. Antigone will
use it contemptuously of the insignificance of human thought in the
face of eternal divine law at 459. As we saw in Chapter 2, the term has
already been used by Creon at 176 and 207 in a way that invites an
audience to be prepared to evaluate his way of thinking as it is tested in
practice. Man (for the subject has narrowed from *anthrôpos*, humanity,
in 332–3 to *anêr*, man, in 348) has 'taught himself the dispositions of
civic order' (355–6); but *orgai* (dispositions) is the plural of the regular
Greek word for 'anger' – an emotion of which Creon has already shown
ample evidence in his response to the news that someone has sprinkled
dust on the corpse of Polynices (244, 280–314), especially in his reaction
to the Chorus-leader's suggestion that the deed may be the work of the
gods (280: 'Stop, before your words fill me with *orgê*'). Man has resources
for everything (360); he advances towards nothing that is to come
without resources (360–1). But the inability of ordinary human beings
to safeguard themselves against future eventualities is proverbial; the
notion that man is resourceful in all respects is immediately contradicted
in the reference to death (361–2), and the sense that one is prepared
for every eventuality is precisely what is described in the next stanza
(365–7) as the kind of cleverness or skill that is 'beyond hope', yet only
sometimes successful.[5]

The ode's ambivalence is underscored by its intertextual relationships
with other prominent Athenian texts.[6] It has two especially prominent
Athenian forebears. One is a passage by the statesman and poet, Solon
(13. 43–76 W).[7] Like Sophocles' ode, this takes the form of a list of
examples of human skill, a *Priamel*. The first, second, and final examples
in both lists are the same: seafaring (Solon 13. 43–6); agriculture and

ploughing (47–8); medicine (57–62).[8] The presence of one item in Solon's list, namely seercraft (53–6), illuminates one aspect of Sophocles' version. Like Solon's seer, Sophocles' 'man' has resources with regard to the future (*Ant.* 360–1); but seers (such as the one we shall encounter later in Sophocles' play) have powers that ordinary men do not. Yet, according to Solon, though a seer can discern the evil that is coming, not even he can avert what is fated. Solon's examples all concern the limitations of the skills that he lists; and the wider context of his remarks is one of the power of fate, the instability of fortune, the ambivalence of wealth, and the prevalence of a phenomenon called *atê* that we shall explore below.

The other major Athenian intertext is the first stasimon of Aeschylus' *Libation Bearers* (585–651).[9] This also begins with a *Priamel*, but more than that, its opening words are closely similar to those of our ode; compare Aeschylus' 'Many (*polla*) are the terrible (*deina*) afflictions of fear …' (585–6) with Sophocles' 'Wonders are many …' (*polla ta deina*, 332). Where our ode then moves from sea to land to sky, the Aeschylean Chorus similarly encompasses earth (personified in 585, as in *Ant.* 338–9), sea, and sky (585–93), before focusing on the 'excessively daring *phronêma* of man' (594–5); 'excessively daring', (*hypertolmon*) answers to 'for the sake of daring' (*tolma*) at *Ant.* 371–2, *phronêma* (here clearly in its negative sense) to the same word at *Ant.* 355,[10] and 'man' (*anêr*) to the same word in *Ant.* 347. The point of the Aeschylean ode, however, is the wicked passions of *women* (596–8), which are then illustrated by a catalogue of bad women,[11] analogues to Clytemnestra, whose just punishment awaits at the hands of her son.

Both these major intertexts raise the issues of right and wrong that arise only in the final stanza of the 'Ode to Man' (365–75), and both might be said to present them within a traditional, 'archaic' moral and theological framework. The 'Ode to Man' combines these influences with a more contemporary-sounding praise of human achievement and progress, but both the ode's intertextual associations and its internal ambivalences suggest that its optimistic orientation is only superficial.[12] It is its closing emphasis on the limits and ambivalence of human ingenuity that contextualize it, within its immediate context, within the play in general, and within wider traditions of Greek thought. Its concluding words, in particular, make the connection between the ode and the immediately preceding action of the play (368–75):

> If he honours the laws of the land [or 'earth': *chthôn*] and the justice of the gods that one swears to observe, he is high in the city; without a city is he who recklessly associates with wrong. May no one who does these things ever share my hearth or my thoughts.

Ostensibly, the Chorus are saying that the preceding reflections on human ingenuity were prompted by the attempted burial of Polynices' body: that action required the kind of daring that demonstrates the negative side of human intelligence. The Chorus assume (as did Creon at 248) that the perpetrator is a man. The audience, however, know that it was a woman, and will see the irony not only in the reference to 'very clever man (*anêr*)' at 348 but also in the ode's evocation of the *Libation Bearers'* powerful ode on the crimes of women. But in that ode, too, doubts about the *phronêma* of men were raised as a counterpoint to the wickedness of women. Sophocles' ode similarly raises the question of whether right, in this instance, lies with the woman or the man. We know that the burial was performed by a woman, not a man; but is that woman a criminal, as in the *Libation Bearers,* or does the daring that the Chorus condemn belong to a man who sought to exert his mastery over Earth, supreme of the gods (338), and over Hades (361)? How stable is his 'windy *phronêma*', and will his *orgai* preserve the city's laws (354–5) or will they fall foul of the 'laws of earth and the justice of the gods' (368–9)? The 'Ode to Man' is a response to the confidence in his own powers that Creon manifested in his opening speech, and to the characteristics that he displayed in his interactions with the Chorus and the Guard, and not only to the supposed ingenuity of the transgressor who buried the body.[13] It invites us to consider Creon's faith in his own understanding, his particular application of political skill, and his specific use of his legislative powers in the light both of contemporary theories which make great claims for such capacities and of a more traditional framework that stresses the fallibility and vulnerability of human rationality.

The first and second stasima compared

The second stasimon (583–625), delivered after Antigone has been revealed as the transgressor whose actions prompted the first stasimon, offers in some respects a different perspective, but in others actualizes many of the implications that were latent in the first.

The ode begins with a traditional speech genre, *makarismos* ('Happy are those who …') and continues in a traditional vein: happiness, *eudaimonia*, is impossible in a house that is shaken by the gods (583–4); in that case, all that remains is *atê*, ruin (584–5). Just such a house is Antigone's, the House of Labdacus, whose generations of trouble are continuing in the sufferings of its surviving members, and particularly in the death penalty that (in the preceding scene) was pronounced on both Antigone and Ismene (594–603). In the second pair of stanzas, the Chorus sing of the inability of men's transgression (and again the word is *andres*, 604–5) to overcome the power of Zeus, and of the ruin, *atê*, that appears (the text is uncertain) especially to attend the rich,[14] and then of the hopes and delusions that lead men (*andres* again, 616) blindly to act in ways that bring disaster (615–20), before concluding with an endorsement of the traditional wisdom that 'sooner or later bad seems good to a man whose mind a god is leading towards disaster (*atê*). He fares but the shortest time without *atê*' (620–5).

The archaic notion of *atê*, prominent in poets such as Homer, Solon, and Aeschylus, is the keynote of the ode.[15] In each of its four occurrences, its immediate reference is to ruin or disaster. But traditionally, and especially in Homer, *atê* is a more inclusive term, covering the disastrous mental aberration that leads people to ruin as well as the ruin that results from such aberration, and in *Antigone*, too, disaster affects the mind as well as one's fortunes ('whose mind a god is leading towards *atê*', 623–4).[16] Similarly, in line 603, the cause of disaster is traced to 'senselessness of speech (*logos*) and a Fury (Erinys) of the mind', phrases which suggest the sense of *atê* as mental aberration.[17] In the final stanza, hope is said to be beneficial in some circumstances (616), but also 'much-wandering' and so prone to delusion (615);[18] for many it amounts to no more that the 'deception (*apata*) of empty-headed passions' (617). Thus, by a popular etymology already familiar in Homer, *atê* (or, in the language of tragic lyric, *ata*) is brought into relation with *apatê*/*apata*, deception.[19] The victim of deception (the Chorus go on) knows nothing until it is too late (618–19),[20] because bad seems good to those whose minds the gods are leading to disaster (620–5). This notion, that divine deception combines with human folly in bringing human beings to destruction, has a pedigree in archaic thought: it is (for example) expressed using both *atê* and *apatê* in a memorable passage of the parodos of Aeschylus' *Persians* and reprised in the subsequent scene between the Ghost of Darius and his Queen.[21] In the second stasimon in general *atê* brings with it a whole set of wider associations (the gap between aims and outcomes, the instability of wealth and prosperity, and the notion that this instability has causes both in humans' own errors, delusions, and transgressions and in the plans of the gods), and it is evident that the concept has its full Homeric or Aeschylean scope.[22]

But *atê* is also a prominent notion in the poem of Solon that is evoked in the first stasimon; it occurs too in the ode from Aeschylus' *Libation Bearers* that is similarly evoked there. The first and second stasima are linked by a series of verbal and conceptual echoes. In particular, their beginnings are closely parallel. They both begin with arresting, proverbial-sounding statements on the human condition, before proceeding to a more specific case. In the first stasimon, the first example of mankind's ingenuity is seafaring (332–7), while in the second, the divine 'shaking' of a house, which entails all kinds of *atê*, is compared to a storm at sea (586–92), reinforced by verbal echoes of the root *pont-* (sea, 335/586) and the word *oidma* (swell, 337/587),[23] the metaphorical winds that represent *atê* in the second perhaps additionally recalling the 'windy thought' of the first (especially *dysanemos*, 591, and *anemoeis*, 353). In the first stasimon the sea represents human achievement; in the second its limits. The second stasimon then moves on to the House of Labdacus, while the next point in the first stasimon is mankind's invention of agriculture, but again the two themes are linked: mankind wears away Earth, supreme of the gods, the immortal (*aphthitos*), the unwearied (*akamatos*),[24] as the plough turns, year on year (338–40), while in the House of Labdacus woe falls on woe in a similar, incessant rhythm; where Earth is immortal and unwearied in the first stasimon, in the second the Labdacids experience further woes over and above those of the dead (*phthitoi*, 595) and it is the 'months of the gods' (607–8), through which the power of Zeus remains undiminished, that are 'unwearied' (*akamatoi*). Earth is the oldest and most august of the gods, but the Labdacids are the gods' victims (genitive plural of *theos* at both 337 and 597); and the agriculture that is a sign of human inventiveness in the first stasimon is echoed in the 'harvesting' of the 'last root' of the House of Oedipus (599–602). There is no escape (597), just as there was none from death, in the first stasimon's most explicit statement of the limits of human resourcefulness (362).

The second stasimon also resembles the first in narrowing its focus from humanity in general to men in particular (*andres*, 604–5, 616; *anêr*, 348), notably so in both cases, given that the event that prompts the first is what the audience know to have been the act of a woman, while the ruminations on the fate of the Labdacids in the second are prompted by the imposition of the death penalty upon its two surviving members, both female. In the first stasimon, speech (*phthegma*) and thought (*phronêma*) were central to man's achievement (354–5), while in the second 'senselessness in speech (*logos*) and a Fury of the mind (*phrenes*)' are the cause of the extirpation of the House of Oedipus (603). In the second stasimon, minds (*phrenes*) can be led, by a god, towards *atê* (623–4), for it is a law (*nomos*, 613) that no mortal transgression can restrain the power of Zeus (604–5); in the first, man's 'city-legislating (*astynomos*) dispositions' (355–6) had to respect both the law of the land and the justice of the gods if he was to be high in his city (368–70). In the first stasimon, man advanced towards the future (*to mellon*) confident that his resources would suffice (360–1); but in the second it is the law of Zeus, the law that confirms his power and dictates that no great wealth (or nothing great) comes to mortals without *atê*, that prevails 'now and in the future (*to mellon*) and in the past' (611–12). For hope (*elpis*) may be no more than 'the deception of light-minded (*kouphonoos*) passions' (615–17), so that a man comes (*herpein*) unawares to disaster (618–20); with wisdom (*sophia*, 620) has it been said, that bad (*kakon*) seems good (*esthlon*) to one whose mind a god is leading towards *atê* (620–4). Just so, in the first stasimon (365–7), man might rely 'beyond hope' (*elpis*) on his wisdom (*sophos*), yet come (*herpein*) now to bad (*kakon*), now to good (*esthlon*). His passionate aims, in the second stasimon, may in the end be as 'light-minded' (*kouphonoos*) as the birds he traps in his nets in the first (342).[25]

Not all of these thematic and verbal correspondences are equally salient; but it does not matter whether the audience catch all or only some of them, for in fact all serve a single overall purpose: the contrast between the potential of human reason and its limits and failings – a contrast that is inherent in the first stasimon itself, but deepened and extended by means of the relation that exists between the first and the second. In picking up a theme that is prominent in the first stasimon's intertexts, and especially in Solon 13, the second stasimon brings in the emphasis on the instability of human happiness, the ambivalence of wealth and prosperity, and the dangers of *atê* in that poem that were omitted, but perhaps still evoked, in the first stasimon.[26]

Delusion and disaster

The extent to which such prominent notions of archaic Greek thought pervade and shape the entire play is often underestimated. The immediate application of the Chorus's words in the second stasimon is to Antigone's family, the Labdacids: theirs is the house which is currently being shaken (583), theirs the ancient sorrows, the interminable and divinely inspired generations of suffering, that have now manifested themselves in the disaster which has overtaken Antigone (594–603). If we follow the apparent direction of the Chorus's argument, so too Antigone must, at least in their minds, have contributed to her plight by her own lack of sense (*anoia*) and under the influence of a 'Fury of the mind'. The application of the second strophic pair (604–25) to Antigone is more of a challenge, but *atê* is still the theme – explicitly, and with reference to objective misfortune, at 613–14 and 624–5; implicitly (and encompassing the term's subjective aspect, i.e. delusion) in the deceptive and foolish variety of hope that brings one to unexpected disaster (615–19) and in the divine deception that makes bad seem good to one whom a god is leading to *atê* (622–4). But if Antigone can, in the first antistrophe, be said to be under the influence of a Fury of the mind that is adding to the generations of suffering in the House of Labdacus, then these statements, at least on the explicit level, can be applied to her or her family too. This must also be the case, at least at the surface level, in the presentation of the view that no great wealth (or nothing great) comes to mortals without *atê* as an eternally valid and vigilant law of Zeus that withstands men's transgression (604–5).

The notion of inherited guilt or suffering is prominent in the poem of Solon that we have already noted as an important intertext for both the first and the second stasimon.[27] But the second stasimon's explanation of Antigone's situation is also thoroughly Aeschylean, with several direct and striking verbal echoes of the great ode that the Chorus sing in the *Seven against Thebes* when it becomes clear that the combat between Eteocles and Polynices will fulfil the curse of Oedipus and furnish a further stage in family's generations of trouble (720–91).[28] Both odes focus on the family's recurrent cycle of suffering (*Ant.* 593–6, *Seven* 739–41); both present these using the image of a sea of troubles (*Ant.* 586–9, *Seven* 758–60); in both, the origin of the suffering lies in some transgression (*Ant.* 604–5, *Seven* 742–3); and both combine references to mental disturbance and the demonic influence of an Erinys, a Fury (*Ant.* 603, *Seven* 722–5, 756–7, 790–1).[29]

In Solon, the innocent may pay for the crimes of their parents and grandparents (Solon 13. 31–2), but in the *Seven* the latest horror, though part of a cycle of suffering that begins with a grandfather's transgression, is also an act of madness that the Chorus abhor. So, too, in *Antigone*, the Chorus seem to see the workings of the 'Fury of the mind' in terms of forms of transgression and delusion that are currently operative in the events that they have just witnessed.

This Aeschylean explanation is not out of step with other evaluations elsewhere in the play. The issue of *atê* in Antigone's family is almost certainly (despite textual corruption) raised in her very first lines in the play (4), and Ismene confirms the theme at 17 (she has had no further news to suggest that she is either more fortunate or more afflicted by *atê*). Ismene's elaboration of this point at 49–60 uses no *atê*-word, but in effect prefigures the Chorus's point in the second stasimon (594–603): she and Antigone are the last of the family, and Antigone's plan to bury the body of Polynices, in defiance of Creon's edict, constitutes a further instalment in the ills that this family has inflicted upon itself. Creon keeps the issue of Antigone's *atê* before us at 485, when he claims that she will not defy him 'without *atê*'. The point that *atê* runs in her family is then rehearsed by Antigone herself at 863–5, where she laments the *atai* of her parents' incest. The consequences of Antigone's actions in burying her brother can be regarded, at least by Creon and the Chorus, as *atê*, and the Chorus, Ismene, and Antigone herself are united in their opinion that *atê* has bedevilled their family in the past. The Chorus's view that there are hereditary reasons for her behaviour and its consequences is one that they put forward more than once elsewhere, both before and after the second stasimon. At 379–80 she is the 'unhappy child of an unhappy father', and at 471–2 she has inherited her father's 'raw' or 'savage' temperament. At 856 they wonder whether her ordeal may be payment for some debt that Oedipus incurred. This touches a nerve (857–8), and she refers to her father's travails, those of the entire Labdacid clan, the *atai* of her parents' incest, and the wretchedness of her own state as a reflection of theirs (859–66).[30] Now, she continues, she goes to join them, 'accursed and unwed' (867). This use of the adjective *araios*, accursed, is the only positive indication in the play that the sufferings of Antigone may have an origin in an actual curse.[31] With the exception of direct references to Oedipus, his wife, and their sons, the play's allusions to the mythological background of the Labdacid family are so sparse and unspecific that one could never be sure that it assumes familiarity with a version in which a curse doomed not only Eteocles and Polynices,[32] but the entire family; yet the basic idea that Antigone's actions and their consequences fall into a pattern that is repeated in the history of her family is well established in the text.

For the Chorus in the second stasimon, *atê* in the sense of 'disaster' has among its causes 'senselessness of speech and an Erinys of the mind' (603), transgression (*hyperbasia*, 605), the 'deception of light-minded passions' (617), failure to foresee the harm that one's actions will cause (618–20), and the confusion of good and bad that afflicts those whose mind a god is leading to disaster (622–4). This language of mental disturbance, misjudgement, and transgression is also widely applied to Antigone. Her proposal to defy Creon's edict exhibits no sense (*nous*), according to Ismene at 67–8 (cf. 'senseless', *anous*, 99); she is 'in love with the impossible' (90, cf. 'hunting the impossible', 92);[33] even Antigone herself refers ironically to the inevitable representation of her actions as a crime (74) and as folly, *dysboulia* (95). Accordingly, when the Chorus see her, the 'unhappy child of an unhappy father' (379–80), being led in as the one who has disobeyed 'the king's laws' (382), they describe the act for which she has been arrested as one of madness (*aphrosynê*, 383). The theme is taken up by Creon. Ismene's intervention in her sister's support is for him confirmation that she has begun to manifest the lack of reason that Antigone has shown from birth (561–2), his use of the adjective *anous* echoing Ismene's own at 99 and prefiguring the Chorus's *anoia* at 603. In the scene that precedes the second stasimon, Creon charges Antigone with 'transgressing the laws' (*hyperbainein*, 449; cf. 605), and Antigone counters with her famously defiant reply (450–70), something that the Chorus-leader sees as a reflection of the character that she has inherited from her father (471–2). For Creon, her behaviour in defiantly justifying her position is a form of *hybris* (arrogant over-confidence that amounts to contempt for others) that compounds the *hybris* that she has already shown in 'transgressing (*hyperbainein*) the laws that had been laid down' (480–3); but this *hybris*, he is determined to show, will lead to *atê* (she will not challenge his power without *atê*, 485).[34]

The link between *hyperbasia*, *hybris*, and *atê* at 480–5 points to the presence of the same set of associations in the ensuing second stasimon (604–14), where the second strophe opens with *hyperbasia* (605) and ends with a reference to the wealth or success that results in *atê* (613–14). *Hybris* is not mentioned, but *hybris* and *koros* are the missing links in the familiar 'archaic chain' that links *atê*, the result, to its causes in the inability to deal appropriately with wealth and success.[35] The chain is equally apparent in the stasimon's preceding stanza: the extirpation of the House of Oedipus has its cause in 'senselessness of speech and a Fury of the mind' (601–3). This is *atê* in both its subjective and objective aspects, both 'delusion' and 'disaster'. In a familiar image, the disaster is presented as 'harvest' – a harvest of *atê*.[36] The presentation of Antigone's actions in terms of *atê* is not only prominent in the scene that precedes the second stasimon, but also involves a wider nexus of characteristically 'archaic' notions with which *atê* is traditionally associated.

The representation of Antigone's actions as irrational and transgressive continues after the second stasimon. It is her behaviour that prompts Creon, addressing Haemon, to reflect in general terms on the dangers of transgression and the importance of obedience (663–5):

No one who transgresses by violating the law or by presuming to give orders to his rulers will get any praise from me.

Equally, in the final scene before Antigone is led away to her death, both she and the Chorus return, in language that repeatedly recalls the second stasimon, to Antigone's transgression, its causes, and its results. The Chorus's lyric iambics at 853–6 link her 'advance to the limit of daring' (853) with her 'fall before the pedestal of Justice' (854–5) and seek a cause for her suffering in her 'repayment' of a debt incurred by her father (856). Antigone, as we have seen, immediately responds with a reference to the sufferings of the Labdacids, including the *atai* of her parents' incest.[37] The latest instalment of those sufferings is Antigone's own death, brought about by her actions in burying Polynices (869–71);

but for the Chorus, though this act manifests *eusebeia*, piety, of a sort (872), it remains a transgression (873–4) rooted in Antigone's passionate and self-willed nature; it is this that has destroyed her (875). This is an interpretation that Antigone disputes in her final words in the play: what divine law has she transgressed (921)? Yet she is apparently abandoned by the gods, and, though pious, has been branded with impiety (*dyssebeia*, 924). As she is led away to her tomb she calls once more on the Chorus, as leading men of Thebes, to witness the injustice of her treatment, 'for revering reverence' (943).

There is thus plenty of purchase in the text of the play for the view enunciated by the Chorus in the second stasimon that Antigone comes to ruin as a result of a transgression that is at once a product of irrational elements in her own character and a reflection of a recurrent sequence of transgressions and sufferings in her family. Both of these factors answer to aspects of *atê* familiar in Sophocles' day especially from the works of Homer, Solon, and Aeschylus. As an account of Antigone's situation, the second stasimon's recourse to the archaic notion of *atê* is by no means a localized perspective; it is a construction that pervades both others' perceptions of Antigone and the self-representation that seeks to contest those perceptions. But this is not the end of the story.

Antigone's complaint that, despite her piety, she has apparently been abandoned by the gods is immediately qualified, in words that bear crucially on the issue of her *atê* (925–8):

> However that may be, if this is fitting in the eyes of the gods, we shall learn through our suffering that we have erred. But if it is these men [i.e. Creon] who are in error, may they suffer evils no greater than those that they are now inflicting, without justice, upon me.

In Homer and in Aeschylus, *atê* is regularly a name for a process in which an error leads to disaster and regret.[38] The association between *atê* and error (*hamartia*) is as old as the speech of Phoenix to Achilles in the Embassy of *Iliad* 9, where the allegory of the Prayers who attempt to heal the damage that (the personified) Ate has done is presented as an amplification of the argument that even the gods accept entreaty from an offender who wishes to make amends for transgression (*hyperbasia*) and *hamartia* (*Iliad* 9.501). The closeness of the association, in archaic poetry and tragedy, is demonstrated in a seminal study by Roger Dawe.[39] But in spite of all that she has said in 806–923 about the horror, pathos, and injustice of her fate, Antigone does not think she is in error and never regrets her deed;[40] her words in lines 925–6 represent a rejected hypothesis that serves as a foil for the eventuality for which she prays, which she regards as more likely, and which does in fact come to pass.[41] Antigone highlights the crucial role of results in the determination of *atê* – a mistake that does not lead to disastrous results is not *atê*. By definition, an agent who is subject to *atê* does not foresee the disaster to come; an observer might, but only results will prove that person correct.[42] Antigone *is* suffering, and she certainly regards her lot as a calamity. There is material here for others to draw conclusions in terms of *atê* on her part, as indeed the Chorus have done.[43] But as Antigone herself represents the situation, the results of her action are not yet in; they will be clear only when we learn what in fact happens to Creon.

This takes us back to the second stasimon. We saw that the Chorus's language of transgression (605) could, given parallels elsewhere in the play, be taken as a reference to Antigone (possibly also including an allusion to further but unspecified transgressions in the history of her family). Similarly, on one level, at least, the notion that no great wealth (or nothing great) comes to mortals without *atê* could be taken as a lesson drawn from the sufferings of the Labdacids. But the eternal laws of Zeus whose transgression brings disaster (604–15) sound more like the principles that Antigone claimed to uphold at 450–7. If Antigone is right about the import of these laws (and Creon's conclusion at 1113–14 – that 'it may be best to end one's life in preservation of the established laws' – suggests that she is),[44] then Creon, and not she, is their violator.[45]

And in fact the association of Creon with the theme of *atê* is even more pervasive and explicit than it is in the case of Antigone. His first reference to the concept comes in that crucial first speech in which he sets out the principles behind his prohibition of Polynices' burial (184–6):

As Zeus who sees all at all times is my witness, I could not keep silent
if I saw *atê* advancing upon the citizens in place of safety (*sôtêria*) . . .

This observation comes in a speech in which Creon emphasizes his
inexperience as a leader (170-4) and expresses his conviction that only
time will reveal a man's – especially a ruler's – character and judgement
(175-7), a maxim attributed to Bias of Priene, one of the Seven Sages of
archaic Greece.[46] The foresight to which Creon aspires in 184-6 is a
traditional mark of the good political and military leader;[47] but it
remains to be seen whether his aspiration will be realized. Taken
together, these statements encourage an audience to focus on the future,
on the consequences of Creon's action in prohibiting burial. This is
where *atê* comes in, for *atê* rests fundamentally upon the relation
between intention, action, and result: *atê* (at least as exploited in the
Iliad and in the plays of Aeschylus) is not simply any calamity, but one
that arises from a catastrophic failure to foresee that disaster is a
potential outcome of one's choices.[48] Creon is determined to speak up
should he see *atê* advancing on his fellow citizens; but *atê*, the disaster
that results from one's own delusion, is not something that one sees
coming. Zeus sees everything and Zeus is the one who knows (184), but
Creon does not.[49] Lines 184-6 establish *atê* as a potential opponent that
may come upon Creon despite his attempts to guard against it; just so,
in the second stasimon, *atê* is something that 'moves towards' the
generations of a family whose house is shaken by god (584-5), no great
wealth (or nothing great) 'comes to' mortals without *atê* (613-14), and
the negative consequences of the harmful *elpis* that is really a deception
(with the play on *atê/apatê* that we have already noted) 'come upon' a
person unawares (618-19). Lines 184-6 thus place *atê* firmly in a
thematic nexus that unites the play's abundant references to good and
bad judgement and their good and bad outcomes. Though we do not at
this stage necessarily reach a firm conclusion that Creon is doomed and
his precepts misguided, we have been alerted to the *atê* that may be
advancing upon Thebes as a result of his actions.

In their personification of *atê*, the link that they suggest between the
quality of Creon's judgement and its potential effects upon the citizens

of Thebes, and their antithesis between *atê* and safety (*sôtêria*), Creon's
words introduce themes that pervade the rest of the play. The association
with safety immediately recurs in Creon's concluding remarks to the
Guard at 304–14. He again raises the issue of the relation between
Zeus's purposes and his own ('If Zeus retains my respect . . ', 304), before
concluding his threat to punish the guards if they do not find 'the
perpetrator of this burial' (306) with a statement of the lesson that he
believes such punishment would impart (310–14):

> in order that you should in future conduct your depredations knowing
> whence profit (*kerdos*) is to be won, and learn that it is not right to love
> profiting from any source. For you would see that more are ruined
> [afflicted by *atê*] as a result of shameful profits than are saved [achieve
> *sôtêria*].

The initial opposition between *atê* and safety now blends into one
between *atê* and *kerdos*, a frequent antithesis that indicates the term's
core sense of 'loss' as opposed to 'profit'.[50] Since *kerdos* is one of the play's
key themes,[51] this is further evidence of *atê*'s deep roots in the conceptual
structure of the play.

Creon's conviction that Antigone will not defy him 'without *atê*' (484–5)
raises the question of whose the *atê* will be. The role of *atê* as a link
between the two is suggested by Creon's description of Antigone and
Ismene as 'two Atai' at 532–3: 'I did not realize that I was nurturing two
Ruins (Atai), to overthrow my throne'.[52] Creon imagines that he has
diagnosed a source of ruin and nipped it in the bud; but in the end he is
ruined, and his royal power is destroyed; he has not yet learned the extent
to which Antigone instantiates his *atê*. The suggestion made by Antigone
herself at 925–8, that her own suffering will be answered by equal suffering
on Creon's part, is here foreshadowed in the notion that Antigone will be
the embodiment of Creon's ruin. If the suffering in Antigone's family is
caused by 'senselessness of speech and a Fury of the mind' (603), Antigone
herself becomes a quasi-demonic agent of Creon's downfall.

The importance of *atê* in that process is underlined in the aftermath
of Creon's belated realization of the truth of Tiresias' warnings. Tiresias

indicates that Creon's thinking has brought harm, not safety, upon his city: 'and it is as a result of your thinking that the city suffers this illness' (1015).[53] Creon did not see this coming. But error (*hamartia*) is common to all mankind, says Tiresias (1023–4); it is only persistence in error, when the *kerdos* of learning from those who give good advice is available, that merits the charge of stupidity (1023–32). *Atê* lurks in the presence both of its antonym, *kerdos*, and of its partial synonym, *hamartia*. Creon thought he could see the difference between *atê* and *sôtêria* (185–6), but it is the blind Tiresias who foresees the disaster that awaits him.[54]

This disaster Tiresias now proceeds to outline, in terms that are redolent of the second stasimon's reflections on the workings of *atê*. As Antigone hoped at 927–8, Creon is to suffer evils parallel to those he inflicted upon Polynices and Antigone (1066–76), thanks to 'the Furies (Erinyes) of Hades and the gods' (1075; cf. the 'Fury (Erinys) of the mind' in 603).[55] These warnings, Tiresias concludes, are like arrows of the heart; they will not miss their target, and Creon will not escape their heat (1084–6) – just as the victim of deceptive hope does not realize his delusion until he burns his foot in the fire (in the second stasimon at 617–19).

Tiresias' warnings alarm the Chorus-leader (1091–4), and Creon shares his concern (1095–7):

> I recognized that too, and it worries me. To give in is terrible, but to stand firm may be to strike one's heart on Ate's net.[56]

If Creon's assumption of power and authority lay behind the catalogue of man's achievements in the first stasimon, then it now looks as though the hunter-fisherman of 343–8 risks becoming the prey. There is still hope, but unless Creon acts quickly, it may be too late, as the Chorus-leader urges at 1103–4:

> Act as quickly as you can, my lord; for the gods' swift-footed Harms cut off the wrongheaded.

But it is too late; hope (to which even the Chorus succumb in the ensuing fifth stasimon, 1115–54) proves illusory, as it often does (615–17);

and Creon's *atê* is confirmed, in the first instance by the Chorus (1257–60):

> Here comes the king himself, a clearly inscribed memorial in his hands;
> if I may say so, his own error (*hamartanein*), no one else's, caused his
> ruin (*atê*).

Creon then repeats the diagnosis, lamenting his 'errors' (*hamartêmata*, 1261–2), the misjudgements that have destroyed his happiness (1265), and his own folly (1269), but also the mighty blow which the god has struck him (1274; cf. 1097), the shaking that the god has given him (1274; cf. 584–5: 'for when a house is shaken by the gods, there is no element of *atê* that does not advance towards the family's members, in all their numbers'). Creon is, after all, one of those to whom bad has seemed good, because a god was leading his mind to *atê*; he has fared but the shortest time free of *atê* (622–5).

The notion of *atê* permeates the play. Its prominence in the second stasimon is a reflection of that ode's central position and significance. That significance is mirrored in the extent to which *atê* itself recurs at each crucial stage of the play's action. The perspective of the second stasimon, complicated though it is, is not a localized one. But only Roger Dawe seems to have noticed that the Chorus-leader's personification of the 'Harms' (Blabai) at 1103–4 represents a transparent evocation of the role of Ate in the allegory of the Prayers (Litai) in *Iliad* 9.[57] The close association between *atê* and *blabê*, harm, is clearly in play in the Litai passage itself: Ate harms people (*blaptein*, *Iliad* 9. 507), and when the *atê* of the original offence gives way to that of the victim who refuses the offender's reparation, that person is harmed (*blaptein*, 512). In addition, the personified Ate of Phoenix's allegory is 'strong and sound of foot' (9. 505), and so can outrun the Litai, who must follow behind to remedy the harm she has done (504–7); just so, the Chorus-leader's Blabai are swift-footed and outrun the imprudent (1103–4).

Atê plays a central role in the plot and thematic structure of the *Iliad*, and Phoenix's allegory in Book 9 is the fulcrum of the balance between the *atê* of Agamemnon, which causes the quarrel and its disastrous results, and that of Achilles, which consists in his rejection of the Embassy and results in the death of Patroclus.[58] In the *Antigone*, the transparent evocation of this salient and emblematic passage comes at the point at which the balance between the sufferings that await Creon and those that he has imposed upon Antigone begins to become apparent. This balance represents the fulfilment not only of Antigone's wish (at 925–8) that Creon's *hamartia* should involve him in suffering no less painful than the suffering she endures as a result of her own alleged *hamartia*, but also of Tiresias' prophecy (at 1064–86) that Creon will be caught in the same evils as he inflicted upon Antigone and Polynices. These evils come upon him after he has rejected Tiresias' earlier advice that, though it is human to err (*exhamartanein*), it is nonetheless sensible (and apparently possible) to heal one's error by changing one's mind (1023–7); here, the words 'he who, once he has fallen into evil, heals himself (*akeisthai*) and does not remain immoveable' in all likelihood constitute another allusion to the allegory of the Litai, in which one who 'transgresses and errs' (*Iliad* 9. 501) can make amends by means of Prayers, which 'come after to heal (*exakeisthai*) the damage' (507). *Atê*-terms are first applied to Antigone's actions and their outcomes, before it becomes clear that the *atê*-sequence of delusion and disaster is exemplified in a more typical form in the case of Creon.[59] The importance of *atê* in linking the fates of Antigone and Creon is underlined by the evocation of a passage that establishes the links between the errors of Agamemnon and Achilles in the *Iliad*, and the *Antigone* thus advertises the extent to which it shares a central theme with that most exemplary of poems.

At the centre of this nexus of links between the putative *atê* of Antigone and the demonstrable *atê* of Creon stands the second stasimon. This song introduces the notion of *atê* in explaining the generations of suffering in Antigone's family, but at another level of meaning accurately diagnoses the causes of Creon's downfall. We noted many of the verbal and thematic echoes that link that ode to evaluations of the conduct of both Antigone and Creon elsewhere in the play.

Among the most significant of these are the recurrent references to the personified, daemonic agents that bring ruin to mortals. The Blabai (= Atai) that the Chorus-leader fears will overtake Creon if he does not remedy his folly in time (1103–4) are prefigured in the Furies or Erinyes who, according to Tiresias, lie in wait for him (1074–6):[60]

> As a result of this, Erinyes of Hades and the gods lie in wait for you, agents of ruin who wreak their destruction after the fact, so that you will be caught up in these very same evils.

The words *lôbêtêres* ('agents of ruin') and *hysterophthoroi* ('who wreak their destruction after the fact') emphasize the harm that these Erinyes cause.[61] The latter term occurs only here in classical Greek. Sophocles' phrase, however, is quoted by the Byzantine archbishop and Homeric commentator, Eustathius, in his note on *Iliad* 9. 506–7, where he observes that, in so far as they are *hysterophthoroi*, the Erinyes of the *Antigone* resemble the Litai in Phoenix's allegory, who see to it that Ate attends anyone who rejects them, 'in order that he be harmed and pay the penalty' (*Iliad* 9. 512). This amounts to saying that Ate herself is *hysterophthoros*, an agent who wreaks destruction after the fact.[62] Eustathius has seen the link between this passage of the *Antigone* and the allegory of *Iliad* 9. That link is confirmed by the similarity between Tiresias' words at 1074–6 and the Chorus-leader's at 1103–4, where the *Iliad* 9 passage is plainly evoked, and it is further substantiated by the way that Sophocles' *hysterophthoroi* ('after-destroying') so clearly recalls Aeschylus' *hysteropoinos*, 'after-punishing', used of Erinys at *Agamemnon* 58–9, but (in a similarly worded passage) of Ate at *Libation Bearers* 382–3.[63] The signs of a virtual equivalence between Ate and Erinys are strong; and so both 1074–6 (with Erinyes) and 1103–4 (with Blabai = Atai), referring to Creon, recall the words of the Chorus in the second stasimon, where they see 'senselessness of speech and a Fury (Erinys) of the mind' as the ruin of the House of Oedipus (599–603). Whether or not there is any sense in which this is to be regarded as an accurate assessment of Antigone's plight, the later reflections of the same theme exploit the latent application of this notion, and of the entire ode, to

Creon. The way in which the *atê*-theme, as applied to Antigone, mutates into the application of the same theme to Creon is aptly summed up in Creon's observation, more accurate than he knows, that in giving a home to Antigone and Ismene he has been nurturing 'two Atai' in his house (533).

Though in most of the actual occurrences of *atê*-words themselves the primary reference is to the concept's objective aspect (harm, damage, or loss), the way in which it is brought into relation with *hamartia* (explicitly at 1259–62, implicitly at 914–15, 925–8, 1023–7; cf. 588, 743–4) illustrates what is in any case apparent at 623–4 and in the second stasimon in general, that *atê* in the *Antigone* is still, as in Homer and Aeschylus, the name of a process in which a harmful state of mind is the cause of a harmful state of affairs. This impression is confirmed by the way in which the *Antigone* activates a large number of *atê*'s traditional associations and connotations. We have already noted the etymological play on *atê* and *apatê* (deception) at 615–25 and the implicit presence of the 'archaic chain' of *olbos* (prosperity), *koros* (satiety), *hybris*, and *atê* at 604–14. Another potential etymological (or folk-etymological) link is with the verb *aêmi*, 'to blow' (of winds).[64] This seems to be active in the Chorus's words in the second stasimon (583–92):

> Blessed are those whose life has not tasted evils. For when a house is shaken by the gods, there is no element of *atê* that does not advance towards the family's members, in all their numbers, as when the swell of the open sea, driven by ill-blowing Thracian blasts, runs over the submarine darkness and rolls the black sand from the depths, and struck by ill winds the headlands groan and roar in response.

The gods' shaking of the house need not specifically suggest a storm, and the description of *atê* as 'advancing' (cf. Creon at 185–6) shows that there are more metaphors than one in play here, but 'shaking' has already been used in a nautical metaphor by Creon at 162–3, and if 'shaken' in 584 is a general environmental metaphor, the sense is soon specified by the storm imagery of 586–92.[65] The storm is a recurrent image of disruption in the play,[66] and if, ultimately, Creon's career is one

of error resulting in disaster, then the image of winds and storms has a
role to play in its presentation.[67] In the second stasimon, the point of
this imagery is to emphasize the force of divinely inspired disaster; but
the cause of that disaster is soon revealed as psychological (603, 615–
25).[68] Just so, Tiresias affirms that the cause of the sickness that afflicts
the city is to be located in the mind of Creon (1015). The imagery of
storms and winds is also used of psychological disturbance.[69] At 929–
30, for example, the Chorus-leader's view that Antigone, in refusing to
give in to evils, has inherited her father's temper (471–2) is recalled in
his observation that 'still the same blasts of the same winds of the soul
possess her'. The notion of psychological winds (a natural image in a
language in which terms for psychological phenomena such as *psychê*,
pneuma, and *thymos* all rest on metaphors of breathing and blowing)[70]
has already appeared in the parodos in connection with the impious
Argive invader, Capaneus (134–7):

> Swung in the balance, he fell and struck the hard earth, the fire-bearer
> who till then had been breathing over us with blasts of hostile winds,
> raging in his mad onrush.

With these winds of unreason we might compare and contrast the
ambivalent 'windy thought' of the first stasimon (354–5). That ode's first
example of the forces that human rationality seeks to control is the sea
(334–7), just as the opening lines of the second stasimon use storm
imagery to express the destruction that is *atê*. The winds of *atê* blow
through the play, before finally sinking Creon, captain of the ship of
state (162–3, 189–90, 994). Creon kept his metaphorical rigging too
tight (Haemon at 715–17), and in the end, found that he had steered his
ship into the harbour of Hades (1284). As the Chorus sing in the fourth
stasimon (951–4), black ships cannot evade the power of fate.[71]

Creon's fate rests on his failure to fulfil the faith in rationality and
progress that is reflected in the first stasimon.[72] The presentation of
his downfall as the ironic fulfilment of the apparent optimism of the
'Ode to Man' is not only illustrated in the image of seafaring. We see
the same movement in the way that Creon's attempt to break the wild,

horse-like Antigone (477–8; cf. horse-taming in the first stasimon at 350–1) fails in the face of the 'self-willed temper' (*autognôtos orga*, 875) that ultimately leads to her suicide; or when we learn from Tiresias that the sickness of the city is caused by Creon's way of thinking (1015) and when he proves unable to 'cure the evil into which he has fallen' (1026–7; cf. medicine at 363–4). It is therefore the 'pessimistic' and 'archaic' second stasimon that is more in keeping with the play's overall dramatic movement and ethos.

Mind, madness, and the nature of happiness

As a major theme, *atê* cannot be dissociated from an even more prevalent network of terms which present the characters' motives and actions in terms of good and bad judgement and its good and bad consequences.[73] This pervasive theme, in turn, encompasses a wider dialectic between the powers of human reason and the irrational forces that limit and undermine it,[74] a dialectic that is exemplified most of all in the antithesis between the first stasimon, with its enumeration of the achievements of human ingenuity, and the subsequent choral odes – the second stasimon tracing ruin to its source in 'senselessness of speech and an Erinys of the mind' (603); the third on the power of Eros to drive people mad (790), to warp their minds to their ruin (791–2); the fourth showcasing, *inter alia,* the madness of Lycurgus in seeking to restrain the frenzy of the female worshippers of Dionysus (the 'divinely possessed women' of 963–4); and the fifth on the power of Dionysus himself, invoked (with his attendant chorus of maddened female worshippers, 1149–54) to help cleanse the city of Thebes of its sickness, but already present, perhaps, in the destruction of the royal house brought about by a woman's rejection of restraint.[75] 'Madness' or irrationality is predicated variously of Antigone, Creon, Haemon, and Eurydice.[76] The first stasimon draws on contemporary thinkers' confidence in the potential of human reason and the possibility of progress; the subsequent odes, especially the second stasimon, and indeed the dénouement of the play in general, confront such attitudes with the much more pessimistic assessments of the power of reason and the capacity for progress that are characteristic of an earlier and more traditional strand of Greek thought.

The *Antigone*'s engagement with such ideas does not amount to a simple privileging of piety over intelligence, but rather specifies the ethical and religious content of 'true wisdom'. A number of the play's reflections on the nature of human intelligence therefore intersect with the theme of *atê* and *kerdos* in another sense, in so far as they contribute to an overall presentation of wisdom as the greatest and folly as the worst of human qualities. Pronouncements of what is best and what is worst for a person or a community – a debate that is characteristic of archaic thought – recur throughout the play.[77] Haemon opens and closes his long speech in the *agôn* with Creon with reflections on this subject: the *phrenes* (wits) that the gods implant in human beings are the greatest of possessions (683–4);[78] the best thing is for a man to be born full of knowledge, but if that proves not to be the case, to learn from those who speak well is also good (720–3). Such a willingness to learn will secure Creon's good fortune, for a father's success is a 'possession' which no other source of pride can surpass in value (701–11): the son's joy in his father's flourishing (and vice versa) is, on the face of it, an alternative candidate for the best thing in life, but Haemon makes it clear that such an end can be secured only by the wisdom whose paramount value he emphasizes at the beginning and end of his speech.[79] The point recurs in the Tiresias scene: Tiresias reflects that good counsel (*euboulia*) is the best of possessions (1050) and Creon agrees that, by the same token, lack of sense is the greatest harm (*blabê*, 1051).[80] Once the seriousness of Tiresias' prophecy has struck home, the Chorus-leader reiterates the value of *euboulia* in the present circumstances (1098) and (as we have seen) warns Creon of the Blabai, the Harms, that overtake the imprudent (1103–4); the allusion to the role of Ate in the *Iliad*'s allegory of the Litai thus brings the rhetoric of the best and worst for human beings into relation with the *atê*-theme.

Once the consequences of Creon's folly have become clear, the general lesson is repeated, first by the Messenger at 1242–3 (Haemon's death reveals to all mankind the extent to which folly, *aboulia*, is the greatest evil for a man), and then by the Chorus in the anapaests that close the play (1347–53):

> Good sense is by far the first part of *eudaimonia*: one must not disrespect the gods in any way. Mighty words of the boastful have paid their debt in mighty blows and taught good sense in old age.[81]

'Good sense' is not value-neutral: what it secures is a form of prosperity that depends on the right relationship with the gods. It may bring the greatest of advantages, for those who understand what is truly advantageous, but its goal is not simply the maximization of advantage. Hence Creon's suspicion, once he has been shaken by Tiresias' prophecy, that it may be best to complete one's life in preservation of the established laws (1113–14) presents not another candidate for the title of 'best thing', but an understanding of what the best thing, good sense, consists in. From the entrance of Haemon onwards, i.e. from the point at which Creon's judgement begins to be questioned even by those who wish him well,[82] opinions are unanimous that good judgement is the best and bad judgement the worst thing. Earlier in the play, however, Creon had expressed different views: in line with his profession at 184–90 that his priority is the city's safety (as opposed to ruin, *atê*, 185), for it is the city that ensures the safety of her citizens (189–90), so at 295–303 he regards money as the worst thing in the world, for money sacks cities and turns citizens out of their homes; at 672–7 he describes disobedience to authority (*anarchia*) in very similar terms. Where at 189–90 it is the successful sailing of the ship of state that brings *sôtêria* to its citizens, at 675–6 it is the citizens' obedience that secures the same end. These views on what saves and ruins a city are, at least implicitly, views about what constitutes *atê*, 'disaster'; they are replaced, in the end, by the view that harm as a state of affairs has its cause in impaired and harmful states of mind that take insufficient account of divine law.

Much of the play's debate about what is valuable in human existence is conducted in terms of the nature of *kerdos*, 'profit'. *Kerdos* is a regular antonym of *atê*; accordingly, the antithesis of *kerdos* and *atê* is drawn into the play's reflections on good and bad forms of wealth and prosperity and on the nature of happiness. Creon himself does not believe that material prosperity is the goal of existence; for him, money is the root of all evil (295–6). He is rather one of 'those who care about power', as the Chorus put it at 873. But Creon's evaluations of others' motives do not rise above the material: even before the Guard has entered with his report of the first burial of Polynices, Creon betrays his suspicion that, if anyone should defy his edict, profit would be their motive (221–2):

> Aye, that [sc. death] is the reward [sc. for disobeying the edict]. But profit accompanied by hope often ruins men.

Here is a form of profit-seeking that entails loss and ruin; there is a link between 'hope' here and the deceptive hope that leads to disaster (*atê*) in the second stasimon (615–25). The antithesis between *kerdos* and *atê* that is implicit in this passage is explicit, and subsumed in the opposition between *atê* and *sôtêria*, in Creon's presentation of the Guards' motivation at 308–14:[83]

> Death alone will not suffice for you, until you are hanged alive and reveal this *hybris*, in order that in future you may conduct your depredations in full knowledge of the proper sources of profit (*kerdos*) and learn that it is not right to love to take profit (*kerdos*) from just any source. For you will see that more men are ruined than saved as a result of shameful profits.

The appearance of *hybris* in 309 brings in the 'archaic chain' of wealth, *hybris*, and *atê* – a sequence that is latent in the second stasimon's assertion that no great wealth (or nothing great) comes to human beings without *atê*.

Creon's suspicions of others' mercenary motives resurface in his confrontation with Tiresias. Tiresias, like all seers, is allegedly motivated only by money and profit (1033–47, 1055, 1061, 1077–8); Creon himself is one of the commodities to be bought and sold (1035–6, 1063). By focusing so single-mindedly (and erroneously) on the material *kerdos* that, in his view, motivates others, but not himself, Creon reveals the limitations of his own outlook.[84] In the end, that outlook brings him to a point at which he is 'rich' only in misfortune (1278) and the only *kerdos* in the midst of his ruin is to be hidden from sight as quickly as possible (1320–7, especially 1326).

Both Tiresias and Antigone offer Creon alternative conceptions of *kerdos*, but he is blind to them. Creon's denunciation of the profit-seeking of seers is itself prompted by Tiresias' suggestion that *kerdos* (1032) can be secured if only he recognizes his *hamartia* (1023–7), remedies the damage (1026–7), and is prepared to learn from one who speaks wisely and with good intent (1031–2). This is the most pleasant thing (1032), since *euboulia* is the greatest of possessions (*ktêmata*, 1050). Antigone, for her part, seeks a *kerdos* that is beyond the ken of men like Creon and the Chorus. For Creon, death is the ultimate sanction (35–6, 221, 308, 488–9, 498, 577, 750, 760–1, 768–80, 936–7); it is the payment (*misthos*, 221) for defying his edict. For the Chorus-leader no one is so stupid as to desire death (220). But Antigone's desire, her *erôs*, for actions that will bring her death, has already been deprecated by Ismene (90; cf. 95–7); and at 460–70 she justifies that desire:

> I knew that I should die – of course I did. Even if you hadn't proclaimed it, I'd have known. But if I am going to die before my time, I call that *kerdos*. For when you live, as I do, in the midst of many evils, how is it not *kerdos* to die? So for me to meet with this fate is a trivial source of pain. But if I had countenanced my mother's dead son being unburied, *that* would have caused me pain; at *this* I feel none. And if you now think that my actions are foolish, one might almost say that I am charged with folly by a fool.

Antigone's willingness to die rather than compromise her obligations to her brother presents a notion of 'profit' that is utterly different from those envisaged by Creon (while ironically confirming his suspicion that, at least in some sense, *kerdos* is the motive of those who oppose him).[85] But it also represents a variation on another traditional tenet of Greek pessimism, that the best thing for mortals is not to be born, and for those who have been, to die as soon as possible.[86]

In presenting the issues in such terms Sophocles draws on a long tradition of archaic moralizing on good and bad ways to acquire material wealth and on material versus non-material forms of prosperity.[87] In the end, the play's dialectic on the best and worst things, profit and loss, benefit and harm, safety and ruin – that is, on *kerdos, atê,* and their various counterparts – represents a sustained reflection on the nature of prosperity (*olbos*) or *eudaimonia* (happiness, 'human flourishing'). Accordingly, *eudaimonia* is the topic which introduces the second stasimon's thoughts on *atê* (582–5):

> Blessed are those whose life has not tasted evils. For when a house is shaken by the gods, there is no element of *atê* that does not advance towards the family's members, in all their numbers.

Here, *atê* seems simply to be *eudaimonia*'s negation: ruin or catastrophe. In the next stanza, however, its origin (in the case of the Labdacids) is traced to its traditional source in the aberrations of the human mind (593–603). In the stanza after that, mental disturbance is replaced by transgression of Zeus's law as the source of *atê* (604–14), but the cause of transgression is then again specified, in the fourth stanza, as (god-inspired) delusion.

As we saw, the second stasimon's presentation of the human propensity to error and destruction proves to be an accurate account of the actions of Creon. When the consequences of those actions are known, both the wider pattern (in which error and its consequences exemplify the instability of human fortunes) and the narrower one (which highlights humans' responsibility for their own suffering, whether directly or through the intervention of the gods to punish transgressors) are emphasized. The former construction is the one put forward by the Messenger at 1155–71:

> Neighbours of the house of Cadmus and of Amphion, there is no human life of any kind that I should ever praise or blame as a stable entity. For fortune (*tychê*) raises up and fortune causes to sink both the fortunate and the unfortunate at any given time; and there is no prophet of what is established for mortals. For Creon was enviable

once, as it seems to me: he saved this Cadmeian land from its enemies, he assumed complete and sole command over the country, and he ruled, flourishing with noble offspring. And now all is lost. When a man's pleasures desert him, I do not reckon him to be alive, but consider him a living corpse. So amass great riches at home, if you will, and live in the manner of a tyrant; but if the joy of these things should leave, I should not buy the rest from a man for the shadow of smoke, by comparison with pleasure.

This evaluation is full of traditional ideas – the impossibility of passing judgement on the quality of a person's life (at least until it is over),[88] the alternation of good and bad fortune,[89] the shadowy, insubstantial nature of human existence.[90] It does not diminish Creon's responsibility or deny that he has perpetrated acts that warrant divine punishment: these aspects are emphasized once Creon himself has returned at 1257.[91] But there, too, considerable emphasis is placed upon his status as an example of the mutability of fortune, the fragility of happiness, and the inevitability of suffering (1265, 1276, 1296, 1337–8). The two strands are maintained in the Chorus's closing anapaests (1347–53, quoted above), with their reference to the role of good sense in *eudaimonia*, but also the dangers of pride and impiety as aspects of human folly.

The Messenger's pronouncement that Creon is now 'a living corpse' (1165–7) shows that the parallelism between her fate and Creon's for which Antigone prayed (925–8) and which Tiresias predicted (1065–76) is now coming to pass. The balance between the fates of Polynices, Antigone, and Creon that these words establish is subsumed in a larger pattern of imagery which presents the shifting balance of human fortunes as an example of a universal pattern. For while the use of the verb *orthoun* (to raise up, to make upright) in 1158 recalls the earlier use of words from the same root with reference to the successful sailing of the ship of state,[92] in this particular context it is part of an image of weighing objects in the balance (the implication of the verb that is translated as 'causes to sink' in 1158), an image that is reinforced by the precise balance of antithetical terms in each of the lines 1157–9 (praise/

blame; raises up/causes to sink; fortunate/unfortunate).[93] This is an image that presents the abstract concept of human happiness as if it were a commodity that could be weighed in the pans of the scales, precisely in order to demonstrate that human happiness does *not* in fact reside in things that one can weigh or count. This is the burden of all the language of *kerdos* in the play, which in the end emphasizes that what is of true value in life cannot be bought and sold. Just so, the Messenger dismisses mere wealth and power ('amass great riches at home, if you will ..', 1168–9), all of which is worth nothing in comparison with pleasure – and again non-material value is expressed in the language of monetary exchange ('I should not buy the rest from a man for the shadow of smoke', 1171).[94]

Causes and explanations

The *Antigone* is a play that emphasizes the role of states of mind and character in choice and in the outcomes of choice, yet the choices that it dramatizes are also presented as depending on factors that lie beyond the agent's control. For the Chorus, Antigone's own 'self-willed temper' (875) has destroyed her; yet they also believe that she is paying for a debt incurred by her father (856, cf. 471–2) and that her actions instantiate a recurrent pattern of suffering in her family (594–8). The Chorus charge Creon with responsibility for his sufferings (1258–60), and he accepts the charge (1261–9), yet he also attributes his *dysbouliai* to a god who struck him on the head and overturned his happiness (1272–6), and sees his troubles as 'fated' (1296, 1345–6). The Chorus concur: 'there is no release for mortals from a disaster that is fated' (1337–8).[95] What was true of the Labdacids, according to the second stasimon (596–8), is apparently true of Creon.[96] Well may we ask (with Winnington-Ingram 1980: 164), what kind of fate this is. As we saw in Chapter 2,[97] Tiresias moves from warning Creon against an outcome that appears to be avoidable to prophesying a state of affairs that has the air of inevitability (996–1032, 1064–90). The text gives us little encouragement to ask whether Tiresias' understanding of possible futures changes between his two speeches, or whether the disaster that he prophesies in his second speech is somehow a consequence of Creon's rejection of the warning contained in the first.[98] Antigone's suffering is apparently part of an inherited pattern from which her family cannot break free; and Creon seems to believe that he himself exemplifies 'the famous dictum that bad seems good to a man whose mind a god is leading towards *atê*' (621–4). What happens to people seems to reflect not only who they are, what they are like, and what they do, but also what is, in some sense, in store for them. Antigone's 'self-willed temper' (875) is reflected in the winds that blow through her soul (929–30) and the Erinys that masters her mind (603); this is what makes her an embodiment of *atê* with respect to Creon (533), who erred his own *atê* (1259–60), but also fell victim to Erinyes and Blabai (1073–5, 1103–4). There are powerful forces that human beings cannot control, both within themselves and in the external world. The world of the *Antigone* is most certainly not, despite the first stasimon's reflection of contemporary theories of human progress, one in which man is the measure of all things, but a more pessimistic and 'archaic' one whose rhythms are substantially resistant to human control.

In so far as the play draws conclusions about all of this, it does so in the case of Creon: his ruin derives from and demonstrates his folly, and so he is a paradigm of *atê* and *hamartia*. For the Messenger, this also makes him a paradigm of the mutability of fortune, but subsumed in that general pattern there are causes that lie in Creon's character and others that seem to lie in more powerful divine and daemonic forces. But what about Antigone? As we have seen in detail, the kind of language that is used of Creon, especially the language of *atê*, *hamartia*, and transgression, is applied to her too; likewise her actions and her sufferings are attributed now to her own character, now to forces beyond her control. We can certainly see Antigone as covered by the Messenger's generalizations on the mutability of fortune; and perhaps one of the reasons that the Messenger generalizes Creon's situation in that way is that the pattern can be applied to Antigone too. Like the *Iliad*, the

Antigone sets the sufferings that arise from error, transgression, and other causes in a wider context of human vulnerability. Antigone and Creon each contribute, by their actions and by the characteristics that their actions express, to what happens to them; but what happens to each underlines the vulnerability that they share with all human beings.

Creon's suffering can be traced with apparent precision to his errors; it has the appearance of condign punishment. Yet these were errors of a kind that anyone might make (as Tiresias points out, 1023–4). But (again) what about Antigone? Is she subject to the same pattern of delusion and disaster? And if this sequence is active in her case, does it really represent the working out of some broader pattern of affliction within her own family? The language of the *atê*-sequence is applied to Antigone, but when it is, there is often a latent application to Creon, before it becomes clear that he represents a definitive case of the delusion that leads to disaster. In that development, Antigone serves as a vector or instrument of Creon's *atê*. So is the use of *atê* and similar language in her case merely a foil for the *atê* of Creon? Antigone herself invites us to conclude that *either* she *or* Creon is wrong, that the *hamartia* of one or the other will be proved by results (925–8 again). Creon's *hamartia* is proved and acknowledged by both the Chorus and himself; Antigone, for her part, is vindicated.[99] Does this mean that the whole question of Antigone's *atê* is just a red herring?

The answer is not clear, because the outcomes of her actions are open to multiple interpretations. First, her vindication may suggest that she is not in error at all; yet her 'self-willed temper' and something about her inheritance from Oedipus (as the Chorus observe) do bring about her death; she does seem to be driven by irrational as well as rational forces. The *atê*-sequence, as we see clearly in Creon's case, typically requires both a disastrous outcome and regret about that outcome, the recognition that the disaster arose from one's own blind folly. Antigone does not quite express this type of reaction; she goes to her living death convinced of the rectitude of her position and in the hope that time will prove her right and Creon wrong. Yet her last words focus on the injustice of her punishment, and she dies apparently abandoned by the gods (921–4, 943). She has no regrets about her action, but her justification of what she has done, especially her statement that she would not have done the same for a husband or a child (904–14), reveals her recognition that the consequences of her action have been dire and that only an exceptional action could exclude regret over those consequences. And while she does not regret what she has done, she does lament the consequences to which it has led, not only for their injustice, but also because the death that awaits her, anomalous, inglorious, and unlamented as it appears, is not at all what she had in mind when she imagined that her death would be (not *atê*, but) *kerdos* (461–2); her suicide by hanging, in the bridal-chamber-cum-tomb to which Creon has consigned her, would exacerbate, rather than alleviate, this impression.[100]

Some modern critics claim that the gods' apparent abandonment of Antigone, their failure to rescue or to reward her, indicates that she is not, in fact, vindicated.[101] This is wrong, for (as we saw) her vindication is clear. But the expectation that justice and piety should be rewarded, and thus the sense that Antigone has suffered for her piety, are not modern moralistic impositions, for the complaint that the righteous are not rewarded is frequent in archaic poetry.[102] Those (both ancient and modern) for whom this question arises have several considerations at their disposal: some would challenge the expectation that virtue should be rewarded, others the conclusion that Antigone is abandoned or that her sufferings are in fact an evil. It might simply be the case that the universe is not ordered in such a way that individual piety is rewarded. Perhaps Antigone suffers because (as the Chorus have suggested) her entire lineage is doomed to disaster.[103] Perhaps her suffering simply represents another aspect of the mutability of fortune, that misfortune can occur through no fault of one's own.[104] Or, to take the second route, one might argue that Antigone is not after all abandoned by the gods, at least to the extent that the complementary sufferings she wishes on Creon (at 925–8, immediately following her complaint at 921–4) do indeed befall him. Her death, one might argue, is not an evil: true, it involves suffering, but her life has in any case been one of suffering; in such circumstances, there can be greater *kerdos* in death than in survival (460–8). The story of Cleobis and Biton in the first book of Herodotus' *Histories* (1. 31. 3–5) vividly illustrates the characteristically 'archaic' proposition that death may be better than life, indeed the best thing that can happen to a human being.

These suggestions are all plausible, to an extent; but there is no way to be sure that any one of them, or indeed any combination of them, constitutes *the* explanation. What happens to Antigone is just that much more resistant to categorical evaluation than are the actions and sufferings of Creon. Whatever story we tell ourselves about the extent to which Creon brought his sufferings upon himself, the fate of Antigone reminds us not to see that story as the only possible pattern. Their fates are in some respects comparable, but only at a certain level of generality. Yet this still matters. The play may eventually forget about Antigone; but much of what eventually proves fruitful in coming to terms with Creon's fate was originally introduced with reference to her situation. It is not at all clear that explanations that go further back than Creon's edict (with all its disastrous consequences) are simply discarded. From one perspective, Antigone is collateral damage in Creon's passage from delusion to disaster; but from another, it is Creon who is collateral damage in the city's final purification from the consequences of generations of Labdacid dysfunction.[105] If there is anything to be said for that explanation, then the interweaving of the fates of Antigone and Creon, rooted in archaic Greek thought though both of those trajectories are, creates a plot that is considerably more complex than what one might regard as the typically 'archaic' or typically 'Aristotelian' sequence that traces the consequences of Creon's *hamartia*. Patterns of archaic Greek thought illuminate the play's complexity, not its simplicity.

4

Love and Death

In this chapter we shall investigate a number of themes centring on two Greek concepts which might be rendered in English as 'love', first *philia* (also translated as 'friendship'), and then *erôs* (erotic passion). In particular, we shall focus on these personal ties in terms of their relationship to the *polis*, and especially in terms of the potential threat that each can represent. The relationship between citizens can be described as a form of *philia*,[1] but more personal varieties of the same relationship can lead to tensions between personal and civic loyalties. Equally, *erôs* can be contained within marriage and contribute to the sustainability of the citizen population; but it is also a powerful motivating force that is capable of much less productive forms of expression.

Friends and enemies

Philia denotes a mutual and reciprocal relationship that almost always has an affective component. That is, though *philia* can be used of the objectively existing reciprocal and mutual obligations between two people or two communities (so that it encompasses ties of kinship, political alliance and allegiance, business partnership, etc., as well as friendship), it normally implies mutual ways of feeling as well as of acting.[2] The notion that you should treat others as they have treated you, i.e. help your friends (*philoi*) and harm your enemies (*echthroi*) is a recurrent ideal in archaic and classical Greece: the Athenian poet and lawgiver, Solon, prayed that the Muses make him sweet to his friends, bitter to his enemies (Solon 13. 5 West); over three hundred years later, the view that helping one's friends and harming one's enemies are central to 'excellence' or 'justice' can be represented as conventional opinion in Platonic dialogues.[3] This is not an aggressive ethic: the notion of reciprocity that underpins it does not sanction unprovoked aggression; but it does assume a strict and straightforward polarity between two distinct categories. But in tragedy (as no doubt often in life) the problem is that the categories fail to remain distinct: rupture of *philia* is ubiquitous and characters may be *philoi* in one respect, but *echthroi* in another.[4] It is a premise of the *Antigone* that *philia* has been violated, and the disruption gets worse as the play gets underway. Polynices and Eteocles, though brothers, were *echthroi*; their sisters, Antigone and Ismene, become *echthrai*, at least in Antigone's eyes. Creon considers his nephew, Polynices, to be an *echthros*, and so enmity is created between Antigone and Creon, and Creon becomes the *echthros* of his own son, Haemon.

The prominence of this theme is apparent from the opening lines of the play: Antigone's first words are a hyper-pleonastic expression of her *philia* with Ismene. The line defies idiomatic translation, but a more or less literal rendering would be something like 'Oh common self-sibling head of Ismene', or even 'Oh common head of Ismene, sharer of the self-same womb'. Antigone's opening speech ends with a series of questions, the last of which is (9–10) 'Or are you unaware that the ills of the *echthroi* are advancing towards the *philoi*?' By this Antigone might mean only that what is proposed with regard to the body of Polynices is the sort of treatment that is appropriate only for an enemy; but it is likely that her words also identify Creon, the source of the proposal, as an enemy.[5] And in either event, the terms *philos* and *echthros* present the issue in personal terms: though *echthros* can sometimes in tragedy refer to an enemy in war (for which the standard prose term is *polemios*), strictly it denotes personal enmity, personal hatred. Antigone thinks of personal relationships, not political ones. The emergency of which she speaks arises because Creon (a *philos* of Antigone and Ismene, since he is their uncle, but perhaps already in Antigone's mind an *echthros*) has decreed different treatment for the corpses of their two brothers (21–38; her use of the dual number emphasizes the status of the siblings as two pairs). Antigone underlines the *philia* between herself and Ismene, and between them and both their dead brothers. But the situation is not so simple: Ismene qualifies and complicates Antigone's categories – some *philoi* come to hate each other, as their own brothers did (12–14, 55–7); they were paired, but in mutual slaughter (duals at 13–14, 55–7); their personal animosity led to the invasion of Thebes by an Argive army (15–16);[6] and their hostility is part of a wider pattern of family breakdown to which both Antigone (2–6) and Ismene (49–57) refer. This interfamilial strife is then replicated as Antigone uses *echthros*-words towards Ismene (86: 'you will be much more hateful if you keep quiet'; 93–4: 'If you say that, I'll hate you, and you will justly be counted an enemy towards the one that died'). Antigone began with inclusive expressions of *philia*, and emphasized the duty to treat all *philoi* alike; yet she quickly declares enmity on Ismene, an enmity that persists on her part, despite some signs to the contrary,[7] in the second scene between Antigone and Ismene at 536–60. From then on, she devotes herself exclusively to one *philos*, her 'dearest' Polynices (73, 81), and as she leaves the stage she refers to herself as the sole survivor of the royal house (941) – Ismene is forgotten. Yet the partiality of Antigone's *philia* is not shared by Ismene. Ismene's words in line 99 (Antigone is 'truly *philos* to [her] *philoi*') endorse Antigone's active devotion to Polynices, but also restate the affection which, she feels, Antigone is still entitled to receive, not least from Ismene herself. Paradoxically, Ismene both endorses Antigone's response to the claims of *philia* – claims that she herself recognizes but feels unable to meet – and offers a more inclusive and less extreme perspective that emphasizes the particularity of Antigone's motivation.

Differing perspectives on *philia*, as on so many other values, divide Antigone and Creon.[8] For Creon, the city must come first: he has no time for anyone who considers a *philos* more important than his homeland (182–3), and he would never make a *philos* of a man who was hostile to his country (187–8), for it is the city that keeps its inhabitants safe, and it is its interests that should determine who one's *philoi* are. For Creon, then, *philoi* are made and unmade for political reasons, a view that would almost certainly strike many in an Athenian audience, familiar as they were with conflicts between personal loyalties and the interests of the state,[9] as entirely laudable. This is the rationale behind Creon's differential treatment of the bodies of Eteocles, the patriot, and Polynices, the traitor. We are reminded that some *philia* relationships are natural, not made, but all are subject to dissolution: Polynices shared Eteocles' blood (he was his *xynaimos*, 198); yet he 'wanted to feed on the common blood' of his fellow Thebans (201–2).[10] Thus, despite his relationship by marriage to Creon (174), he is no friend of his, nor of the Theban *polis*.

The threat to Thebes that Polynices posed arose out of familial strife that eventually became fratricidal. Both the Chorus (in the parodos) and Creon (in his opening speech) use language that suggests distaste for the brothers' hostility and its effects,[11] and yet the '*miasma* of their murder at each other's hands' (172) will continue to afflict the city as result of Creon's exposure of the body: the source of the city's sickness lies in Creon's mind, says Tiresias at 1015, but even after Tiresias' warning Creon is (at least initially) contemptuous of the dangers of *miasma* (1042–4). The pollution that Creon causes (and that threatens the city) has antecedent causes in the pollution of mutual fratricide that threatened the city, and that itself has roots that go further back in this family with its history of parricide and incest. Creon himself sets out to put the city first, the family and all other sources of loyalty second; yet ultimately the city will require deliverance from the dangers that he himself has created.

The origins of this development can perhaps be glimpsed in Creon's opening speech. First, his power derives from his 'closeness in kinship to the dead' (174). One does not need to know more than the minimum about the mythological background (no more, for example, than one could glean from Aeschylus' Theban trilogy) to see that the succession of rulers that he recounts (Laius, Oedipus, Eteocles, and Polynices, 165–74) is not an inspiring set of precedents. Creon proposes a clean break with the past, but also emphasizes an unbroken line of succession that legitimizes his power, and inserts himself in the Labdacid succession.[12]

His principles are to put the city first, all other loyalties second. Yet his political power derives from a familial connection (he is related to the Labdacids by marriage). Kinship ties give him the power, he thinks, to override ties of kinship. Whether or not the audience wonder at this stage whether Creon really does represent the end of the disruption and danger posed by the Labdacids, they learn soon enough that he does not. As for the principles on which Creon bases his first act as ruler, he himself tells us that principles are all very well, but only time will tell how they hold up in practice (175–7). The test will be the success of his edict. The principles on which the edict rests he refers to as the laws (*nomoi*) by which he strengthens the city (191); the edict itself is 'sibling' (*adelpha*, 192) to these. But the proclamation itself, with its differential treatment of Eteocles and Polynices (194–206), serves to underline that the tie between siblings can be sundered.[13] Such has been the pattern, not only in the brothers' case, but also in that of Antigone and Ismene: so will there be a rift between Creon's principles and his edict? For the attentive, the potential for conflict between siblings that Creon's use of *adelpha* activates is a clear sign of possible divergence between the *nomoi* to which he subscribes – admirable enough to be quoted by Demosthenes a century later – and the proclamation (*kêrygma*) that he takes to express those *nomoi*. This is a potential that Antigone famously activates in her contemptuous distinction between mere proclamations (*kêrygmata*) and the unwritten laws (*nomima*) of the gods at 453–5.

The opposition of Antigone and Creon comes to life in their confrontation at 441–525. Her very first line in the play had emphasized the closeness of blood-ties, especially through the link with the mother's body: the regular Greek term for 'sibling' (*adelphos/adelphê*) itself means 'from the same womb', but Antigone's compound *autadelphos* emphasizes yet further the 'self-sameness' of the womb from which she and Ismene emerged.[14] This is the same womb that both produced Oedipus and received his seed; and Oedipus is mentioned in the very next line as the source of the 'evils' that Antigone and Ismene share.[15] She uses the word *autadelphos* again at 503 in expressing the strength of her commitment to Polynices,[16] and makes the same point elsewhere in the same scene, in referring to her inability to look on as 'the deceased [who was born] from her mother' remained unburied (466–7). Her motivation is expressed in equally visceral terms at 511: what she has done, she says, is 'to respect those who emerged from the same gut'.[17] Antigone's word here, *sebein*, to respect or revere, is another of those terms over which she and Creon disagree:[18] Antigone favours locutions that apply *sebas* and *eusebeia* to loyalty to one's kin and the gods,[19] while Creon deploys them with reference to respect for the city and its laws, and ultimately for his own power.[20]

Antigone's familial and religious values and Creon's political ideals remain opposed as their stichomythia continues (512–14):

> CREON: Was the one that died on the other side not also of the same blood (*homaimos*)?
> ANTIGONE: *Homaimos* of one mother and the same father.
> CREON: Then why do you honour a recompense that is impious (*dyssebês*) in his eyes?

Creon reverts to the basic fact of Eteocles' loyalty and Polynices' treachery (as also at 516, 518, 520), while Antigone restates the common sibling bond and the laws of Hades (517, 519, 521). There is no meeting of minds; persuasion and resolution are impossible, given who these people are, as well as the principles they espouse. In the confrontation itself, neither obviously 'wins'; but though Antigone's penultimate shot ('Who knows whether these things [i.e., depriving the undeserving dead of the privileges accorded the deserving, 520] are ritually pure in the underworld?') sounds agnostic, it is in fact a pertinent reminder of the limitations of human knowledge about the wishes of the gods, and its force is later vindicated when Creon's differential treatment of the bodies proves to be anything but pure.

But this does not quite conclude their exchange. Before that happens, Creon restates both the polarity of friends and enemies and the primacy of the political criterion for each (522):

> The *echthros* is never a *philos*, not even when he dies.

To the extent that Tiresias later condemns the prolongation of enmity beyond the grave (1029–30), this statement is proved wrong. Antigone counters with her most famous line of all (523):

I was born to join in love (*symphilein*) not in hatred (*synechthein*).

On one level, the line once again opposes kinship-*philia* to Creon's politically determined *philia*, for its basic point is that ties of kinship are given at birth, while enmities are socially constituted and so (normally) acquired as one's social identity develops.[21] But as a statement of the absolute primacy of kinship ties, its universal force is immediately undercut by the very next scene of the play (536–60), in which Ismene's love drives her to attempt to share her sister's fate, but is coldly rejected by Antigone. We note especially Ismene's repeated use (in 537, 541, and 545) of the preverb *syn-* ('together') that Antigone had emphasized in her aphorism at 523, and Antigone's cruel dismissal, 'I do not love a *philos* who is *philos* in words alone', at 544. The *philia* towards Ismene that Antigone was born with can, it seems, be dissolved, in the same way as was that between Eteocles and Polynices; they were joined in hatred, not in love, even if they both loved Antigone. Antigone may be proved right, but her behaviour and her principles are at variance here, and it may take more than principle to explain her devotion to Polynices as opposed to Ismene.[22]

Just as Antigone's commitment to the primacy of kinship ties begins to appear questionable, so problems arise in Creon's elevation of the interests of the state as the criterion for all other forms of relationship: he both fails to secure the interests of the state in practice and learns the importance of the ties that he disparaged. If Antigone's use of visceral language for kinship ties, emphasizing shared blood and the sharing of the same womb, underlines the intensity, but also the partiality, of her commitment, Creon's use of the same language emphasizes the importance of the bonds that he affects to disparage. Already at 198 his description of Polynices as Eteocles' *xynaimos* (brother, literally 'blood-sharer') highlights the equality in their status as full brothers that is fundamental to Antigone's argument. His words at 486–90 then begin to illustrate a dangerous contempt for such ties:

But whether she is my sister's child or closer to me in blood (*homaimonestera*) than my whole circle of Zeus Herkeios, she and her sister (*xynaimos*) will not evade the worst of deaths. For indeed I accuse her equally of planning this burial.

In this case, Creon makes no distinction between the two sisters (*xynaimoi*). He later recognizes that there is a distinction to be drawn (771); but ultimately his intended treatment of both Antigone and Ismene is identical: having reprieved Ismene, he unsuccessfully attempts to reprieve Antigone (1112, 1204–25). In this way, his treatment of the sisters at first contrasts with, but ultimately replicates, his treatment of the brothers: in the face of Antigone's arguments to the contrary, he maintains the rectitude of treating *xynaimoi* differently in death (512–13); but in the end Polynices is duly buried (1196–1204). But the children of Oedipus are not only kin to each other; they are also kin to Creon – his sister's blood runs in their veins. This is the tie he says he will ignore at 486–90. Indeed, he says, not even a closer blood-tie than this would weigh with him in the exercise of his political and judicial power. But the form of words he uses also brings into question his relation towards the gods who underwrite such relationships: not even if Antigone were closer in blood (*homaimonestera*) than all who worship Zeus at Creon's hearth would it make a difference. All Creon's references to Zeus sound an ominous note. At 184, his reference to 'Zeus who sees everything' underlines the leap in the dark that he, as an ordinary mortal, one who does not see ruin coming until it is too late, is taking. At 304, his use of the conditional ('if Zeus retains my respect') raises a genuine question about whether he is showing respect (*sebas*) for Zeus. At 1040–3 he claims that fear of *miasma* would not induce him to bury Polynices, even if Zeus's eagles carried the corpse's flesh as food to his throne. Antigone's distinction between the pronouncements of Zeus and those of Creon at 450 is warranted. But his references to Zeus Herkeios (and the blood-ties that bind those who worship him) at 486–7 and to Zeus Xynaimos (as the subject of Antigone's constant harping) at 658–9 serve the further purpose of forging a link between Creon's disparagement of kinship ties (and of the gods whose power is invested in them) and the pain that he eventually suffers because he does so. First, what the Chorus call 'shared-blood strife' (*neikos xynaimon*, 793–4) breaks out between Creon and his closest blood-relative, the aptly named Haemon; then the son attempts to kill his father, before turning his sword in anger against himself (1232–9). 'Haemon is dead,' announces the Messenger (1175), 'bloodied by his own hand' – *Haimôn . . . haimassetai*. And Creon learns what blood-ties can mean to a person.

But the ties of *philia* that exist between blood-relatives are not the only ones that Creon disparages. Creon's answer to Antigone's declaration that she was born to join in love, not in hatred, is the following (524–5): 'Then go below and love them (*philein*), if you must love (*philein*).' Creon has no time for Antigone's talk of *philia*. By 'them' he is referring to Polynices and Eteocles, but the prospect of *philia* in Hades introduces a new theme that is immediately developed with the arrival of Ismene (526ff.). She is incredulous that Creon would condemn to death the girl who is betrothed to his own son (568, 574), especially since the couple are so well suited (570).[23] The marriage of Antigone and Haemon, then, would fulfil the ideal of 'like-mindedness' between man and wife that Odysseus commends to the young Nausicaa in the *Odyssey*.[24] But Creon invokes another association, the agricultural imagery of the Athenian formula of betrothal,[25] when he observes that the role of wife is one that can be filled by any number of women: 'Others have furrows that he can plough' (569). And so 'Hades is the one who will put a stop to this marriage' (575).

We soon hear the views of the bridegroom. The closeness of the bond between Haemon and Antigone has been suggested by Ismene at 570 and 572. As Haemon enters, the Chorus raise the possibility that his arrival is motivated by resentment at the treatment of his fiancée and the loss of his marriage (626–30). Creon's first words to his son then pose the alternatives of frenzied rage on behalf of his bride or unconditional *philia* towards his father (632–4). In effect, Creon is setting *philia* between father and son against the irrational passion that the Chorus will identify, in the song they sing after Haemon's departure, as *erôs*.[26] But if Creon thinks that

Haemon feels *erôs* for Antigone (as is suggested by 746, 750, 756, 760–1), he also wants him to reject her as a *philos* (639–62). A son should have the same friends and enemies as his father (639–44); filial disloyalty merely gives the father's enemies an opportunity to mock (645–7). Sexual pleasure would be a poor motive for contravening these values (648–51); 'for', he explains (652–3), 'what wound could be worse than an evil *philos*?' Creon thus sees Antigone as his enemy and demands that Haemon reject her as a *philos*. His justification for this lies in Antigone's disobedience (663–76), which Creon condemns in terms that appeal in general to the citizen body's sense of itself as a community of hoplite warriors, standing shoulder to shoulder in the line of battle, ideals that were reflected in the oath that young Athenian warriors swore when they entered upon the first stage of their military service.[27] In Athenian political terms, this pushes many of the right buttons. Perhaps even the personalization of these principles, as Creon reveals that they serve the needs of his self-image as a man who is both a strong leader and a strong head of household (655–62), a man who cannot be bested by a woman (678–80),[28] strikes a sympathetic chord with some in the original audience in a way that it does not for us. But the political justifications are surely undercut by the claim that the city's leader must be obeyed in small things and great, right and wrong (666–7),[29] a sentiment that he follows up with a series of rhetorical questions: 'Is the city going to tell me how to rule?' (734); 'Am I to rule in my own interests or someone else's?' (736); and 'Isn't the city considered to belong to its ruler?' (738).

Again in this scene Creon disparages Antigone's attachment to religious and familial duty: her invocations of Zeus Xynaimos are to no avail; he will kill her (658–9). But familial duty is what he demands of Haemon, and out of that duty he expects Haemon to 'spit this girl out like an enemy and let her marry someone in Hades' (653–4); a bad woman is a 'cold thing to embrace' (650). By the time he calls Haemon 'inferior to a woman' (746) and 'a woman's slave' (756) he realizes that Haemon has made his choice, and that father and son have become enemies. Haemon has not spat Antigone out, but does finally spit in his father's face (1233), before he clings 'in a feeble embrace' to the cold, dead body of Antigone (1236–7) and dies, 'obtaining his nuptial rites in the house of Hades' (1240–1).[30] Creon's words have come back to haunt him.

The choice that Creon tries to force on Haemon, that he should put his ties to his father before marriage, strongly resembles that already made by Antigone when, as an unmarried maiden and out of loyalty to her brother, she chose an action that would lead to her death. Both Antigone's choice and Creon's ultimatum to Haemon put natal before conjugal family. In Antigone's final scene she stresses her lack of *philoi* in this world (847, 876–82) and the abundance of *philoi* in Hades (863–71, 892–903), and justifies her choice of death over life by setting higher value on a brother than on a husband or children. Just as Creon said that Haemon could find other furrows to plough, so Antigone observes that the role of husband is one that can be filled by any man, and that children can be replaced, by means of a new husband if necessary; but when one's parents are dead, brothers are irreplaceable (904–15). Many have wished to eject these lines from the text.[31] They are in some ways poorly expressed, and the argument they advance fits better in its other fifth-century outing (at Herodotus 3. 119) than it does here.[32] But we have the evidence of Aristotle that they were in the text of the play as it existed in the fourth century;[33] and even without that strong indication of their genuineness, their contribution to some of the major themes of the play is such that they must be original.[34]

Creon, as representative of the *polis* and in line with his perception of the city's needs, seeks to control two inter-related institutions, of the *oikos* (household) and of marriage, whose regulation is integral to the health of a well-functioning *polis*. But Creon's conception of the *polis* turns out to be limited, and he uses his power not to integrate the institutions of the family and marriage, but to repress them. He suffers in proportion to his acts when his *oikos* is wiped out and he loses both his closest blood-relative and his wife. Creon learns what blood-ties mean when Haemon, with his significant name, proves himself to be the complementary opposite of Antigone, putting his bride before his father, in contrast to her preference for a brother over marriage, husband, and children. He learns what marital ties mean when Eurydice emerges as a counterpart to Antigone, killing herself out of grief for her son, and cursing the husband whose decisions as military and political leader cost her both her sons (1301–5, 1312–16). The parallel between the tragedies of Antigone and Creon is something we have discussed extensively above; but there is more to be said about the way that the fate of Creon's *oikos* comes to mirror that of Antigone's.

Sex and death

Antigone comes from a family in which, even if we consider only her own generation and that of her parents (the only ones to feature substantially in the backstory that is alluded to in the play itself), breakdown in relations between blood-relatives and failure of marriage have been prominent. Her own idiosyncratic devotion to one category of *philia*, and to one *philos* in particular within that category, is also represented in terms not of *philia* but of *erôs*. According to Ismene, Antigone is 'in love with the impossible' (90). On the face of it, this is simple hyperbole, using a very strong word (*eran*), normally associated with the powerful force of sexual attraction, to make a point about the irrational vehemence of Antigone's (non-sexual) determination to defy Creon's edict. But why that word, here, of the daughter of Oedipus and her devotion to a member of her own family? Ismene's observation is part of her answer to Antigone's statement that she 'is pleasing those whom [she] should please most' (89). There are pleasures other than sexual, but, naturally enough, an Athenian wife would be expected to please her husband in all kinds of ways,[35] and Creon uses a word from the same root when he warns Haemon not to lose his senses on account of the pleasure to be found in marriage (648).

Antigone's words in line 89 recall something she had said just a few lines before (73–6):

> I shall lie with him, *philos* with *philos*, having committed a holy crime.
> I have to please those below for longer than those up here: there I shall lie forever.

For death to be figured as sleep, and for the verb 'to lie' to be used of both, is nothing unusual. But though Polynices is the only relative that Antigone has to bury, he is not (as she herself observes later, 897–9) her only relative in Hades. What is so special about her relationship with him? Why is he in particular the one with whom she will lie, *philos* with *philos*, like husband and wife? It is a son and daughter of Oedipus that we are talking about here: in her final scene (at 864–5) Antigone laments her mother's incestuous 'lying' (*koimêmata*) with the child she herself produced. The notion of two members of this family lying together cannot be free of this association.[36]

The hint of an erotic aspect to Antigone's devotion is sustained by the Chorus-leader's observation, in response to Creon's request that the Chorus should not side with his opponents, that 'no one is so foolish as to be in love with (*eran*) death'. But Antigone disobeys the edict, exercising a choice of death over life (555), because for her death is better than life (461–7); in the confrontation with Creon that follows her arrest she goes so far as to goad him over his delay in implementing the penalty (497–9). Creon's injunction, that she should demonstrate her *philia* in Hades (524–5), is not something that she rejects. She looks forward to renewing *philia* with her father, her mother, and her brother after her death (897–9).[37] Antigone herself stresses her anomalous situation, her fixation with death,[38] when she tells Ismene that her soul (*psychê*) has long since died, to permit her to serve the dead (559–60). Even before her entombment, then, Antigone is, like Creon at the end of the play (1167; cf. 1288, 1325), a living corpse. Creon's remark at 777, that Hades is the only god she worships, is both sarcastic and a sign of his own neglect of Hades' claims, but it is not wholly without foundation. Antigone's final scene perhaps gives another perspective,[39] but even there it is the manner of her death and its injustice to which she draws attention. Otherwise, death itself appears to hold an attraction for her, and in just one or two places that attraction is expressed in erotic terms or in ways that suggest a particular affection for Polynices. None of this amounts to an explicit indication that Antigone harbours or harboured incestuous desires for her brother. But the closeness of their bond is presented in ways that remind us that her family has a history of introversion and that both she and her brother are the products of incest.

We shall turn to the 'marriage of death' theme in detail below. But there is one aspect of that theme that illustrates both the play's recurrent associations between sex and death and the parallelisms that emerge between Antigone and her family, on the one hand, and Creon and his on the other. This is the Messenger's description of Haemon's death (1234–41):

> Then the poor fellow, angry at himself, tensed himself, just as he was, over his sword, and drove it half its length into his side. Still in his senses, he clung to the maiden in a feeble embrace, and, breathing hard, he emitted a quick stream of bloody drops onto her white cheek. He lies, corpse embracing corpse, obtaining his nuptial rites in the house of Hades, poor lad . . .

Penetration takes place, but of the male. Antigone's body remains inviolate; she has killed herself by hanging and knows nothing of Haemon's presence. The image of the female soaked in the male's blood as a perversion of sexual climax draws upon Clytemnestra's memorable description of her murder of Agamemnon at Aeschylus, *Agamemnon* 1389–90. And Haemon lies, 'corpse around corpse', as Antigone wanted to lie with Polynices, *philos* with *philos* (73). Both Antigone and Haemon achieve marriage in Hades, but while Haemon is united with Antigone, Antigone is arguably united with Polynices, in a bizarre triangle of love and death.

Marriage and death

As we noted, at least part of the aberration that Antigone represents lies in her being the product of an incestuous union. Incest is one extreme on the spectrum of ways that marriage can depart from the norms of Athenian ideology. The other extreme, from the Athenian point of view, is also represented in Antigone's family, in Polynices' marriage to the daughter of Adrastus, king of Argos. In the period in which *Antigone* was first performed, Athenian law prohibited not only (as it had probably always done) marriage between close blood relations, but also marriage between Athenians and members of other communities. Athenian marriage was moderately endogamous: cousins could and often did marry, but marriage between individuals of citizen and non-citizen status was prohibited.[40] The extremes of both endogamy and exogamy were avoided. In the house of Labdacus, on the other hand, the existence of both is highlighted by Antigone herself. In response to the Chorus's conclusion that she is paying the price for a debt incurred by her father (856), she sings (863–71):

> O the ruin (*atai*) of my mother's bed, my poor mother's incestuous couplings (*koimêmata*) with my father, from what parents I, poor wretch, was born. I make my way to dwell with them, accursed, unwed, as you see. O brother who made a fatal marriage, your death destroyed me, though I am still alive.

Oedipus married his mother; Polynices married an Argive, not a Theban. Two failed marriages, one at either extreme of the spectrum of endogamy and exogamy, have destroyed Antigone's own marriage and left her with nothing but a marriage of death.[41]

Antigone's predicament arises from a failure in funeral ritual, a failure that is then compounded, as Tiresias will point out (1069), in Creon's attempt to lodge a living soul in the world of the dead, a disruption of the norm that amounts, in effect, to giving Antigone herself a funeral in which she is the only mourner. But this failure in turn leads to a failure of marriage ritual, as we have already noted with respect to Haemon's 'nuptial rites', above. Creon plays a substantial role in this failure; but so too does Antigone herself. She laments her marriage to death (816), but her decision to defy Creon's edict was also a choice of natal over conjugal family (905–14), a decision to die rather than to marry. The coalescence of the two themes is represented in Antigone's departure scene, as the two rites of passage, wedding and funeral, are vividly conflated. As we saw, Creon's reference to her finding a *philos* in Hades (524–5) immediately preceded Ismene's introduction of the theme of Antigone's wedding to Haemon (568–75). In the scenes that follow, these two perspectives (death as a kind of marriage and death as a replacement for marriage) remain intertwined.

Creon is the first to refer as such to Antigone's death as her marriage at 654: 'Let her marry someone in Hades.' But Creon is Antigone's *kyrios*, and in suggesting an alternative husband for her he is, albeit sarcastically, exercising his right to arrange her marriage. Before the marriage to death scene is played out before our eyes at 806ff., the Chorus sing a hymn to Eros (781–800). Though one might not get this impression from modern textbooks, *erôs* is central to the Athenian wedding and to the ideal of marriage that it promotes, as can be seen from the regular appearance of Erotes and other erotic imagery in wedding scenes on Athenian vases.[42] Songs invoking Eros or Aphrodite, too, most likely formed part of fifth-century Athenian wedding celebrations;[43] thus, while this particular song stresses the destructive aspects of *erôs* and in particular looks back to the conflict between Creon and Haemon, it also heralds the entrance of the 'bride', Antigone, at 801, quite possibly wearing her wedding dress.[44] Marriage is a prominent topic in her song. Hades, 'who puts all to bed',[45] is leading her alive to the shores of Acheron, as a bridegroom leads the bride from her father's house to her new home. She will have no share of marriage and no one will sing her wedding song,[46] but instead she will be bride to Acheron (810–16).

The fact that the conflation of wedding and funeral ritual is being visually and physically dramatized on stage is underlined by her lament at 916–20:

> And now he leads me, laying hands on me like this, without marriage bed or wedding song, with no share of marriage or of the rearing of children, but rather I, the ill-fated one, make my way like this, bereft of friends, alive to the hollows of the dead.

Here, Antigone's wedding is absent ('without marriage bed . . .' etc.), but also present in the detail of the hands that are leading Antigone to her tomb. Whoever these hands belong to (presumably an attendant rather than Creon himself, though Creon remains the effective agent), the action will no doubt have been more appropriate to imprisonment than to marriage. Yet even the typical gesture of leading the bride to her new home, a hand on her wrist, constitutes a reflection of the abduction imagery that permeates the Athenian wedding.[47] Antigone's walking, led by another, to her new home conveys an underlying image of the passage from life to death, but visually it will much more obviously have recalled the Athenian wedding.[48]

The place where Antigone is entombed is twice called a *nympheion*, a bridal chamber (by Antigone herself at 891, and by the Messenger at 1205), and so the ritual that is played out before the audience in Antigone's departure scene is concluded by the leading of the bride to the chamber in which, in the normal scheme of things, the marriage would be consummated. In the choral ode following Antigone's departure (944–50), Danae's bronze tomb is also described as a bridal chamber (*thalamos*), in which the marriage her father tried to prevent is in fact consummated. Just as Acrisius, father of Danae, imprisoned his daughter to prevent her marriage, so Creon imprisoned Antigone in order to marry her to death rather than to Haemon. In his case, too, the attempt fails. Antigone's marriage achieves a consummation of sorts, at least in the sexualized suicide of Haemon. But by then Antigone is dead, having hanged herself in her bridal-chamber-cum-tomb with what is very probably her bridal veil (1220–2). Veiling and unveiling were important aspects of the Greek wedding,[49] but Antigone has used her veil before Haemon arrives, and has used it to asphyxiate herself, dying in a way that draws no blood. This is a woman's and especially a virgin's death,[50] found in myth and in medical sources in association with virgins who reject marriage (contrast the suicide by the sword of a wife and mother, Eurydice, at 1282–3, 1302, 1315–16, a violent death that results from decisions taken by Creon, *stratêgos*, ruler, husband, and father).[51] It is thus significant that it is Haemon, not Antigone, who is said to complete his 'nuptial rites' (1240–1). Antigone remains a virgin, one who prefers her natal family to life with a husband, to the end. The marriage that she achieves is not marriage with Haemon. Like the virgin buried in her wedding dress, she is married only to death. Her *autognôtos orga* (self-willed temper) remains with her to the end.[52]

Marriage is a difficult transition to negotiate. An individual moves from one *oikos* to another; the new *oikos* admits a stranger. There are many things that can go wrong, at many different stages of the process.[53] Wedding ritual acknowledges the dangers of the transition precisely in order to overcome them; but myth, and tragedy which draws on myth, realize the potential for disaster that is encompassed by ritual. In tragedy, marriage ritual tends to be subverted, and marriages are often disastrous. The association between marriage and death is part of the negative tendency of marriage ritual, reflecting the 'death' of the maiden who becomes a wife, a pattern encapsulated above all in the myth of Persephone, but in a large number of other sources too, from mythical to medical. In the *Antigone*, the negative tendencies of ritual and myth are dramatized in the presentation of Antigone herself, whose resistance to marriage recalls the anxiety of the post-pubescent maidens whose symptoms are described in the Hippocratic treatise *On Virgins*,[54] according to which virgins who do not have sex soon after puberty are subject to the collection of blood within the body, which takes hold of the heart and causes insanity. The girl has visions, which lead to impulses to kill herself by strangulation or drowning (thus shedding no blood); or, if she has no visions, she falls in love (*eran*) with Death. The prescription is intercourse and childbirth.

Back to the *polis*

The Athenian *polis* controlled both funerals and weddings, the former largely so that social divisions and tensions should not be exposed through ostentatious funerals and extravagant forms of mourning,[55] the latter in order to determine admission to and exclusion from the citizen body. In both cases, the *polis* regulates the activities of the *oikos*. In this play, past disruption of ties of *philia* and *erôs* within the *oikos* produces further disruption in wedding and funerary ritual. Norms are transgressed and categories confounded. Both Antigone's devotion to her natal family and Creon's failure to take both natal and conjugal ties sufficiently seriously end in disaster, and two *oikoi* are destroyed. Two young people fail to fulfil their social roles as adults, and are married only in death. A marriage that has produced two adult male sons dissolves with the suicide of the wife, after both her sons have died without issue.[56] The norms of the *polis* and the legitimacy of its control over private households are justified by their breakdown in this play, but the rights of the *oikos* are also vindicated, and the dangers of repression and rigidity on the part of the *polis* are demonstrated. The *Antigone* confronts the latent fears and anxieties that surround a community's social institutions and magnifies them, so that the practices of the *polis* in controlling those anxieties in everyday life are legitimized. As is frequently the case, the traditional norms and practices familiar to the contemporary Athenian audience are refracted by their breach in the heroic world of Thebes.[57]

Though the play does dramatize oppositions between loyalty to the *polis* and loyalty to one's *philoi*, between *polis* and *oikos*, it will not do simply to map these polarities on to the opposition between Creon and Antigone. If Creon is more clearly a failure, in terms of his stated aim of securing the city's interests (for, in the end, he is the problem, not the solution: 1015), so too Antigone's behaviour represents a failure – of a child to become an adult, of a girl to become a woman, and of a woman to become a mother. No citizen in the audience hoped for leaders like Creon, or daughters like Antigone. Though her aims and her actions are vindicated, she represents a consequence and a continuation of the disruption and dysfunction that has beset her family for at least three generations. The gap between (on the one hand) an audience's appreciation of her ideals, her devotion, her aims, and her courage and (on the other) its recognition of the deviation from the norm that she represents is not just a matter of the gulf that always exists between what audiences want to see when they watch drama and what they want to see when they return to their everyday worlds, but rather a gap that exists within the dramatic structure of the play itself, between the surface sweep of events and some of their deeper undercurrents.

In her conflict with Ismene and her attachment to Polynices, even though this is not actually incestuous, Antigone recalls the problems that have bedevilled her family: conflict between *philoi* (Eteocles and Polynices, Oedipus and his sons, Oedipus and Laius), and incest. Antigone's status as a Labdacid, and the generations of trouble within her family, are stressed at several points in the play (49–60, 379–80, 471–2, 594–603, 856–65).[58] The similarity in character between Antigone and her parents, especially Oedipus, is ironically raised in the prologue, at 37–8, where she urges Ismene to show that her nature is true to the nobility of their parents. For the Chorus (471–2) Antigone has indeed inherited Oedipus' character, but it is a 'raw' or 'savage' one. We see similar patterns in Creon's family too: the conflict between Creon and Haemon mirrors that between Laius and Oedipus and that between Oedipus and his own sons: Creon takes Haemon's words at 751 ('Then she will die, and her death will kill another') as a threat of parricide (752), and in fact Haemon does attempt to kill his father at 1231–4. For Eurydice, on the other hand, Creon is a child-killer (1305), a point that Creon himself has already made by presenting Haemon's death as a case of internecine killing (1263–4). As Creon blames himself for the death of his son, so he blames himself for that of Eurydice (1319). In her suicide, however, she reminds us of the unnamed wife of Oedipus (53–4).[59] In lamenting (probably) the 'empty bed' of her son, Megareus (1302–3), she recalls Antigone, compared to a mother bird finding her 'bed' empty of nestlings at 423–8. Creon's *oikos*, like that of the Labdacids, is destroyed; Creon's concerns at the end of the play become as focused on his family as were those of Antigone at the beginning.[60] It is not that Creon was wrong to give primacy to the *polis*, and should have focused on the *oikos* all along, but more that his conduct towards both *polis* and *oikos* has endangered the one and ruined the other. On the one hand, Creon did fail to give the claims of family their due; but in doing so he also endangered the state by taking a stand in an ongoing internecine quarrel, becoming embroiled in a struggle with his niece, and by alienating his own son.

If Antigone is the last in a doomed and problematic lineage, Creon proves himself the true successor of Laius, Oedipus, and the brothers Eteocles and Polynices (165–74). He does so both as the last in a line of problematic leaders and, as it were, as an honorary member of the Labdacid dynasty – his own claim to rule lies in kinship (by marriage), and the manner of his rule replicates the familial strife that is the Labdacids' chief characteristic. The city's claims remain valid throughout the play, but the deliverance that the Chorus hailed in their address to the new day's dawn (101–5),[61] the forgetfulness of trouble that they hoped to celebrate in the worship of Dionysus (148–54), comes late, only after they have invoked Dionysus once more, this time to come and purify the city of its sickness (1140–5); if there is purification, it requires that the city be purged both of the Labdacids and of Creon's family.[62] The city's deliverance can come only when the disruption, whatever its nature, that afflicts both of these families has run its course. The second stasimon, therefore, with its reflections on the generations of disaster that may affect a family and its latent application to Creon, is the central node that connects the play's presentation of the rights and wrongs of its main characters' actions with the social, civic, and ritual themes that we have explored in this chapter. As an explanation of error, failure, and the ruin that results, the *atê*-sequence applies, in the end, more obviously to Creon than to Antigone; but at a deeper level, the ruin that has afflicted the Labdacids provides a context not only for Antigone's fate, but also for Creon's.

5

Reception

Sophocles' *Antigone* is very much a play for today. The South African actor John Kani, who collaborated with Athol Fugard and Winston Ntshona in one of the most iconic modern adaptations, speaks for many in saying that '*Antigone* addresses itself to any corner of the world where the human spirit is being oppressed'.[1] A recent example is *Antigone in Shatila* (aka *Antigone of Syria*), performed by Syrian women now living in the Beirut refugee camp of that name.[2] For the Greek Prime Minister, Alexis Tsipras, in a speech to the European Parliament in summer 2015, 'Sophocles, in his masterpiece *Antigone*, taught us that there are times when the supreme law, which is even superior to the laws of people, is justice.'[3] Antigone has become an icon of principled resistance in defence of universal rights. But she has not always been, and the story of her transformation is a long and intriguing one.

Probably no other Greek tragedy has as rich an afterlife in terms of theatrical production or literary adaptation. But *Antigone* is one of a more select group of tragedies whose influence is not limited to these domains: only *Oedipus the King* can rival its place in intellectual history. This chapter discusses only a few of the most striking examples of this huge afterlife. Its subject is the reception of Sophocles' play (rather than the wider mythological saga to which it belongs), and so those works which respond primarily to later reworkings of the Antigone story (by Euripides, Seneca, or Statius) are not discussed in detail. After a brief account of the ancient reception, I concentrate on *Antigone*'s influence from Hegel to the present day. This inevitably omits even some of the most important modern receptions.

Ancient reception

The Greek world

Signs of *Antigone*'s impact on subsequent tragedy first appear in Sophocles' own *Oedipus the King*, first produced perhaps in the late 430s or early 420s, where Antigone and Ismene are deployed for emotional effect at the end of the play. They enter at Oedipus' request (1459–75), and a reference to Oedipus' sons (1459–61) is enough to remind an audience of the fraternal strife to come and its consequences for the two girls on stage. Whether or not the passage is authentic,[4] it shows that, after *Antigone,* the consequences of Oedipus' death for his daughters, their suffering in connection with their brothers' enmity, and the role of Creon in their futures had become part of an audience's horizon of expectations with respect to the Oedipus story.

Discussion of Antigone's role in Euripides' *Phoenician Women,* tentatively dated to around 411–409 BC,[5] can be hampered by suspicions about two of the main scenes in which she appears.[6] Recent scholarship has on the whole favoured authenticity.[7] In her first appearance Antigone, like Helen in the *Iliad,* looks down from the city's walls on the battlefield below, and the major figures on the opposing side are identified (88–201). She reappears at 1270, summoned by her mother in an effort to prevent the duel between her brothers. Mother and daughter depart for the battlefield (1283), and their failure, followed by Jocasta's suicide, is reported by a Messenger (1335–1479). Antigone then returns (at 1485) and is joined in lamentation by Oedipus (1539ff.). The play's final scene features Antigone's defiance of Creon, first over his banishment of Oedipus and then over the denial of burial and her marriage to Haemon (1639–82). Unable in practice to defy Creon over the burial of Polynices, she accompanies Oedipus into exile. Euripides' inclusion of Antigone's defiance (especially at 1650–9) testifies to the contribution of Sophocles' *Antigone* to the tradition of Theban mythology.[8] Like her Sophoclean counterpart, this Antigone is forced to transcend the norms of maidenly behaviour, but she does so in a less extreme and more gradual fashion.

The *Phoenician Women* was a very popular play in antiquity.[9] It inspired works of the same title by the Roman tragedians Accius and Seneca, and was a major source not only for Statius, but also for later adaptations such as Racine's *La Thébaïde ou les frères ennemis* (1664) and Jane Robe's *The Fatal Legacy* (1723).[10] Perhaps the first sign of its influence is in Sophocles' own *Oedipus at Colonus*, produced by the playwright's grandson (also Sophocles) in 401 BC, several years after its author's death. At the end of *Phoenician Women*, Oedipus remembers a prophecy that he should die in exile in Attica, at Colonus, an area sacred to Poseidon (1703–9); this is his destination as he departs with Antigone. Their arrival, and the events surrounding Oedipus' death, are the subject of *Oedipus at Colonus*. The story may have appeared first in the Euripidean play, then in the Sophoclean, though some believe that the end of Euripides' play has been remodelled under the influence of *Oedipus at Colonus*.[11]

Whereas *Antigone* turns on Antigone's devotion to her brother, *Oedipus at Colonus* depicts her devotion to her father. Like Polynices, Oedipus is denied burial in his home territory (399–407, 591, 599–603, 784–6). He too is 'unburied' (*ataphos*, 1732), but in a different sense – he has no grave, and the spot at which he died is to be known by no one (1758, 1760–7). Antigone's desire to see her father's grave (1725–8, 1733, 1756–7) is thus frustrated. Devotion to all her *philoi* alike is Antigone's defining feature in this play.[12] She intervenes decisively at 237–53, when the Chorus reject Oedipus' supplication in horror at his past. Her intervention is crucial again at 1181–1203, where she begs Oedipus to give a hearing to the appeals of Polynices, himself now an exile and a suppliant. In contrast to *Antigone*, in this play Antigone and Ismene support each other throughout.[13] But Antigone is unable to reconcile Oedipus and Polynices (1254–1396); and she similarly fails to dissuade Polynices from mounting his expedition against Thebes, though it will mean the death of both brothers (1414–46). Oedipus and Polynices are alike in insisting that a *philos* who has harmed one in the past must forever be regarded as an *echthros*.[14]

Oedipus at Colonus is careful to leave room for the events of *Antigone*. As in *Phoenician Women*, Polynices makes a specific request that his sisters should see to the burial of his body (1405–10, 1435). On departing, he prays (in vain) that his sisters' lives should be happy and fortunate (1435, 1444–6). The issue of Antigone's future and of her return to Thebes is then raised repeatedly at the play's close (1737–8, 1742–3, 1748–50); at 1769–72 she expresses a determination to return and prevent the fratricide. But the kinsmen to whom she is so devoted have already made this impossible; and the outcome is foreshadowed in the play's characterization of Creon as a crude villain. Like *Phoenician Women*, *Oedipus at Colonus* presupposes an audience whose dominant impression of the earlier Sophoclean Antigone is of a character motivated by duty and devotion to family. At the same time, the two later plays resemble each other in softening the edges of that earlier incarnation, so that, despite the extraordinary circumstances in which she finds herself, their Antigone conforms more closely to traditional ideals of Athenian maidenhood.[15]

The classic status of Sophocles' *Antigone* receives further confirmation in the closing scenes of Aeschylus' *Seven against Thebes*, where Antigone (accompanied by Ismene) declares her determination to defy Creon's prohibition of the burial of Polynices. Though the trilogy of which this is the final play was produced in 467 BC, most scholars believe that Antigone played no part in the original version and the closing scenes in which she is present were added after the production not only of Sophocles' *Antigone* but also of Euripides' *Phoenician Women*.[16] Antigone's defiance of the Herald's prohibition (1005–53) illustrates not only the integration of Antigone's deed into the tradition of the Theban saga, but also the salience in the popular imagination of the characteristic assertiveness of her stance.[17]

As well as his *Phoenician Women*, Euripides also (at roughly the same stage of his career) composed an *Antigone*.[18] Twenty fragments, mostly gnomic in character and so of limited use in reconstructing the plot, survive in quotations by later authors. An ancient *hypothesis* to Sophocles' *Antigone*, however, suggests that Euripides' version involved Haemon as Antigone's accomplice in the burial of Polynices, and that this led to their marriage; it also refers to the birth of their child,

Maeon.[19] A later *Antigone*, by Astydamas, is known to have been produced in 341 BC,[20] winning the first prize at the Dionysia in that year. Scholars speculate that either Euripides' or Astydamas' *Antigone* is the source for a version in Hyginus, *Fabula* 72, where Heracles appears as a mediator on Haemon's behalf, after Creon has discovered that he and Antigone have had a son, despite Creon's original order that Haemon should kill Antigone as punishment for burying her brother's body.[21]

Antigone is not an especially popular subject in ancient art: *LIMC* catalogues sixteen possible depictions.[22] According to Oliver Taplin, 'There is not one single vase-painting that can be probably related to [Sophocles'] *Antigone*.'[23] This is very likely correct: there are items that depict Antigone's involvement in the burial of Polynices, but these seem to derive from versions other than Sophocles'. The only candidate as a depiction of the confrontation between Antigone and Creon is a Lucanian nestoris of around 380 BC in the British Museum,[24] in which two guards present a woman (with appropriately downcast eyes, as at *Ant.* 441) to a seated figure in oriental headgear. There are no inscriptions, and a reference to Sophocles' play, or even to the confrontation between Antigone and Creon, does not seem inevitable.

Antigone at Rome

The strongest evidence for the reception of Sophocles' version of the *Antigone* story is the version of Accius (born *c.* 170, died *c.* 80 BC).[25] Only six short fragments of his *Antigone* survive, but they are enough to suggest a relatively faithful adaptation.[26] Seneca's *Phoenician Women* is undated, but appears to have been left unfinished:[27] it is only 664 lines long and has no choral parts. In the first of its two discrete sections, Antigone is, as in *Oedipus at Colonus*, in exile with her father. In the second, as in Euripides' *Phoenician Women*, she and her mother attempt to avert the fratricide.[28] There is nothing that suggests direct adaptation of Sophocles' *Antigone*; but Seneca may have intended to complete the unfinished work with a final act dramatizing the confrontation between

Antigone and Creon over the burial of Polynices.[29] The play would thus have ended as, in its surviving form, it begins, with the demonstration of Antigone's *pietas* (loyalty to kin): *pietas* and its breakdown in the House of Labdacus are the central themes.[30]

Familial duty is also Antigone's defining characteristic in Statius' *Thebaid* (published *c.* AD 92), an account of the destruction of the House of Labdacus from Oedipus' curse to Theseus' burial of the Argive dead. *Phoenician Women* and other Euripidean tragedies (especially *Suppliant Women*) take their place among its many poetic models and influences.[31] The question of Statius' use of Sophocles is more controversial, but an awareness of *Antigone* cannot really be denied.[32] This is confirmed above all by the presentation of the burial of Polynices in Book 12 as a contest between Polynices' wife, Argia, and Antigone for the latter's Sophoclean role. As Argia cradles the body in her arms, she asks (12. 330–1), 'Did you move none of your kinfolk to tears? Where is your mother? Where is Antigone, whose reputation is famous?' (332–3). This question refers not to Antigone's place in the plot of Statius' *Thebaid* so far, but to the literary tradition, especially Sophocles' *Antigone*.[33] No sooner has Argia posed her question than Antigone appears (349), bent on the same task, and indignant at encountering a rival: 'Whose body are you searching for', she asks (365–6); 'And who do you think you are to do so on *my* night?'[34] Argia and Antigone then join forces: they drag Polynices' body to a burning pyre which proves to be that of Eteocles (409–28); even in death, the brothers cannot be reconciled, and the flames arising from their corpses part in never-ending hostility (429–46). The two women are then apprehended by Creon's guards, and the issue of the ownership of the Sophoclean Antigone's role arises once more.[35] Like Antigone in Sophocles' play (*Ant.* 443), they 'openly confess that they flouted Creon's orders' (452–4); like Sophocles' heroine they exhibit a brave but irrational desire for death (456–7); and, rather like Antigone and Ismene in their second confrontation (*Ant.* 526–60), they each claim responsibility. As with Antigone and Ismene in Sophocles' play, mutual respect (460) quickly turns to hostility (462).[36]

At 12. 459 Antigone claims that her *pietas* led her to act, Argia her *amor*. The quasi-erotic aspect of Antigone's devotion to Polynices in Sophocles' play, rooted in their incestuous origins (see Chapter 4), has become Argia's legitimate love for her husband. True, Polynices and Antigone are bound by an intense mutual affection,[37] and this does provoke jealousy in Argia (12. 394–7): Polynices found it easy, she says, to abandon her in Argos in the hope of returning to his beloved sister, the sole focus of his desires. But the suggestion of a quasi-conjugal relationship between Polynices and Antigone is not otherwise salient, and even if Polynices did love her more than his wife, there is no sign that she loved him like a husband. Though her *pietas* does – in a highly Sophoclean manner – lead to conflict when confronted with the *amor* of Argia,[38] *pietas* remains, as in Seneca's *Phoenician Women,* her defining characteristic.[39] Argia, by contrast, is the woman whose conduct, like that of the Sophoclean Antigone, represents a female appropriation of masculine values (12. 177–9): she 'abandons her sex' to undertake a 'huge task', in a 'sudden passion' (*amor*) for 'non-feminine virtue' (*virtus,* cognate with *vir,* man).

It is Statius' version of the Antigone-myth that – together, sometimes, with the *Phoenician Women* of Euripides and Seneca – leaves the strongest impression on later versions of the Theban myth from the Middle Ages until the later eighteenth century.[40] It is the ultimate source for the twelfth-century *Roman de Thèbes,* in which Antigone dies of lovesickness following a competition for her affections between Parthenopaeus, one of the Seven against Thebes, and the King of Nubia.[41] In Dante's *Purgatorio* 22. 109–14 (*c.* 1314) Virgil explains to Statius that the souls of his characters, Antigone, Argia, and their sisters, Ismene and Deipyle, are with those of other pagans in Limbo.[42] Antigone then disappears until the sixteenth century, resurfacing notably in the Christianizing version of Robert Garnier, *Antigone: ou la piété* (Paris, 1580), a lyric drama drawing on (chiefly) Renaissance translations of Sophocles' Theban plays, the *Phoenician Women* of Euripides and Seneca, and Statius.[43] Argia does not feature in Garnier, but her Statian role as Antigone's accomplice is replicated in a number of later versions, including Jean de Rotrou's tragedy, *La Thébaïde* (first performed Paris, 1637; published 1639),[44] several eighteenth-century operas,[45] and Vittorio Alfieri's tragic *Antigone* of 1783. In the latter, having joined with Argia to bury Polynices, Antigone is condemned to death by Creon. Sophocles' original begins to assert itself when she refuses Creon's offer of a reprieve if she will marry Haemon. She is killed, and Haemon kills himself.[46]

The history of Antigone's characterization in the post-Sophoclean tradition, from Euripides to the eighteenth century, is one of the softening of her rough edges, the heightening of the love interest in the plots in which she appears, and the accentuation of her status as a paradigm of familial piety. Almost as soon as she was created, Sophocles' Antigone was transformed, and it is other characterizations, not Sophocles', that dominate in the following centuries. A decisive break with this tradition comes in the early nineteenth century, when the features of the modern Antigone begin to be established.[47] The origins of this change are complex, but it clearly belongs against the background of Enlightenment thought regarding the position of the individual in society and of the political circumstances of the years before and after the French Revolution. The rise of German philhellenism in this period is crucial.[48]

Our Antigone: Hegel and after

Antigone among the philosophers

As a student in Tübingen from 1788–93 Friedrich Hölderlin (1770–1843) was – along with his fellow students, Hegel and Schelling – an enthusiastic supporter of the French Revolution. His translation of Sophocles' *Antigone* was published along with a version of *Oedipus the King* in 1804,[49] but ridiculed by his contemporaries for its occasional mistranslations and the strangeness of its language, especially for what were regarded as risibly unnatural attempts to render Greek idioms in German:[50] the translation of Ismene's question in line 20 – 'Was ist's? Du scheinst ein rotes Wort zu färben' (more strikingly literal than Constantine's 'What is it? You seem to dye your words with red') – in particular provoked the ridicule of Heinrich Voß (son of Johann Heinrich Voß, the translator of Homer), his severest early critic.[51] In the twentieth century, however, the translation came to be regarded both as a key work in Hölderlin's *oeuvre* and as a landmark in the modern reception of Sophocles' play, praised for its boldness, its religiosity, its developed and idiosyncratic vision of 'the tragic', and above all for the power of its poetic language.[52]

Hölderlin's interpretation emerges especially in the dense and difficult notes that he penned to accompany his translation.[53] In his view, Antigone and Creon are alike: where Antigone recognizes God 'through lawlessness', Creon represents 'the pious fear in the face of Fate, and with it the honouring of God as something set in law'.[54] Each has his or her own 'Zeus': '*My* Zeus did not dictate that law,' says Antigone in Hölderlin's version of line 450, the passage with which he opens his interpretation of the play in his Notes.[55] Hölderlin sees this balance in terms of a more abstract antithesis between 'formlessness' (or the 'anti-formal') and the 'formal' (or 'all too formal'), otherwise expressed in terms of the 'aorgic' versus the 'organic'.[56] This opposition in turn implies another that Hölderlin – partly anticipating Nietzsche – draws elsewhere between the 'Apollonian' (associated with the 'anti-formal' or 'aorgic') and the 'Junonian' (associated with the 'formal' and 'organic').[57] It is this element in particular that Hölderlin sought to emphasize in his translations. He wrote that he sought to bring out 'the element of the Oriental' that the Greeks had repudiated,[58] everything that is the opposite of the supposedly all too rational culture that he associated with the Germany of his own day.[59] Antigone's 'highest trait', according to Hölderlin, is the 'holy madness' that is allegedly evident in her recognition that she, like Niobe, has matched herself against the gods and thus exemplifies 'a superlative of human spirit and heroic virtuosity'.[60] 'Madness' in general, and especially the madness that it takes for a human being to assert him- or herself against the divine, looms large in Hölderlin's version (as indeed it does in Sophocles' play).

For Hölderlin, upheaval in the mind is reflected in society. Tragedy in general and the *Antigone* in particular reflect 'the spirit of the times'.[61] The opposition between Antigone and Creon takes place at 'a time of unrest', of 'national reversal', in which 'even a neutral person ... will be forced ... to be present to an infinite degree in the religious, political and moral forms of his or her country ... The rational form here developing tragically is political, indeed republican, because between Creon and Antigone, the formal and the anti-formal, the balance is held too equally'.[62] Thus, in Hölderlin's translation of lines 79 and 907, Antigone's act becomes one of *Aufstand* ('revolt'). Hölderlin's notion of revolution is not narrowly political; but the *Antigone* is now once again, in a sense that had not been true since the days of Sophocles and Demosthenes, a political play.

Hölderlin's version has its own afterlife, not only (from 1919) on the German stage (and occasionally elsewhere),[63] but notably also as the basis for Bertolt Brecht's 1948 adaptation and as the libretto for Carl Orff's 1949 operatic version, whose score and instrumentation sought to enhance the 'orientalizing' elements of Hölderlin's text.[64] Hölderlin's *Antigone* also takes on a particular importance in the thought of Martin Heidegger, who played a substantial role in establishing the status that Hölderlin now enjoys as a philosophical poet.[65] According to George Steiner, 'The consequences of Hölderlin's hermeneutic metamorphosis of Sophocles are, necessarily, reciprocal. We read, we experience Sophocles differently after Hölderlin.'[66]

Several aspects of Hölderlin's approach to *Antigone* in particular and tragedy in general reflect the intellectual background he shared with the philosopher, G. W. F. Hegel (1770–1831), an even more significant figure in shaping modern approaches to the play.[67] One does not have to read very far in scholarship on the *Antigone* to encounter references – usually in passing and often in inverted commas – to the 'Hegelian' interpretation.[68] This is often misrepresented as the view that the play dramatizes a clash of right against right, family against state. That this is an over-simplification is apparent even from the 'canonic text' that Steiner identifies as the source of 'the notion of tragedy as a conflict between two equal "rights" or "truths", a passage in Hegel's posthumously published *Lectures on the Philosophy of Religion*:[69]

> The collision between the two highest moral powers is set forth in a plastic fashion in that supreme and absolute example of tragedy, 'Antigone.' In this case, family love, what is holy, what belongs to the inner life and to inner feeling, and which because of this is also called the law of the nether gods, comes into collision with the law of the State. Creon is not a tyrant, but really a moral power; Creon is not in the wrong; he maintains that the law of the State, the authority of government, is to be held in respect, and that punishment follows the infraction of the law. Each of these two sides realizes only one of the moral powers, and has only one of these as its content; this is the element of one-sidedness here, and the meaning of eternal justice is shown in this, that both end in injustice just because they are one-sided, though at the same time both obtain justice too. Both are recognized as having a value of their own in the untroubled course of morality. Here they both have their own validity, but a validity which is equalized. It is only the one-sidedness in their claims which justice comes forward to oppose.[70]

The passage is one of several in which Hegel expresses admiration for the *Antigone* as a model of classical tragedy.[71] Creon is 'not a tyrant' in so far as he represents a legitimate interest, the legal, ethical, and religious community of the *polis*. He is 'not wrong' in his positive and genuine commitment to the state. But he is wrong (he 'end[s] in injustice') in his treatment of what Antigone stands for. Antigone, too, represents a legitimate principle, but does so in a way that leads her to violate an opposing and equally legitimate principle. The argument thus operates at the level of principle, not of the conduct of the two characters as individuals. It is no argument against it to say that it glosses over the motivations of Creon and Antigone as they are actually represented in the play.

The terms in which Hegel expresses himself in this passage have a substantial hinterland in his philosophy, especially in the *Lectures on Aesthetics* and the *Phenomenology of Spirit*.[72] The (posthumously published) *Aesthetics* emphasize in particular the notion of 'collision'. Ancient tragedy dramatizes conflicts of principle within (as in *Oedipus Tyrannus*) or between individuals, as in *Antigone*, where the opposition 'between ethical life in its social universality and the family as the natural ground of moral relations' plays itself out in further antithesis between man and woman, living and dead, individual and state, human versus divine law, light versus darkness, and 'upper' versus 'lower' gods.[73] In this process of conflict, there is always an element of reconciliation, as the one-sidedness of the heroes' opposing positions is overcome. This is the 'eternal justice' mentioned in the first passage quoted above.[74] Reconciliation may be a feature of the tragic plot itself, as in Aeschylus' *Eumenides*.[75] But in a play such as the *Antigone* reconciliation and eternal justice are purely features of the audience's reflection on the dialectic that the play's conflicts have instantiated.[76]

In the *Phenomenology of Spirit*, published in 1807, these oppositions appear not merely as the stuff of tragedy, but as dynamics of human history:[77] Hegel's engagement with the *Antigone* has clearly informed his view of the development of consciousness.[78] Despite being referred to only twice,[79] the play lies behind substantial sections of the work, providing a model for Hegel's account of relations between individual and state, state and family, man and woman in ancient Greek society. But one familial, male-female relationship stands out among all others – that between brother and sister. Relationships between husband and wife, parent and child, are not complete in themselves – in these, each party wants something from the other, and they are subject to change and dissolution. A woman's relationship towards the husband or the child is not about this particular person, but about a role that may be played by more than one individual. The relationship between brother and sister, on the other hand, is biological, but stable; unlike husband and wife, 'they do not desire one another; nor have they given to one another, nor received from one another, this independence of individual being; they are free individualities with respect to each other'. Because of all this, Hegel argues, the sister's relationship to her brother is one of mutual recognition of individual selfhood: 'The loss of a brother is thus irreparable to the sister, and her duty towards him is the highest.'[80] The argumentation is substantially that of Antigone at lines 905–15 of Sophocles' play. These lines, which Goethe had wished to declare spurious,[81] are central not only to Hegel's view of the play in the *Phenomenology*, but also to the *Phenomenology*'s view of the relations between man and woman, family and state, as aspects of ethical life.[82]

At every stage of his thought, Hegel's account of the clash between Antigone and Creon is complex and nuanced. Antigone's right always involves wrong, and yet Hegel's greater admiration for her than for Creon is apparent – nowhere more so than in his *Lectures on the History of Philosophy*,[83] where 'the heavenly Antigone, that noblest of figures that ever appeared on earth',[84] joins a very select company, one that includes Socrates and Jesus Christ, of those whose individual suffering gave rise to spiritual progress.[85] Hegel's interpretation of the *Antigone* is of enormous influence; his framework permeates German scholarship on tragedy, and hence the interpretation of tragedy more generally, from his day to our own.[86] With Hegel, Antigone enters the history of philosophy. His engagement with the text adds impetus to the upsurge in interest in the play and in the figure of Antigone herself in the decades following the French Revolution, and is the main reason why Antigone looms so large in the continental philosophical tradition.

One early sign of this influence is a fascinating vignette in the first volume of Søren Kierkegaard's *Either/Or* (1843).[87] Kierkegaard creates an Antigone who is both ancient and modern, 'a daughter of sorrow' with 'a dowry of pain as her outfit', and in some sense an avatar of the author himself.[88] Like her ancient counterpart, she is the product of a doomed and accursed family; but this is a 'secret' of which only she is aware; she is not even certain that Oedipus himself was aware of it (p. 161). For her, 'life does not unfold like the Greek Antigone's: it is turned inward, not outward. The stage is inside, not outside; it is a spiritual stage' (p. 157). Antigone's secret, and the grief that it generates, demonstrate her love for a father who is still held in high esteem; but it is also the cause of her anxiety and the source of her alienation. She is in love, and 'the object of her love … is not unaware of it' (p. 162). But this leads to two tragic 'collisions': between her love for her father and her love for herself; and between her love for her father and her love for her beloved. Marriage would require her to confide in her husband; but that would be to betray her father. Yet if she keeps her secret, she sacrifices her life, her love, and her happiness. Since she cannot betray her father, and because she does not wish to perpetuate the guilt that she has inherited from him, she cannot act on her love. She is unable to choose (pp. 163–4): 'Only in the moment of her death can she confess the fervency of her love; only in the moment she does not belong to him can she confess that she belongs to him.' Her father and her lover both cause her death (p. 164).

Martin Heidegger (1889–1976) approaches the *Antigone* through the lens of Hölderlin's translation.[89] Heidegger's interest in the play centres in particular on the 'Ode to Man', which he discusses at length in two Freiburg lecture courses – one on metaphysics, delivered in 1935 (Heidegger 2000), and the second on Hölderlin's hymn, *The Ister*, in 1942–3 (Heidegger 1996). The *Introduction to Metaphysics* explicitly takes the 'Ode to Man' out of context in order to explore, in Heidegger's characteristically abstruse idiolect, what it discloses of Sophocles' supposed intuitions regarding such key Heideggerian concerns as the nature of being and the question of what it is for human beings to be in the world.[90] The 1942–3 lectures retain these concerns, but also place the ode in the wider contexts of Sophocles' play as whole and of Hölderlin's poetic and intellectual engagement with the Greeks.[91] In both, the keynote lies in Heidegger's translation of the term *deinon* (in the ode's opening sentence) as *unheimlich* – uncanny, but also (etymologically) unhomely (*unheimisch*). In the *Ister* lectures, the uncanny is resolved into several aspects, as the fearful, the powerful, the inhabitual – each of which is in itself ambivalent.[92] Human being is all about humans' attempt to attain the 'homely' in a world which demonstrates yet limits their achievements. Man finds his way through everything (*pantoporos*), but ultimately can find no way out (*aporos*); his very resourcefulness is his downfall. He dominates, but also forfeits the *polis*, his 'site', the home of Being and of Being Homely (*hypsipolis/*

apolis). He 'comes to Nothing' – to catastrophe, to *atê* – because of what he is, but also because of what the world of being is – because of the inherent contradictions, the unity of opposites, in each. In seeking, but failing to find, the homely in the face of the unhomely, man is the unhomeliest, the most uncanny of all. In these 1942–3 lectures, Hölderlin's project, of becoming truly German (homely) through encountering the Greeks (the unhomely), becomes an aspect of the experience of mankind as Heidegger finds it in the 'Ode to Man'.[93]

Heidegger's conviction that the conflicts that it presents are a matter of highly abstract questions of being in the world belongs with his resistance to ethical and political readings of the play; this in turn represents a wilful refusal to consider the genuine moral and political issues that an alternative reading of the play would raise for the society – and the party – of which he was a member.[94] Heidegger joined the Nazi Party in 1933, remained a member until the end of the war, and never unequivocally condemned the atrocities of the regime. His depoliticization of the play incorporates it within a vision of the triumph of German culture. For most of the twentieth century (as we shall see below) Antigone is a hero of resistance; Heidegger's approach is all the more remarkable for its imperviousness to the play's anti-authoritarian potential. This is not an isolated phenomenon: revivals of Sophocles' original were especially popular in German theatres under the Third Reich.[95] Though the motivation of some may have been covertly subversive, they were clearly not perceived as such by the authorities.[96] 'Our' Antigone is not the only one possible; though she is not entirely a product of the post-war period,[97] that is when she truly comes into her own.

Though references to Hegel are scarce in Heidegger's discussion, his reading of the play is a target throughout. Similarly anti-Hegel and at least superficially influenced by Heidegger is the celebrated interpretation of Jacques Lacan,[98] expounded in three seminars in 1960 and published in 1986 in the seventh volume of *Le Séminaire de Jacques Lacan* (*L'éthique de la psychanalyse, 1959–1960*).[99] Far from being an exploration of the conflict between state and family or between divine and human law,[100] much less the opposition of two principles of equal value, the play according to Lacan presents an Antigone who goes 'beyond the limits of the human' in pursuit of 'the pure and simple desire of death as such'.[101] In his opposition to Antigone's desire, Creon stands for the order of law and morality (the 'Symbolic Order'), but is a second-rate, unheroic figure;[102] he is the one who manifests an Aristotelian *hamartia*, in contrast to Antigone, whom Lacan associates with *atê* in a sense that excludes *hamartia*,[103] and who attempts to bury Polynices not out of obedience to the unwritten laws of Zeus, Dike, or the gods, but simply because she is who she is and he is who he is, for the sake of the act as such and the desire, the death wish, that it expresses.[104] Antigone's heroism stems precisely from her refusal to give ground on her desire.[105] This is what leads Lacan to comment on her 'splendour':[106]

> [O]ver and beyond the dialogue, over and beyond the question of family and country, over and beyond the moralizing arguments, it is Antigone who fascinates us, Antigone in her unbearable splendour. She has a quality that both attracts us and startles us, in the sense of intimidates us; this terrible, self-willed victim disturbs us.[107]

Antigone's act is 'ethical' (as opposed to 'moral'), because it is performed for its own sake, as an act of self-legislation (Lacan returns several times to the Chorus's description of Antigone as *autonomos*) that makes no concessions to conventional morality or external sanctions. And it is 'beautiful' precisely because it has this existential character, with no taint of utility. Yet it is individual rather than universalizable, and its individuality is inhuman and pathological in character: Creon 'is, like all executioners and tyrants at bottom, a human character. Only the martyrs know neither pity nor fear. Believe me, the day when the martyrs are victorious will be the day of universal conflagration. The play is calculated to demonstrate that fact.'[108]

The influence of Lacan's account is apparent not only in the work of self-confessed Lacanians, such as Slavoj Žižek, but also within classical studies[109] and as a focus of philosophical discussion. Jacques Derrida's 'often wildly self-indulgent and arbitrary' commentary on Hegel in his 1974 work *Glas* both resembles and distances itself from Lacan in its critique of the 'phallocentrism' of both Hegel and Lacan in their idealization of Antigone and of the anti-Semitism that is the complement of Hegel's philhellenism.[110] In the same year, Luce Irigaray published *Speculum de l'autre femme*, in which she too assails the phallocentrism inherent in Hegel's exclusion of Antigone from the civic, the political, the rational, and the ethical, a criticism that she extends elsewhere to Lacan.[111] In Judith Butler's 2000 monograph, *Antigone's Claim*, Irigaray joins Hegel and Lacan as a target, for she too allegedly presents Antigone as an opponent of politics from a pre-political standpoint, of kinship, 'blood', and maternity.[112] Butler argues against Lacan on the purity of Antigone's desire and against Hegel on the absence of any incestuous overtones in her attachment to Polynices.[113] The fact that Antigone's situation is so thoroughly conditioned by her incestuous origins, she claims, undermines any straightforward identification of her position with 'the family' in opposition to 'the state'. As incest undermines the family as a normative structure, so the defiance of Antigone, a product of incest who affirms her attachment to her dead brother rather than assuming the role of wife and mother, destabilizes the 'heteronormative' family. Thus Antigone, '[a]lthough not quite a queer heroine', opens up the possibility of 'other ways of organizing sexuality'.[114]

Philosophers' continued fascination with Antigone remains a dialogue with Hegel and his legacy in continental thought, as witnessed by Hutchings and Pulkkinen's 2010 collection on Hegel, Antigone, and feminism, the volume by Wilmer and Žukauskaitė on Antigone in postmodern thought that appeared in the same year,[115] and other recent studies that take Hegel and his critics as a point of departure.[116] The philosophical Antigone is a creature first of the profound influence that Sophocles' play had in the development of Hegel's philosophical system and then of the desire of Hegel's successors to appropriate this authoritative text in expounding their own philosophies and politics. In all this, Antigone has become a kind of talisman in a dialogue that is less with Sophocles than with each participant's philosophical predecessors.[117] The philosophical Antigone is by no means all that there is to the contemporary afterlife of Sophocles' play. Yet there is one decisive consequence of the turn to *Antigone* in Hegel and his contemporaries that should not be minimized: after Hegel, the Antigone who is admired, criticized, discussed, and (mis)appropriated is not the composite figure who emerged from Euripides, Statius, and their mediaeval and early-modern followers, but Sophocles' Antigone.

Antigone on the modern stage

This shift is also one that takes place on stage. A decisive step was taken in a production first mounted ten years after Hegel's death, at the Court Theatre in the New Palace at Potsdam on 28 October 1841. This was Ludwig Tieck's staging of the recent translation by Johann Jakob Donner, with incidental music by Felix Mendelssohn-Bartholdy.[118] Productions of Greek tragedy were not new to the German stage: Goethe himself had staged *Antigone* in Weimar in 1809 and after; but this was an abridged and adapted version.[119] A production of a version of Sophocles' text, complete and without additions, offered something new. Though not actually an opera (with one minor exception, Mendelssohn's music accompanies only those parts of the original that would have been sung or chanted), it marks a decisive shift away from previous musical dramatizations of the Antigone story, with their happy endings and their eclectic adaptation of a range of classical models.[120] Its musicality is central to its aesthetic as a self-consciously 'authentic' revival of the ancient dramatist's art. Both Donner's translation and Mendelssohn's music were based on the metres of the Greek original;[121] the music differentiates between choral song, recitative, and actor's lyric in ways that respect, without entirely replicating, the dispositions of Sophocles' play.[122] The historicizing impetus extended also to other aspects of the production – a chorus of fifteen (or rather sixteen, since their leader was additional to their number), and set-design, staging, and costumes based on the archaeological knowledge of the day.[123] But there were limits: the actors were not masked and women played the female roles.[124] The production was a major success, revived in Berlin and Leipzig in 1842, before being widely performed in other German cities and abroad (including Paris in 1844, and London, Dublin, Edinburgh, and New York in 1845).[125] Hegel had apparently believed that the experience of Greek tragedy could not be adequately translated to the modern stage;[126] Donner-Tieck-Mendelssohn, in the majority view of their contemporaries, proved him wrong.[127]

In contrast to the striving for authenticity of that production, the *Antigone* of German Expressionist poet and playwright Walter Hasenclever, written in 1916 and first performed (and published) in 1917, is rooted in the historical circumstances of its time.[128] Hasenclever's Creon is an authoritarian absolutist, coldly impervious to the suffering of his subjects; elements of his script are apparently drawn from the speeches of Wilhelm II.[129] First Antigone, then Haemon enlist popular support until, with both dead and the city in flames, Creon is made to see the error of his ways: Tiresias calls up a nightmare tableau of war's victims, and Creon abdicates, accepting his responsibility for the city's destruction. The mob have had their fill of the powerful and make to storm the palace, when a voice from the grave reminds them of their guilt and ephemerality, and brings them to their knees. Throughout, Antigone's motives are love and humanity: the 'unwritten law' she obeys is called 'Love'; she bids Creon honour the dead, because all human beings die, and so all are brothers (II.2). She has the support not only of Haemon, but also of Ismene, as the sisters offer themselves in sacrifice in the name of all women, 'yoked and subservient' (III.2). It is Hasenclever's play that inaugurates Antigone's career as a twentieth-century icon of radical, feminist, and pacifist resistance.

Roughly contemporary is the *Antigone* of Jean Cocteau, first performed on 20 December 1922 in Paris, with incidental music by Arthur Honegger, sets by Pablo Picasso, and costumes by Coco Chanel.[130] This was an austere and deliberately alienating production, marked in particular by Cocteau's drastic abridgement of Sophocles' original. What remains of the text is faithfully translated, but much has been jettisoned, especially from the choral elements: Cocteau's version is less than half as long as Sophocles'. Cocteau likened it to an aerial photograph, a bird's eye view that would allow hitherto unnoticed qualities to become apparent and permit audiences to experience a familiar text as if for the first time.[131]

Cocteau's exclusion of the political is in marked contrast to the version composed in Paris in 1930 by the exiled Portuguese intellectual, António Sérgio de Sousa, a social-democratic opponent of the dictator, António de Oliveira Salazar, whose regime ruled Portugal from 1926 to 1974. In this version, Creon is an out-and-out tyrant and Antigone his principled democratic opponent. As in Hasenclever, Antigone and Ismene are closer than in Sophocles, Antigone's opposition has Christianizing aspects, and the stage is peopled with various quasi-choral groups. Antigone and Haemon die, but Creon is overthrown by a popular uprising, and the play ends with a scene of democratic reconciliation inspired by Aeschylus' *Eumenides*.[132]

Cocteau's version takes on additional resonance through its use as the basis for the libretto to the opera by the Swiss composer, Arthur Honegger.[133] Honegger began in 1924 to develop his music for Cocteau's 1922 production into a full-scale three-act opera. Its first performance (in Brussels, 28 December 1927) similarly featured sets by Picasso and costumes by Chanel. Honegger's *Antigone* is widely regarded as his masterpiece,[134] but its main interest for us lies in its triumphant revival, in the occupied Paris of 1943, in a production that was repeated regularly until the liberation in 1944.[135] Performance of a modernist *Antigone* in Nazi-occupied Paris confounds easy assumptions regarding the attitudes of the occupying power to the avant garde and the potentially subversive,[136] and confirms what we noted above about the surprising popularity of *Antigone* in Nazi Germany itself. Neither Cocteau, who inspired the revival, nor Honegger wished to highlight the work's subversive potential. The opera's score, 'the empathetic, vocally heroic, treatment of Créon', and the production itself can be regarded as emphasizing the tragedy of Creon rather than the heroism of Antigone.[137]

The *Antigone* of Jean Anouilh premiered on 4 February 1944 and similarly ran until the liberation. The first production to be staged when the theatre reopened on 27 September 1944, it continued into 1945 and was revived for several further seasons. Thus, in Paris in 1944, as the Allies planned the invasion of France for June of that year, there were no fewer than three *Antigone*s in the theatres: Honegger's, Anouilh's, and the first attested production of Garnier's 1580 *Antigone, ou la piété*.[138] Anouilh's play had been completed and approved by the censors in 1942, but its production was delayed, and so Honegger's version beat it to the stage.[139] Anouilh was well aware of the potential of Antigone as a symbol for the Resistance.[140] By 1944, the risk of subversive, anti-authoritarian responses to the production was one that concerned the German authorities.[141] For some audiences and critics, both before and after the liberation, Anouilh's play did present an occasion for celebrating the Resistance.[142] This understanding gained ground after the war, and became for many years the standard interpretation.[143] Yet the initial production's sole review in the underground press was deeply hostile, taking the play's nihilism as tantamount to connivance with fascism;[144] and it was extremely popular in collaborationist, fascist, and pro-German circles.[145]

Both pro- and anti-Resistance interpretations typically see Anouilh's Antigone as a symbol of the Resistance and Creon as representing the Vichy regime of Marshal Pétain (or his head of government, Pierre Laval).[146] Such allegorizing approaches do find their place in contemporary reviews; yet, especially among collaborationist and pro-fascist responses, a more complex interpretation emerges, in which Creon's necessary maintenance of order is balanced by the 'purity' and 'grandeur' of Antigone's defiance.[147] Witt and Fleming have traced these and similar terms as keywords of a movement that Witt calls 'aesthetic fascism'; according to them, whether or not Anouilh's Antigone offers an apology for Vichy collaboration (and they are both inclined to believe that it does),[148] it manifests a less directly 'political' form of fascism that celebrates purity, sacrifice, and the beauty of suffering by contrast with the mediocrity of bourgeois contentment, conformity, and the compromises of politics.[149]

Anouilh gives his play an expository prologue, spoken by the actor who plays the Chorus, and a bourgeois domestic setting, in which

Antigone interacts with her Nurse, Ismene, and Haemon; but from the Guard's report to Haemon's departure after confronting his father, he follows the Sophoclean sequence fairly closely. Haemon's exit is followed by Antigone's final scene, a dialogue with Jonas, one of Anouilh's three Guards, in which she dictates a farewell letter to Haemon; but even this scene, with Antigone's hesitations, has its roots in Sophocles; as if to underline its relation to the original, Anouilh has Antigone quote *Ant.* 891–2, 'Hail, then, my grave, my marriage bed, my underground home!'[150] After the suicide of Eurydice (pp. 58–9), Creon is left alone; but where in Sophocles he is left to contemplate the fulfilment of Tiresias' warning, in Anouilh he carries on with his duties as head of state (p. 60). Because Tiresias has been omitted, Creon's presence at Antigone's tomb is not due to his desire to rescue her and avoid the disaster; rather, he is leaving after having Antigone walled up alive when he hears Haemon's voice from within the tomb (p. 58). In Anouilh's play, Creon's attempt to save Antigone comes earlier, in the *agôn* between the two that, at fully one third of the play (pp. 30–49), is even more central in Anouilh than in Sophocles.

But Antigone cannot be saved – a given of the plot that is highlighted throughout by metatheatrical references to tragic inevitability and the fixity of roles.[151] Yet Creon comes close: he demonstrates that neither Polynices nor Eteocles was the hero of Antigone's imagination (pp. 41–4), and she turns to go back to her room (pp. 44–5). It is in urging her, as she goes, to look forward to a conventional future of bourgeois domesticity that Creon makes his mistake, and she chooses death (p. 47). As in Sophocles, Antigone's conception of happiness leads her to choose death over life. Her fixation with death is a major theme in Sophocles too, but in Anouilh it has – along with her refusal to grow up – become the ultimate reason for her self-sacrifice.[152] She dies, but without really knowing why (pp. 56–7).

Some argue that it is Creon who wins the contest with Antigone and comes off best in the play overall.[153] True, he does undermine Antigone's reasons for resistance, so that her death may appear gratuitous. True, Antigone doubts her decision at the very last moment. But Creon himself recognizes that his attempt to save Antigone was a trial of strength, and he lost (p. 49). However arbitrary Antigone's opposition may be, the mere possibility of opposition that cannot be coerced into conformity demonstrates the weakness of power. This is her victory; and Creon's defeat, for a ruler whose conduct in office is determined by the need to control how things appear to the public, is substantial.[154] Though it is perhaps its historical circumstances and the controversial nature of its reception that give Anouilh's play its prominence in the reception-history of *Antigone*, the work is of great interest for the audacity with which it reconfigures the plot, as well as many of the motifs and themes, of Sophocles' original. Whatever its politics, it ranks as one of the most thought-provoking of twentieth-century adaptations.

Out of the same historical background comes the *Antigone of Sophocles* by Bertolt Brecht, written in less than a fortnight towards the end of 1947 and first performed, after a month's rehearsal, in the small town of Chur in Switzerland on 15 February 1948.[155] On the advice of Caspar Neher, his set-designer, Brecht chose to adapt Hölderlin's 1804 translation,[156] leaving around half of Hölderlin's lines entirely or almost entirely as he found them, while substantially revising or omitting the rest.[157] His own additions, after the style of Hölderlin, though occasionally even more archaizing and obscure, are considerable. The result is a transformation of Hölderlin and a further departure from Sophocles,[158] one which purports to 'rationalize' the original, uncovering 'the underlying popular legend' beneath all the supposed accretions of fate and religion, yet still drawing on the 'barbarism' supposedly characteristic of Greek tragedy.[159] Sophocles exists in Brecht's adaptation both as a classic and as a model from which modern tragedy must distance itself. Hölderlin's affinity for the 'Oriental' in Greek tragedy serves Brecht's purpose, but his use of Hölderlin's text also allows him to align himself with a strand of German philhellenism untainted by Nazism.[160] Brecht's aspirations for the work as a model for a new kind of tragedy emerge from his development of its staging and production into the first of his 'model-books', published with photographs by Ruth Berlau in 1949.[161]

The 1948 production began with a Prelude set in Berlin, April 1945. Two sisters return home from the air-raid shelter to find signs of their brother's return from the front. But the brother has deserted, and when the sisters leave for work, they find him hanging outside from a meat hook. One prepares to cut him down, while the other attempts to dissuade her. An SS man appears and questions the sisters about their connection to 'the traitor'. The first denies all knowledge, but the other is still holding the knife. Will she act? Should she? And what would it mean, in the context of Berlin 1945, if she did?[162]

In the play itself, Eteocles and Polynices have been fighting on the same side in an aggressive war for 'the grey metal' of Argos (pp. 10, 43–4) – the importance of Argos' mineral wealth as a motive for the Theban invasion is a central theme. Eteocles 'did not fear the fight' (p. 10), and is treated as a hero; Polynices is not to be buried because he deserted (pp. 10, 14, 22). Polynices is a traitor only in so far as he is, in Creon's view, a coward; he is killed not by Eteocles, but by Creon himself (pp. 25, 30, 41, 46), and the motive for his desertion is the meaningless loss of his brother in a war of Creon's devising (p. 41). This has triggered a more extensive rebellion in the army, which Creon puts down by hanging 'in public the many [that] this aggrieved' (p. 46). Though the Chorus of Elders still sing a victory song on entering (p. 12), and Creon encourages them to exult in Thebes' 'total' victory over Argos (and in the mutilation of *all* its exposed corpses, p. 13), the war is not in fact over: here the role of Tiresias is not to warn Creon of his folly in exposing Polynices and burying Antigone alive, but to expose Creon's assurances that the war is won (pp. 13, 31, 41) as lies (pp. 38, 41–2). Ultimately, the Elders too rebel (pp. 44–5).

Creon's confidence rests on his sons. The elder, Megareus, will return to stamp out opposition at home (p. 45).[163] But Megareus, it emerges, is dead, having failed to secure the allegiance of an army disaffected by Creon's treatment of Polynices (pp. 45–6). With an Argive invasion imminent, Creon places all his hopes in Haemon (p. 47), so that his attempt to release Antigone is merely an expedient to secure his surviving son's compliance. But Haemon kills himself over Antigone's corpse. Creon laments his death, but only as the 'sword' who should have saved Thebes (p. 50). There is no Eurydice in this version, and no sympathy for a Creon who finally departs to await his own downfall and that of his city (p. 50). Brecht's attitude towards Creon is thus clear enough, even without the salutation *mein Führer* (retained in translation, p. 15) or the repeated references to Thebes' 'stormtroops'. The Prelude sets up an analogy between Creon's wish that Thebes be destroyed with him (p. 50) and the last days of Hitler; the failure of his aggression against Argos, and the immediate turn in the tide of the war that this entails, turn Argos into Stalingrad.[164]

Brecht's attitude towards Antigone is less clear. The 1948 Prelude suggests that Antigone's choice, and the possibility of a similar choice in Berlin in April 1945, are to be the focus of the drama that follows; but in the play itself there is emphasis on the complicity of those who have acquiesced in Creon's war. This includes the Elders, who supported Creon as a bulwark against the 'rapacious populace' (p. 43) and out of economic self-interest (pp. 36–7, 41, 43–5). But according to them, Antigone too is complicit: 'she also once / Ate of the bread that was baked / In the stony dark'; only when her only family suffered 'did the child of unseeing Oedipus / Remove the long since threadbare blindfold from her eyes / To look into the abyss' (pp. 37–8).[165] Both Creon (p. 24) and the Elders (p. 51) see Antigone's resistance as helping 'nobody but the enemy', and she herself regards defeat as safer than victory under Creon (p. 24). Her defiance, she affirms, is only an 'example' (p. 21). This may be admirable, but it comes too late. Her resistance makes her a martyr, but also a victim;[166] it becomes a means by which the self-destructive potential of Creon's thirst for power is realized. Brecht undercuts the exemplarity of the grand moral gesture by emphasizing its practical consequences and highlighting a distinction between the internal divisions of the ruling class and the more fundamental opposition between rulers and ruled.[167] Antigone's act mirrors not the opposition of Hitler's inveterate opponents among the German resistance – from whom Brecht wished to dissociate her[168] – but something more like the conspiracy of July 1944, led by the aristocratic Claus Schenk Graf von Stauffenberg.[169]

The Brechtian or what one might crudely describe as the 'left-wing' vision of Antigone has not held absolute sway in the years following World War II. Brecht's 1948 production was followed in 1949 by Orff's primitivist, ritualist, and apolitical operatic setting of Hölderlin's translation.[170] Yet Brecht's play, created at a time when Antigone could be an object of contention between left and right, is a major factor in appropriating her for the left. Much of this has to do with the politics of the post-war theatre, but perhaps more important is Brecht's influence as a dramatist and theorist. Brecht's *Antigone* has made the association between Antigone and anti-authoritarian resistance almost automatic; that association, in turn, fosters an erroneously over-schematic misconception not only of Brecht's play, but also of Anouilh's. Our Antigone is fundamentally shaped by the Antigones of World War II and its immediate aftermath.

The link that Brecht's play draws between Berlin under the Nazis and the dilemma of Sophocles' heroine is reflected in Rolf Hochhuth's 1963 novel, *Die Berliner Antigone*,[171] which Steiner (1984: 143) summarizes thus:

> Implicated in the 1944 plot against Hitler, Anne's brother has been hanged and consigned to dissection. But just after the air raid his remains have been removed, carted through fire and ruin, and given loving burial. Now Anne is to be beheaded and her own body is to take the useful place of her brother's. How can the judge even dare hint to the Führer that the intolerable young woman is secretly affianced to his son, that the latter is threatening mutiny if the sentence is carried out?

The role of Brecht's version in the post-war adoption of Antigone as an icon of radical resistance is further attested by its adaptation by Judith Malina, premiered in Krefeld in 1967 and performed in sixteen countries in the twenty years thereafter by the New York Living Theatre.[172] The legacy of World War II in the modern reception of *Antigone*, meanwhile, is apparent in the film *Germany in Autumn* (*Deutschland im Herbst*), first shown (in March 1978) just over four months after the events that inspired it. A collaborative enterprise, led by such luminaries of the New German Cinema as Alexander Kluge and Volker Schlöndorff, the film documents the funerals of the industrialist and former SS officer, Hanns Martin Schleyer, kidnapped and murdered by the terrorist Red Army Faction, and of three of the RAF's leaders, Andreas Baader, Gudrun Ensslin, and Jan Carl Raspe, who committed suicide in prison following a failed bid to secure their release via the hijacking of a Lufthansa airliner. Schleyer's funeral, attended by the great and the good of the Federal Republic (including several ex-Nazis), is shown at the beginning of the film; those of the terrorists, facilitated by the Mayor of Stuttgart in the face of widespread opposition, at the end. Prominent among those seeking a decent burial for the terrorists was Ensslin's sister, whose role as an Antigonesque figure is highlighted by the fact that the funerals of Baader et al. are preceded by a fifteen-minute vignette (written by Heinrich Böll and filmed by Schlöndorff) in which a group of television executives consider whether to broadcast a production of Sophocles' play as part of a series designed to introduce young people to the classics, before deciding that it is simply too topical. The Mayor of Stuttgart whose intervention made the terrorists' funerals possible was Manfred Rommel, son of Field Marshal Erwin Rommel, commanded by Hitler in 1944 to commit suicide or be publicly proclaimed a traitor. Earlier in the film, the state funeral of Rommel senior is juxtaposed with that of Schleyer in 1977.[173] As in Sophocles, the theme of parents and children is pervasive: archaic Greek themes – inherited guilt, generational conflict, one generation's curse on its successors – take on a new resonance.[174] Footage of Rommel's funeral is also interspersed with black and white newsreel of the assassination, in 1938, of King Alexander of Serbia, attributed in voice-over to German secret services. The simple polarities of patriot and traitor, state violence versus terrorism are thus undercut, here and throughout, as Antigone-like figures and scenarios recur.[175]

Germany in Autumn was followed by a spate of theatrical *Antigone*s – three at the Berliner Theatertreffen in May 1979 alone.[176] Since then, the conception of *Antigone* as *the* iconic drama of political resistance has dominated. Productions and adaptations of Sophocles' play have been used to denounce tyranny and defend the right to dissent all over the world – in the Argentina of Griselda Gambaro's *Antígona furiosa* (1986);[177] in Soviet-dominated Eastern Europe (especially in the years before the revolutions of 1989);[178] as a critique of the normalization of violence in contemporary Mexico;[179] and in many other countries.[180] The play's iconicity is demonstrated by a sequence in Andrzej Wajda's film *Katyn*, in which a woman, Agnieszka, dismisses her sister's objections and erects a tombstone which records that their brother was murdered in the wartime massacre that was in fact perpetrated by the Soviets, though the Communist authorities blamed it on the Nazis. In one scene, Agnieszka sells her hair to the theatre in Cracow as a means of raising money. As her hair is cut, an actress recites, without attribution, some lines from her part in the theatre's current production. As Agnieszka collects her money from the box office, a poster for that production, of Sophocles' *Antigone*, appears in the background – alluding to Wajda's own 1984 Cracow production, staged under martial law and foreshadowing the triumph of Solidarity.[181]

This vision of *Antigone* is a worldwide phenomenon, but there are notable clusters – not only in Europe, but also in Africa and Latin America. We end with a look at two of the most striking concentrations: in Africa, and in Ireland.

Africa

Greek drama, and especially *Antigone*, has played a significant role in the ways in which poets and dramatists in Africa and in the African diaspora have appropriated and reconfigured the canonical works of the colonial powers.[182] Among the most prominent African *Antigones* are *Odale's Choice*, by the Barbados-born playwright Edward Kamau Braithwaite, first produced in Ghana in 1962,[183] and Sylvain Bemba's 1988 Congolese version, *Noces posthumes de Santigone* (first performed in 1990 and translated in the same year as *Black Wedding Candles for Blessed Antigone*).[184] *Odale's Choice* offers a pared-down version of Sophocles' plot: Odale defies her uncle Creon (the only non-Africanized name in the play) to conduct a rudimentary burial of the body of her brother Tawia, killed by Creon himself. Odale is to be pardoned and exiled, rather than executed; but she insists that she can accept no reprieve unless Tawia is properly buried, and Creon orders that her body be exposed beside that of her brother. In *Black Wedding Candles for Blessed Antigone*, Melissa Yadé, an African student studying in England, is playing the part of Antigone in a production in Birmingham, when she learns that her fiancé, Titus Saint-Just Bund, revolutionary leader of the fictitious country of Amandla, has been killed in a coup. Explicitly identifying herself with Antigone, she returns to Amandla, denounces and dominates the 'New Leader' who has ousted Titus, and declares her determination to ensure that he receives a proper burial. She buries the body, and boards a plane back to Britain, but is killed (as we learn from the narrator), along with all other passengers, when the plane crashes into the sea. More recently, Sophocles' heroine has provided the inspiration for *Bintou*, by Koffi Kwahulé from Côte d'Ivoire.[185] Set in the French *banlieues*, the play presents the eponymous character's unsuccessful defiance of her uncle's insistence that she undergo female genital mutilation.

The two most celebrated African *Antigone*s, however, are *The Island*, by Athol Fugard (in collaboration with its original performers, John Kani and Winston Ntshona), and *Tegonni*, by Femi Osofisan. *The Island* (first performed at The Space, Cape Town, on 2 July 1973) is set in South Africa's notorious Robben Island prison, where opponents of the apartheid regime were incarcerated.[186] Two prisoners, John and Winston, return to their shared cell after back-breaking labour and beatings. After tending each other's wounds, they resume their rehearsals for a two-man performance of Sophocles' *Antigone*, to be presented at the prison's annual concert, with John as Creon and Winston as Antigone. As the rehearsal proceeds, Winston becomes increasingly uncomfortable with his role as a female character. John receives a summons to the governor's office, where he learns that his ten-year sentence has been commuted to three. Winston, sentenced to life, will remain to face a living death on the Island. Finally, however, it is Winston's role as a woman that allows him to overcome the crisis that John's impending release occasions. In the final scene, the performance of 'The Trial and Punishment of Antigone' itself, contemporary South Africa merges with ancient Athens as John/Creon prosecutes Winston/Antigone as an enemy of the apartheid state, addressing the audience as if they were united against 'subversive elements' or, as he calls them, 'rats' (pp. 73–4, 77). In pronouncing sentence, he proclaims (p. 77):

> Take her from where she stands, straight to the Island! There wall her up in a cell for life, with enough food to acquit ourselves of the taint of her blood.

Assimilated to Antigone's, Winston's sentence indicts the regime that condemned him. In his last words as Antigone, Winston further assimilates her situation to his own (p. 77):

> Brothers and Sisters of the Land! I go now on my last journey. I must leave the light of day forever, for the Island, strange and cold, to be lost between life and death. So, to my grave, my everlasting prison, condemned alive to solitary death.

Antigone's defiance now defines Winston's view of himself, and he speaks Antigone's words in his own person (p. 77):

> [*Tearing off his wig and confronting the audience as Winston, not Antigone.*]
>   Gods of our Fathers! My Land! My Home!
>   Time waits no longer. I go now to my living death, because I honoured those things to which honour belongs.

The fear of feminization that marks Sophocles' Creon is in this version transferred to the character playing Antigone. Winston's reluctance to undertake the female role uncovers sexual tensions between him and John, as sharers of the same cell, almost as a married couple (p. 65); but it also demonstrates a misogyny that suggests a parallel between these oppressed black men and their oppressors. Winston's conversion implies an analogy between his status as a mere 'boy' in apartheid South Africa (p. 60) and the abjection of women in which he and his fellows participate. By the end of the play, all members of the audience are potentially 'Brothers and Sisters of the Land', united in recognition of injustice; opposition to one form of oppression implies opposition to all.

This is an adaptation that in its own development, production, and performance enacts the dissent that has become the *Antigone*'s defining feature for modern audiences.[187] Not only did it have to overcome censorship and surveillance in order to make it to the stage, but it has a background in actual performances of *Antigone* on Robben Island itself. One of these featured a member of Fugard's all-black theatre company, arrested while rehearsing the part of Haemon in a 1965 production of the play. In another, Nelson Mandela himself took the part of Creon.[188]

Tegonni: An African Antigone, by the Nigerian writer Femi Osofisan, was first produced at Emory University in the United States, in autumn 1994.[189] Nigeria was then in turmoil, following the annulment of democratic elections which would have installed Chief Moshood Abiola as President, and the assumption of power by General Sani Abacha in the previous year.[190] In the programme notes to the original production Osofisan related *Tegonni* not only to the late nineteenth-century colonial context in which it is set, but also to the contemporary situation (p. 108).[191] The published text (first edition 1999) is dedicated to the memory of the 'martyr', Abiola, who died, on the day set for his release from prison, in 1998.

The action unfolds in the imaginary town of Oke-Osun in northern Yorubaland, under British colonial rule. Tegonni is a Yoruba princess, daughter of the late ruler. The play makes extensive use of Yoruba song, dance, myth, and symbolism; Greek, Yoruba, and other traditions coalesce in exploring an even more fundamental myth: the myth of freedom (p. 96). The play proper opens with the appearance, on a raised platform, of the Yoruba water goddess, Yemoja, in her boat, surrounded by splendidly attired female attendants, who dance and sing in her honour. Early scenes focus on the wedding of Tegonni to the British District Officer, Allan Jones. The town poet, chronicler, and master drummer, Isokun, is initially reluctant to sanction the marriage, but is persuaded by

Tegonni's friends. A more serious obstacle is the colonial governor, Lieutenant General Carter-Ross, who has ordered that the wedding procession be blocked by the corpse of Tegonni's brother, Oyekunle, a popular successor deposed at Carter-Ross's behest and killed in mutual fratricide by the more compliant and subservient Adeloro. Oyekunle's deposition clearly recalls Abiola's. The transformation of Tegonni, at first surrounded by her friends in exuberant celebration of her wedding, into an Antigone-figure is signalled by the appearance of the mythological Antigone herself. Her presence brings a metatheatrical insistence on the inevitability of the plot that recalls Anouilh, but also underlines that the Antigone-myth, the myth of freedom, is a myth of eternal recurrence. In a later scene, in which Antigone tests Tegonni's resolve, both unite in the conviction that 'oppression can never last'.[192] 'Again and again', she says, 'it will be overthrown.' But this is necessary, the play implies, because oppression also continually returns. A range of cultural traditions, Osofisan suggests, coalesce on the same point: oppression will never be defeated, and in practice resistance may seem futile, but poetry, literature, drama, and myth give us the resources to keep trying. The metaphors through which they do so are colour-blind, as Antigone herself observes (p. 17).[193]

Following Antigone's entrance, her attendants play the role of Carter-Ross's soldiers in guarding the body and barring the passage of the wedding party, whose traditional wedding song mutates into a dirge. Carter-Ross's edict is then conveyed in a letter read by District Officer Jones. For the first of several times, Jones pleads on Tegonni's behalf; but Carter-Ross, a father-figure as well as a tyrant, is motivated much more by opposition to the mixed marriage than by the desire to make an example of Oyekunle. The marriage is a sign of hope that both the indigenous community and the occupying British oppose. But Jones's acquaintance with Tegonni goes back to the protection he gave her when her own community threatened her bid for equality and economic autonomy (pp. 12–13, 26, 28, 56, 99).[194] These are among the many ways in which the play, despite the brutal portrayal of Carter-Ross, avoids a simple polarity between good Africans and wicked colonialists.

Tegonni fulfils her ritual obligations and is arrested, but is freed by masked ritual performers, only to be recaptured when she, also masked, returns to confront Carter-Ross. From her initial arrest onwards, the prospect of a reprieve if only she will apologize in public is repeatedly held out. A set-piece apology is arranged, but Tegonni in the end stands by her decision to bury her brother. Melodramatically, Jones rushes in to declare his love.[195] Carter-Ross has an apparent heart attack and is carried off by his aide-de-camp; but shots ring out and Tegonni falls. In the final tableau, Antigone descends from Yemoja's boat and revives Tegonni; they kneel before the goddess as the boat begins to depart.

Ireland

Antigone has also had a particular appeal in Ireland. Tom Paulin's *The Riot Act* was first presented by Field Day Theatre Company at the Guildhall, Derry, on 19 September 1984.[196] This is a version that stays close to the original both in plot and in dialogue; only in the occasional abridgement of the choral odes does it begin to diverge from Sophocles. It draws its power partly from its association with the political circumstances in which it was performed, but also from the link that its language – thanks to Paulin's flair with the cadences and idioms of Ulster speech – makes with those circumstances. It is this use of language, rather than any direct allusion to contemporary events, that is Paulin's 'primary means of giving a specifically Northern Irish locale for the play's action'.[197] At the play's heart is a gloriously satirical portrayal of Creon as 'a kind of puritan gangster, a megalomaniac who spoke alternately in an English public school voice and a deep menacing Ulster growl'.[198] His opening speech is a masterly send-up of the clichéd insincerity of the modern political class. As in Sophocles, the fourth stasimon's description of Lycurgus ('Lycurgus, he disliked music and strong drink, and when the crack was good he was bitter', p. 48) also reflects on Creon, and we discern a recognizable Ulster type: encouraged by the Chorus's reference to Creon as 'the big man' (p. 15), many have detected a caricature of the Reverend Ian Paisley.[199] For some, it is 'a rather heavy-handed caricature'.[200] Antigone, for her part, undergoes a significant degree of airbrushing. The rift with Ismene is softened. We take the famous expression of shared love at face value (p. 30). For the Messenger, Antigone is 'that brave wee girl' (p. 58). This is an Antigone who requites Haemon's affection (p. 34),[201] and achieves a genuinely mutual union with him in death (p. 59):

> and Haemon, he was holding her,
> dead gentle in his arms.
>
> . . .
>
> Poor lad, he's with her now.
> They loved each other.

The Riot Act is certainly a one-sided *Antigone*;[202] but it is also a remarkably vigorous one. Paulin was developing an analogy between Antigone and the Northern Irish civil rights movement that had already been drawn by the writer and politician Conor Cruise O'Brien.[203] For Paulin, O'Brien's preference for Ismene-like behaviour, and especially his association of Antigonesque resistance with 'all those funerals', meant 'that the Unionist state is virtually absolved of all responsibility and Creon's hands appear to be clean'.[204] His conviction that *Antigone* was 'a play that belonged in Ireland' (2002: 166) took on additional resonance after the IRA hunger strikes of 1980–1, the second phase of which led to the deaths of ten republican prisoners and raised issues about the rights of the relatives to bury their kin without state interference.[205]

Brendan Kennelly's *Antigone* received its first performance in Dublin on 28 April 1986.[206] As in Paulin, Antigone's heroism is never in doubt, and Creon is in the wrong from the outset.[207] What Creon opposes above all is love, in formulations that subsume Sophocles' original *erôs* and *philia*, but also have strong connotations of Christian *agapê*. 'I have no wish to school myself in hate,' says Antigone (p. 24, Kennelly's version of Sophocles' line 523), 'I want to love.' It is love that Antigone dies for (p. 25) and love that Creon kills (p. 38). Love, in the third stasimon, is 'the truest crime … always dying, yet never completely dead' (p. 34). Mutual love binds Antigone and Haemon (p. 26),[208] and so Creon 'killed [his] son's love' (p. 48) in more ways than one.

Though Kennelly's is not a Christianizing play, Ireland's Christian heritage asserts itself in the emphasis not only on love, but also on the word. Kennelly has written of his admiration for the Gospel's pronouncement 'In the beginning was the word …'.[209] The relation between word and deed, voice and silence, openness and secrecy pervades the play.[210] Each character has his or her own 'word', but from Creon's edict onwards, words have the power of deeds. Ultimately, they even become agents: in a much-expanded scene centring on Eurydice, words know 'no mercy'; they turn Eurydice's 'living beauty / Into the very picture of death'; they fly 'like lunatic birds'; the Messenger's 'words of murder' strangle Eurydice's words of prayer (pp. 44–5). Just so, Creon recognizes that his words killed his son (p. 47). The power of the word, of the voice that breaks the silence, of word as action and agent, is possibly the play's dominant theme.

Kennelly has also said that he sees his play as a 'feminist declaration of independence'.[211] If Creon fails as a ruler because his notion of kingship is based on patriarchal autocracy, he fails as an individual especially because, in failing to know woman, he fails to acknowledge the potential of the feminine to illuminate his own identity – his horror of feminization is thoroughly Sophoclean, but even more central in Kennelly.[212] Antigone's words (p. 35) are addressed to the Chorus, but framed as applying to men in general:

Mock me, if you will.
I do not doubt that you are able.
You are used to flattering men.
But I am a woman
And must go my way alone.
You know all about men,
You know all about power,
You know all about money.

But you know nothing of women.

What man
Knows anything of woman?

If he did
He would change from being a man
As men recognize a man.

If I lived,
I could change all the men of the world.

A daughter (as the Chorus character expresses it, p. 38), is

> the light of life
> The better part of a man's blood
> The transformation of crude manhood
> Into a creature to be loved by men
> She is the reason for his being
> She opens him up to himself
> Through her he may know himself
> And know more deeply the proud pain of love.

The 'black hole' in which Antigone is imprisoned represents the negation of love and man's failure to understand woman.[213]

Kennelly's *Antigone* is less obviously related to contemporary Irish politics than *The Riot Act*; for Anthony Roche, it is 'the least obviously Hibernicized' of the several 1980s Irish versions.[214] Yet

> it is no accident that all three [of Kennelly's versions of Greek tragedy] were written in the mid- to late 1980s, when Ireland was convulsed by debates and referenda having to do with the rights of women and control of their own sexual identity in relation to abortion and divorce.[215]

Seamus Heaney's *Burial at Thebes*, first performed at Dublin's Abbey Theatre on 5 April 2004, is – at first sight – even less Hibernicized.[216]

Like Paulin's, this is a version that stays close to Sophocles' original throughout, transformed only in so far as its poetic voice is Heaney's – intimate, direct, and rooted in the natural world. It also shares a political background with Paulin's version. In a published lecture, Heaney draws a comparison with the hunger strikes of 1981, when a former neighbour, Francis Hughes, was the second hunger striker to die, and the British authorities insisted that his corpse must be returned to his home village under police escort.[217] But he also goes further back, to the rise of the civil rights movement in the 1960s, to his own role in the protests as a young lecturer in Belfast, and to the writings of Conor Cruise O'Brien that had earlier provoked Paulin's reaction.[218]

Heaney also sees his version as a reflection of more recent, global political issues, specifically the 2003 invasion of Iraq by a US-led, UK-supported coalition. In his most forceful statement of the link between the Iraq War and *The Burial at Thebes*, he draws an analogy between Creon and George W. Bush, 'a Creon figure if ever there was one, a law-and-order bossman trying to boss the nations of the world into uncritical agreement with his edicts'. Hence he sees his version of Sophocles' 'Ode to Man' 'as a sort of open letter to George Bush'.[219] These resonances have been taken up by critics,[220] and they have left their mark on the play: both the issue that led to the IRA hunger strikes (the UK government's denial of political status to IRA prisoners) and the treatment of captives in the US-led 'War on Terror' surface in Heaney's adaptation of lines 517–18 (pp. 23–4):

ANTIGONE: Polyneices was no common criminal.
CREON: He terrorized us. Eteocles stood by us.[221]

Heaney also spoke out repeatedly against Bush's insistence on a binary division between supporters of the war and enemies of freedom.[222] This finds a more substantial echo in the play. Antigone's words in the prologue are a virtual quotation of Bush (p. 3):[223]

'I'll flush 'em out,' he says.
'Whoever isn't for us
Is against us in this case.'

Behind Creon's repeated references to 'patriotism' (pp. 10–11) and Antigone's to the fear of 'sounding unpatriotic' (p. 23) lies the 2001 USA Patriot Act, widely perceived as permitting the erosion of civil liberties in the name of state security and an inspiration for Giorgio Agamben's exploration of the same mechanism, the 'state of exception', in other contexts.[224]

But Heaney is also reluctant to make Creon 'a cipher for President Bush',[225] and wishes to acknowledge that Creon 'has a point, and a responsibility'.[226] He seems torn between the attraction of contemporary political resonance and a desire to be true to what he sees as the essence of Sophocles' tragedy. He finds a bridge between these positions in his observation that Antigone's defiance of Creon is 'a gesture that is as anthropological as it is political'.[227] Hence his title: burial provides a theme that unites ancient Greece and the globalized world of the twenty-first century – the 'common handful of clay' (p. 3) that Polynices is initially denied.[228] But Heaney's focus on mourning and burial was also inspired by an eighteenth-century Irish poem, Eibhlín Dubh Ní Chonaill's 'Caoineadh Airt Uí Laoghaire' (Lament for Art O'Leary), written to express a woman's grief and outrage at the killing of her husband by English soldiers at the instigation of the Sheriff of Cork.[229] The importance of the lament in the Irish tradition is unobtrusively kept before us by the repeated use of the verb 'to keen' (from Irish *caoinim*).[230] The inspiration provided by Eibhlín Dubh's lament roots the play more deeply in the history of Anglo-Irish relations, with its resonance of a time before English rule was overthrown.[231]

Heaney's verse is splendid; but many feel that it does not make a convincing play.[232] The poet seems to be in two minds, both about the possibility of contemporary political resonance and about the rights and wrongs of the conflict. Despite the partial assimilation of Creon and Bush, Heaney also wants Creon to be a tragic figure worthy of an audience's sympathies. And despite his expression of a balance, in which 'Creon's sufferings weigh heavily and evenly in the scales' (2004a: 76), Heaney has also loaded the dice heavily in Antigone's favour. Much of the harshness of the Sophoclean original is effaced; the rightness of her cause is never in doubt; and she excites the unmitigated admiration not only of Haemon ('*She was heroic!*' p. 31), but also of the Chorus (p. 37):

> Steadfast Antigone,
> Never before did Death
> Open his stone door
> To one so radiant.
> You would not live a lie.
> Vindicated, lauded,
> Age and disease outwitted,
> You go with head held high.

In his published accounts of his aims in writing the play Heaney both overstates and seeks to play down its contemporary political resonance. Its uncertainties seem to have been compounded by the original production,[233] and reviews were poor.[234] Whereas Conall Morrison's contemporary version builds the politics of the Middle East into the production itself, Heaney's relies substantially on extra-textual support in order to impress its political implications on its audiences.

Conclusion

Our Antigone, in the theatre and in contemporary thought, is a dissident. Whether Creon's position represents 'us' or 'them' is a bigger issue for Sophocles' original audience than it is in most modern productions.[235] The most emblematic modern versions react directly to very specific contemporary political circumstances. Unlike Athol Fugard or Andrzej Wajda, Sophocles did not have to defy the authorities and risk his liberty to get his play on stage. He was awarded a chorus by the city's leading magistrate, trained them at state expense, and saw his *Antigone* performed in a civic theatre before a mass popular audience at a state-funded religious festival. As far as we know, there was no immediate political issue to which Sophocles was reacting. His Antigone does challenge authority; but Antigone the freedom-fighter is a creation of the play's modern afterlife. The political aspects of Sophocles' play lie elsewhere, partly in general considerations about the nature of justice and the potential of human reason, but also in fundamental issues of political authority and the pressures of leadership – the frequent gulf between ideals and their implementation in practice; the tendency of power to seduce the powerful; the overlap between personal and principled motivations; the desire to dominate rather than to listen. Sophocles' *Antigone* justifies Athenian beliefs in the rights of all citizens to be heard, to play a part in ruling as well as in being ruled, and questions the confidence of the rising democracy in the potential for progress through the exercise of reason alone.

Both our *Antigone* and Sophocles' are thoroughly political; but not in the same ways. Though it is inevitable that we should read the original through the iconic versions and representations that have formed our modern experience of the play, we also need to strive to recover what is distinctive about the immense work of art that inspired this tradition. The *Antigone*, as we have it in Greek, is by no means universal in all the issues that it raises; there is a great deal that is period- and culture-specific. Yet the political aspects of the original are such that they can be applied to recurrent political issues. The emphasis that Sophocles' traditional ethics place on the limitations that constrain us all, even the powerful, can be used to give a voice to the disempowered, in a variety of political and cultural contexts. It is at least partly because Sophocles' *Antigone* is not a response to a specific fifth-century crisis that it can respond to nineteenth-, twentieth-, and twenty-first-century crises.[236]

Notes

Chapter 1

1 Thucydides 1. 115. 2–3.

2 Ion of Chios 392 F 6 *FGrHist*, Androtion 324 F 38 *FGrHist*.

3 Contrast Jebb (1900: xlv–xlvii).

4 From the inscription known as the Parian Marble, 239 A 60 *FGrHist*.

5 For the election of generals 'after the sixth prytany', see the Aristotelian *Constitution of Athens* (*Ath. Pol.*) 44. 4. For the implications, see Woodbury (1970: 217–24); cf. Jouanna (2007: 766 n. 64).

6 See Lewis (1988), esp. pp. 35–43. Sophocles in fact was the victor at the Dionysia of 438: see Euripides, *Alcestis*, hypothesis ii; Lewis (1988: 43). If (like Jouanna (2007: 43–51)) we want to accommodate *all* the ancient evidence regarding Sophocles' career as *stratêgos*, then we also need to reckon with a (later?) *stratêgia* as a colleague of Nicias (Plutarch, *Nicias* 15. 2 = T 26 Radt) and another alongside Thucydides (*Life* 1 = T 1. 5 Radt), earlier if this is the son of Melesias, later if it is the historian. Cf. Develin (1989: 104).

7 See Scullion (2002: 85–6).

8 First production and victory: Plutarch, *Cimon* 8. 8–9, though some think that Plutarch has confused first recorded victory with first production: see Radt (1988: 13–16); Scullion (2002: 87–90); cf. C. W. Müller (1984: 60). The total number of his plays is given as 130 (*Life* 18 = T1. 76–7 Radt, citing Aristophanes of Byzantium), with either seventeen (ibid.) or seven of these being judged spurious (hence the figure of 123, *Suda* σ 815 = T 2. 9 Radt): see Sommerstein (2012: 191–2). Sophocles died in 406 or very early 405 (Aristophanes, *Frogs* 76–7 etc.); *Oedipus at Colonus* was produced posthumously in 401 (*Hyp. OC* ii. 1–3).

9 The ability (from, it is normally assumed, the 430s onwards) to produce plays at another festival, the Lenaia, as well as at the City Dionysia, may explain an increase in productivity, in Euripides' case as well as Sophocles'. See Finglass (2011: 3–4). On tragedy at the Lenaia, cf. Pickard-Cambridge (1988: 40–2, 108, 125, 359–61). For considerations of the frequency with

which tragedians might compete at the dramatic festivals, see C. W. Müller (1984: 60–77).

10 See Bethe (1891); Robert (1915); Baldry (1956); March (1987: 121–54); Gantz (1993: 488–522); Mastronarde (1994: 17–30); Griffith (1999: 4–12).

11 For Polynices as a traitor, cf. Creon at 198–202, 280–9, 514–20.

12 Polynices' Argive marriage is referred to in passing at 870.

13 See M. L. West (2003: 6–10, 38–59).

14 Numbered 222A in Campbell (1991: 136–43).

15 On order and content see Gantz (1980: 158–9), (1993: 296, 521, 523); Zimmermann (1993: 81–7). There is a conspectus of attempts at reconstruction in Radt (1985: 116).

16 See esp. Hesiod, frr. 192–3 M-W (Oedipus' funeral, Polynices), Pindar *Olympian* 2. 37–45 (476 BC: the first occurrence of Laius' name, killed by Oedipus in fulfilment of a Delphic oracle; the mutual slaughter of his sons; the success of Polynices' son, Thersander, presumably one of the Epigonoi – also first here), *Nemean* 9. 18–27 (474 BC: Adrastus, Amphiaraus, and the first expedition, ending in seven pyres at Thebes), *Olympian* 6. 12–17 (472 or 468 BC: ditto). On the last two passages, cf. below, this chapter, at note 23.

17 See *Thebaid* frr. 1–3 in M. L. West (2003) for Oedipus' curse, the brothers' enmity, and the Argive alliance.

18 Pausanias 9. 5. 10–11 argues that the word 'immediately' (*aphar*) at *Odyssey* 11. 274 ('immediately the gods made [Oedipus' parricide and incest] known to humans') precludes any children of that union, and he adduces the version of the *Oedipodeia*, in which a second wife is the mother of Oedipus' children (whom Pausanias assimilates to the four offspring familiar from Sophocles). Cf. below, this chapter, at note 36.

19 *Odyssey* 11. 275–9. For other signs that Oedipus may have continued to rule at Thebes after the discovery of his deeds, cf. *Iliad* 23. 677–80, Hesiod, *Works and Days* 162–3, with Gantz (1993: 501–2).

20 See *Oedipodeia* fr. 1 in M. L. West (2003) (= Pausanias, above, n. 18). On this version, and on Pherecydes fr. 95 in R. L. Fowler (2000), cf. below, this chapter, at note 37. In *Antigone*, however, the point that Oedipus' offspring are the product of an incestuous union is repeatedly mentioned, but not extensively elaborated upon (see 1, 53, 513, 863–6), which suggests that it must already have been the dominant tradition in Sophocles' day, even if it goes back only as far as Aeschylus' Theban trilogy, as suggested by March (1987: 138, 140); cf. Baldry (1956: 31).

21 Stesichorus 222(b) *PMGF* = 222A in Campbell (1991: 136–43), lines 218–34.

22 As in Euripides' *Phoenician Women*, in which both Oedipus and Jocasta survive to witness the results of their sons' enmity.

23 Pausanias (1. 39. 2) saw their tombs on the road from Eleusis.

24 See G. Müller (1967: 239–40); Brown (1987: 212); contrast Kamerbeek (1978: 182); Griffith (1999: 308). Lloyd-Jones and Wilson (1990a: 143–4) argue for a lacuna rather than interpolation. Eteocles has already been buried, apparently (*Ant.* 23–5), even if 194–7 make it sound as if the burial has still to take place. We are not encouraged to speculate as to why Antigone appears unconcerned that one of her brothers has been buried in her absence, though that is certainly the implication of the early part of the play. On one interpretation of lines 898–903, favoured by Brown (1987: 198–9), Antigone does say that she participated in giving Eteocles, as well as her parents, due burial rites, including the washing and dressing of the body; but it is more likely that 'brother' at 899 means Polynices; 'washing, dressing, and pouring funeral libations' in 900–2 refers (mainly or wholly) to the funerals of the parents, before Antigone returns to the subject of Polynices' funeral in 902–3: see Griffith (1999: 276–7).

25 The curse goes back to *Thebaid* frr. 2–3 in M. L. West (2003); arrangements meant to forestall conflict appear first in Stesichorus 222(b) *PMGF* (cf. Hellanicus fr. 98 Fowler), though they may have existed also in the *Thebaid* (so Mastronarde (1994: 27)).

26 Regardless of how this may have been treated in the lost plays of the tetralogy. The *Seven* refers to a 'transgression' on Laius' part, which at least includes, and may be no more than, his refusal to heed an oracular warning against having a child (742–57); see M. L. West (1999: 40). In support of an earlier transgression for which the oracle is punishment, see Lloyd-Jones (1983: 120–1), (2002: 10–11). For a recent discussion, see Sewell-Rutter (2007: 28–33, 61–7).

27 The first reference to the Labdacids as a clan is Pindar, *Isthmian* 3. 16 (undated, but earlier than *Antigone*).

28 The play can, of course, be highly allusive in its references to other, non-Labdacid myths, as in the fourth stasimon (944–87); but that is a different issue.

29 For the impression that Creon's power goes further back than the assumption of command on the deaths of Eteocles and Polynices,

cf. 289–92, together with his complaint in the Tiresias scene itself that he has 'long' been a target for the corrupt practices of seers (1033–6).

30 As at *Oedipus Tyrannus* 1418; see Jebb (1900: 178) on 993–4, Brown (1987: 208) on 993–5.

31 Thebes' founder, Cadmus, killed a dragon sacred to Ares at the site of his new city. The Spartoi sprang spontaneously from the furrows where Cadmus, on Athena's advice, had sown the dragon's teeth. Five Spartoi survived the conflict that followed, and these joined Cadmus in founding the new city: see Pherecydes frr. 22 and 88 in R. L. Fowler (2000); Apollodorus 3. 4. 1–2; Gantz (1993: 468–9).

32 See Griffith (1999: 350–1) on 1302–3; Cingano (2003: 71–2). In the *Phoenician Women*, the other son of Creon is called Menoeceus. The specific detail of his voluntary self-sacrifice may be a Euripidean invention, as argued by Mastronarde (1994: 28–9). If we follow Bothe in emending the manuscripts' reference to Megareus' 'famous bed' in *Ant.* 1303 to 'famous lot', i.e. his death in battle (so Brown in his edition), this would further support an allusion to such a version; others, however, prefer Seyffert's 'empty bed' (Lloyd-Jones and Wilson 1990b; Griffith 1999).

33 See Brown (1987: 208) on 993–5; Mastronarde (1994: 29).

34 Specifically on the myths of Antigone herself, see Petersmann (1978); Zimmermann (1993). On the role of Antigone, Ismene, Creon, and Haemon in earlier versions of the Theban saga, see Cingano (2003).

35 It is possible that the body of Polynices was somehow singled out in the *Eleusinioi*, if that is indeed the focus of a fragmentary reference to the decomposition of a corpse (singular) at fr. 53a in Radt (1985); cf. Griffith (1999: 6 and n. 25).

36 So Fraenkel (1964); Dawe (1967); Hutchinson (1985: xliii–xlv, 190–1, 209–11); Gantz (1993: 520); Zimmermann (1993: 96–112). Contrast Lloyd-Jones (1959).

37 Fr. 95 in R. L. Fowler (2000). See now the discussion in R. L. Fowler (2013: 403–8).

38 Pherecydes was famous in 455/454 BC, according to Eusebius; his handling of the genealogy of the family of the Athenian statesman, Cimon, in his fr. 2 (cf. fr. 60) dates him to a period before the ascendancy of Cimon (*c.* 460s BC), according to Jacoby (1947: 31), but to the time of Cimon himself according to Huxley (1973). For the Pherecydes fragment as the earliest extant source to name Antigone, see Zimmermann (1993: 89–96).

39 See note 2 above.

40 See Zimmermann (1993: 94–5, 118); Griffith (1999: 10); Cingano (2003: 77–8).

41 Also depicted on two sixth-century vases, *LIMC* Ismene I, numbers 3–4. See Gantz (1993: 513–14); Zimmermann (1993: 68–70, 91); Cingano (2003: 74–5); R. L. Fowler (2013: 407).

42 Fr. 3 in M. L. West (2003); cf. scholiast on Euripides, *Phoenician Women* 1760, citing an author named Pisander. See Cingano (2003: 70–1). On the identity of this Pisander, see Lloyd-Jones (2002: 2–4, 9).

43 See *Odyssey* 11. 269–70; Pindar, *Isthmian* 4. 61–4 (father of Megara, wife of Heracles); Hesiod, *Shield of Heracles* 83–5 (welcomes Amphitryon, father of Heracles, to Thebes); *Oedipodeia* fr. 3 in M. L. West (2003) (father of Haemon, the Sphinx's victim); Aeschylus, *Seven against Thebes* 474 (father of Megareus, a descendant of the Sown Men); cf. Cingano (2003: 81–4).

44 See Gantz (1993: 530). Tiresias first appears in the *Odyssey* (10. 490–5, 524, 537, 565; 11. 29–50, 88–151, 164–5, 478–9; 12. 266–76; 23. 251–3, 322–3).

45 With the very probable exception of Creon's wife, Eurydice: see Griffith (1999: 9).

46 In favour of Sophoclean invention, see Baldry (1956: 33–4); G. Müller (1967: 21–4) is more cautious. For Antigone as a feature of pre-Sophoclean tradition, see Zimmermann (1993: 88–96, 115–16, 200, 225–6, 294–5, etc.). On Sophocles' innovative use of traditional material, cf. Zimmermann (1993: 115, 120); Griffith (1999: 8–10). It is always possible, though not demonstrable, that some details attested in later, unSophoclean versions also go back to pre-Sophoclean traditions: see Petersmann (1978: 82–96); Gantz (1993: 520–1); Zimmermann (1993: 225, 233, 255, 259, 262, 266, 275).

47 Tragedy regularly gives females, especially young females, a reason to be out of doors: cf. pseudo-Aeschylus, *Prometheus Bound* 133–5, Euripides, *Children of Heracles* 474–7, *Phoenician Women* 87ff., *Iphigenia at Aulis* 185–91. For norm, cf. *Trojan Women* 649–53. For the argument that this fact in itself already marks Antigone as transgressive, see Sourvinou-Inwood (1989a), and cf. Chapter 2 below.

48 Cf. Seale (1982: 85); Griffith (1999: 22). In conventional terms, Antigone is, as Creon claims (578–9), a woman 'on the loose'; in another conventional image, she is an unruly horse (477–8), to be curbed by the bit; on these points, cf. e.g. Gould (1980: 40, 53, 57–8).

49 See Griffith (1999: 11); cf. Garvie (2005: 39).

50 Griffith (1999: 165) on 223–6.

51 See Griffith (1999: 2 and n. 7) on this and other signs of *Antigone*'s comparatively early date.

52 For the perceived problem, see Jebb (1900: 86) on 429; Drachmann (1908); Rouse (1911). B. H. Fowler (1967: 150 n. 48) gives an extensive list of discussions, from 1931 to 1964; cf. Hester (1971: 27 n. 1) for the years 1911 to 1971 and Tyrrell and Bennett (1998: 22 n. 45) for 1911 to 1990.

53 See Brown (1987: 150) on 249–58, drawing on Bradshaw (1962); cf. Whitehorne (1983: 132). Contrast the argument of Adams (1931), McCall (1972), and Tyrrell and Bennett (1998: 69) that the first burial was, as the Chorus-leader says at 278–9, the 'work of the gods', and that of Honig (2013: 156–70) that it was the work of Ismene.

54 For those who perceive a problem, this is in fact the best solution. For a full and persuasive statement, see Whitehorne (1983: 129–33, 139–40); cf. Hester (1971: 27–9).

55 See Nicolai (2010: 182–3).

56 We assume, in tragedy as in life, that body language expresses the mind; see Budelmann and Easterling (2010), esp. pp. 300–1 on this passage.

57 For further speculation on the meaning of Antigone's posture in this scene, see Mueller (2011); on the protocols of looking and looking away that lie behind it, cf. Cairns (2005a).

58 See Griffith (1999: 22): '688–700 suggest that he [Haemon] has come from elsewhere in the city'.

59 The common assumption that a line has dropped out between 690 and 691 would make the speeches exactly equal; but approximate parity in length is enough to demonstrate the formalistic tendency of such scenes.

60 Bain (1981: 14) supports the former view.

61 On such 'mirror scenes' in tragedy, see Taplin (1978: 122–39). On their use in *Antigone*, cf. Seale (1982: 91–2, 103, 106).

62 So Jebb (1900: 145); Linforth (1961: 220); Kamerbeek (1978: 143); Bain (1981: 4–5, 14); contrast Kitto (1956: 167–8, 170); Brown (1987: 184) on 760.

63 According to A. Suter's formal criteria 'Antigone's scene before she is taken to the cave to die is not a lament' (Suter (2008: 159)); but for the essential point, see Seaford (1984: 253–4); Brown (1987: 190); Dué (2012: 247–8). On the conflation of funeral and wedding motifs, see Goheen (1951:

37–41); Seaford (1987: 107–8); Ditmars (1992: 109–14); Rehm (1993: 63–4); Griffith (1999: 267, 273). Cf. Chapter 4 below, pp. 107–10.

64 For the suggestion, see Goheen (1951: 38); Seaford (1987: 113).

65 For the 'rule' and the departure from it at *Ant*. 885ff. see Bain (1981: 2, 24–9).

66 See Kitto (1956: 173) and contrast Seale (1982: 101).

67 On Creon's presence onstage during the second, third, and fourth stasima, see Kitto (1956: 165–73); Griffith (1999: 24).

68 Cf. G. Müller (1967: 227) on the effect of Tiresias' surprise entrance, and Riemer (1991: 20) on the contrast with *Oedipus the King*.

69 Cf. 18–19, with comments above, p. 12.

70 Knox (1979: 175); Brown (1987: 224) on 1258. Cf. and contrast Seale (1982: 105).

71 In favour of the *ekkyklêma*, see Seale (1982: 106); Brown (1987: 225–6) on 1293. Against, see Griffith (1999: 349–50) on 1293. If line 1239 ('You can see; [the body] is no longer in the recesses') suggests that the body is no longer in the palace, then this does not suit the convention that the *ekkyklêma* is used to reveal *interior* tableaux. But on the assumption that the *ekkyklêma* was used, the line might also indicate that the body has been moved from an inner to a more accessible area of the house.

Chapter 2

1 See Bowra (1944: 65); Reinhardt (1979: 64–5); Segal (1986: 137–9). Cf. the overview of Carter (2012: 111–16).

2 Diller (1956); Knox (1964).

3 See e.g. Diller (1956: 82); Kirkwood (1958: 52); Knox (1964: 73–5, with 62–90 in general on the extent to which Antigone and Creon each exhibit The Heroic Temper); G. Müller (1967: 12); on 'yielding' (*eikein, eikathein*: *Ant*. 472, 718, 1029, 1096) in Sophocles, see Diller (1956: 72, 75–7); Knox (1964: 15–17). Against the view that Creon is primarily to be thought of as a failed hero, see Gibert (1995: 105–9); cf. Hester (1971: 39).

4 See Scodel (2010: 7–13).

5 Aristotle, *Poetics* 6, 1449b24–5; cf. J. Jones (1962: 21–9); Heath (1987: 90–111).

6 Such as the three early 'diptych' plays of Sophocles, *Ajax*, *Women of Trachis*, and *Antigone*. See Heath (1987: 92–5). On the 'diptych' structure, see Webster (1936: 102–3); Waldock (1951: 49–61); Kirkwood (1958: 42–55).

7 See e.g. Gellie (1972: 30); Heath (1987: 94–5).

8 For a forceful statement of entirely the opposite point of view, see Sourvinou-Inwood (1989a), (1990). Cf. the extreme pro-Creon stance of Calder (1968).

9 For these claims, see Heath (1987: 75), with further discussion of the terms at 90–8. For contrary views, see most recently Liapis (2013: 87–8, 90–1).

10 See Sourvinou-Inwood (1989a: 146).

11 Creon's assumption in 248 and its echo at 348 thus initiate the themes of male versus female, the norms of manliness, and the question of who *is* the man, which all then recur later in the play, especially in Creon's confrontation with Antigone and in his determination to demonstrate his power by making an example of her (484–5, 525; cf. 648–52, 678–80, 740–1, 756).

12 See further Chapter 3 below.

13 Cf. Holt (1999: 675–6).

14 Von Fritz (1962) argued that the Chorus (793–4) are wrong to see Haemon's opposition to Creon as motivated by *erôs*, as such a motive would undermine his arguments in the previous scene. But this is a false antithesis; and ample evidence of the truth of the Chorus's diagnosis is provided by Haemon's subsequent behaviour. As Winnington-Ingram puts it (1980: 92), 'Did he threaten, and then commit, suicide because he thought his father was behaving as a bad king?' For more on *erôs*, see Chapter 4.

15 See Kitto (1956: 163, 167, 176–7); Winnington-Ingram (1980: 97; cf. p. 101 on the fourth stasimon).

16 Plus the considerably more enigmatic example of Cleopatra, wife of Phineus, whose relevance as an example here is obscure and disputed: see the various commentaries, and, for speculative accounts, Winnington-Ingram (1980: 98–109), Sourvinou-Inwood (1989b).

17 See Gantz (1993: 113–14).

18 Cf. Winnington-Ingram (1980: 101–4).

19 Cf. 986–7, of Cleopatra.

20 See Hesiod, *Catalogue of Women* fr. 135 M-W = fr. 241 in Most (2007); Pherecydes frr. 10, 12 Fowler. See further Gantz (1993: 299–303, 310).

21 See esp. 999–1022, 1068–76.

22 Tiresias' emphasis is in fact different: he first urges Creon to remedy the disruption he has caused by leaving the corpse unburied (1015–32), with the general assurance that this will be better for the city (1015) and for Creon himself (1025–7, 1031–2). When Creon rejects that advice, Tiresias then states (categorically and not hypothetically) that Creon's actions will cost him a son of his own and cause his house to resound with lamentation (1064–79). His first utterance is a warning, and presupposes that the situation can yet be retrieved, while the second is a statement of fact, albeit about the future. Cf. below, Chapter 3, pp. 88–9 and n. 98.

23 See Griffith (1999: 329, 331) on 1192–1243 and 1206–8.

24 For this pattern, cf. Heath (1987: 95), comparing Sophocles' *Women of Trachis* and Euripides' *Hippolytus* and *Andromache*.

25 The word is used again in the Hymn to Eros at 794, of the 'kindred strife' that the god has provoked between Creon and Haemon. At 198 it refers to the relationship between Eteocles and Polynices; cf. the synonym *homaimos* at 512–13.

26 For the political image of *metoikia* (i.e. the status of resident aliens at Athens) that she evokes in these lines, cf. 867–8, 890, and see Knox (1964: 114–15); Seaford (1990: 78–9). In the first stasimon (370–1), the Chorus described anyone who boldly disregarded divine justice as 'without a city' (*apolis*); in a sense, between the communities of the living and the dead as she is, this seems to be Antigone's fate; but in the end, it may also be Creon's.

27 Thus the news does to him what Tiresias said he was doing to Polynices (1029–30).

28 For a full and detailed review of opinions on the rights and wrongs of Creon's and Antigone's positions, see Hester (1971), esp. 11–18. In the past twenty or so years, much discussion has centred on support for or opposition to the extreme anti-Antigone viewpoint put forward by Sourvinou-Inwood (1989a) and (1990). See e.g. Foley (1995); Holt (1999); Scodel (2010: 106–19); Liapis (2013).

29 Cf. Parker (1983: 43–4). For plentiful evidence of the obligation to bury the dead and the importance of the family in funerary ritual and the care of the dead in fifth-century Athens, cf. various authors in Patterson (2006a); see also Whitehorne (1983: 135–7).

30 See Segal (1971); cf. Vernant (1991). For Rosivach (1983: 197), by contrast, non-burial and mutilation are 'normal practice', 'if not the norm, at least a frequent occurrence'. On the seminal importance of the encounter of Achilles and Priam in *Iliad* 24, cf. Steiner (1984: 242–3).

31 See Linforth (1961: 190–3, 195); Gellie (1972: 33); Whitehorne (1983:133–5); Tyrrell and Bennett (1998: 57–9, 65, 129–30); cf. more recently Shapiro (2006). On the text of *Iliad* 1. 4–5 and its interpretation, see Redfield (2001: 457–8, 467–9).

32 See Whitman (1951: 86–7); Linforth (1961: 193); Garvie (2005: 18–19). See especially *Ajax* 1332–45.

33 For a good general assessment, see Morwood (2007: 8–14). On the importance of the myth of Theseus' intervention to bury the Seven in Athenian self-definition, see Bennett and Tyrrell (1990), reprised and expanded in Tyrrell and Bennett (1998: 5–28, 40–2, 61, 71–2, 76–7, 86, 91, 106, 110–11, 115–18, 120–1, 131–2, 135); cf. Harris (2004: 38–9). Tyrrell and Bennett argue that the prominence of this theme in public eulogies of the Athenian war-dead in particular (e.g. Lysias 2. 7–10; Demosthenes 60. 8; cf. Isocrates 4. 54–9, 64, 10. 31, 12. 168–74) is an important factor in guiding an audience's response to Antigone; cf. Segal (1995: 122–3). Denial of burial fails also in Aeschylus' lost plays *Eleusinioi* (on the Seven against Thebes) and *Ransom of Hector*: see Sommerstein (2009: 56–7, 262–9).

34 See Cerri (1979: 42–3, 79–81).

35 See Parker (1983: 45–8). The relevance of this for the *Antigone* is widely discussed: see e.g. Hester (1971: 19–21, 55), with references to earlier discussions; Rosivach (1983); Whitehorne (1983: 137–9); Sourvinou-Inwood (1989a: 137–8, 147); Tyrrell and Bennett (1998: 131); Holt (1999: 663–8); Patterson (2006b: 33–9).

36 The same law is cited at Xenophon, *Hellenica* 1. 7. 22, in the context of the trial of the generals responsible for the failure to rescue the shipwrecked at Arginusae in 406 BC. The presentation of the issue at Euripides, *Phoenician Women* 775–6 and 1629–30 precisely reflects the Athenian position by limiting the prohibition of Polynices' burial to Theban territory, as also seems to be the case at Aeschylus, *Seven against Thebes* 1014 (see Hutchinson (1985) on that line).

37 Pseudo-Plutarch, *Lives of the Ten Orators* 834a–b.

38 See Plato, *Laws* 873c, 874b, 909c, and esp. 960b (omitting the specification 'beyond the borders'); cf. Griffith (1999: 30 and n. 91).

39 Cf. Holt (1999: 665).

40 The issue is complicated by textual uncertainty in a crucial passage (Xenophon, *Hellenica* 1. 7.20, the 'decree of Cannonus'). For the range of views, see MacDowell (1978: 254–5); Parker (1983: 47 n. 52); Allen (2000: 218–22); Todd (2000: 33–4, 37–9).

41 As it was in Georgian Britain. The Murder Act, passed by the UK parliament in 1752, forbade the burial of those executed for homicide and required that their remains be publicly dissected or displayed (an apparently popular spectacle). The Act was repealed in 1836; public executions were not banned until 1868. See Gatrell (1994: 267–9).

42 See MacDowell (1978: 254); Sourvinou-Inwood (1989a: 147), (1990: 27–8).

43 Cf. Griffith (1999: 31 n. 94).

44 See Sourvinou-Inwood (1989a), especially 137–8, (1990: 21–3); cf. Holt (1999: 668). For Creon's own religiosity, see Knox (1964: 99–102); M. W. Blundell (1989: 128–30); Griffith (1999: 47).

45 See Hester (1971: 20–1). Contrast Sourvinou-Inwood (1989a: 147): Polynices' 'achievement of proper burial' is 'a corrective excess'.

46 See Griffith (1999: 276) on 900–3; cf. Garland (1985: 24, 28–30, 32–4, 37).

47 Cf. Sourvinou-Inwood (1989a: 139–40); Hame (2008).

48 The abnormality of the circumstances in which Antigone finds herself – especially in the absence of a male relative to conduct the burial – is emphasized by Foley (1995: 139); cf. Patterson (2006b: 37). Antigone's act is still one of rebellion, as Hame points out (2008: 11), but the crucial issue is the presentation of that act in the play itself.

49 See MacDowell (1978: 84–9); Just (1989); Patterson (1991); S. Blundell (1995: 113–29).

50 It is often assumed that Demosthenes' quotation proves positive characterization; but it does not. This is not just because Demosthenes may be quoting out of context, as is often the case; but also because he wants to have things both ways – though Creon's words at 175–90 are 'fine and advantageous' (19. 246), Creon himself is a tyrant (in the pejorative sense of the word, 19. 247), played not by the lead actor (protagonist), but by the tritagonist, Aeschines the bit-part player: see MacDowell (2000: 305). Demosthenes not only denigrates Aeschines' profession as an actor, he also invites his audience to associate him with any negative impression that they may have of Creon as a ruler in Sophocles' play. The passage is certainly evidence that 175–90 represent uncontroversial Athenian ideals,

and this is a relevant consideration, but they do not prove that positive ideals are matched by positive characterization; the quotation is perfectly compatible with the espousal of positive ideals by an unsympathetic character. Cf. Harris (2004: 28); Ferrario (2006: 81–2); Hall (2011: 57–9). For similar sentiments to Creon's in a near-contemporary political context, see Pericles at Thucydides 2. 60. 2–4 and compare *Ant.* 188–90.

51 See Sourvinou-Inwood (1989a), esp. 135; (1990); (1991b). Similar views more recently in Liapis (2013), esp. pp. 82–6. For Brown (1987: 9), the root of the error lies in our familiarity with the model of the Christian martyr, specifically invoked by e.g. Jebb (1900: xxv). Similarly, Hester (1971: 13) lists seventeen scholars who allegedly 'see the *Antigone* as a martyr-play with Antigone herself as almost a Christian saint'; to the anachronistic figure of the martyr, Holt (1999: 658–9) and Sourvinou-Inwood (1990: 11) would (respectively) add those of the 'heroic dissident' and 'proto-feminist heroine'.

52 As Foley points out (1995: 132), Sourvinou-Inwood treats the fifth-century audience 'as an undifferentiated collectivity' with a 'unified cultural ideology'; cf. the earlier warnings against such assumptions in Goldhill (1986: 89–92). For her part, Sourvinou-Inwood regards such observations as 'clearly fallacious' (1990: 13); but her position, that we must choose between (a) a construct that purports to represent the views of 'all or most fifth-century Athenians' and therefore gives us the attitude of 'Sophocles and his contemporaries' and (b) 'the hidden assumption that it is . . . "better" to privilege our own arbitrary readings', is itself a clear example of the fallacy of false alternatives.

53 On tragedy's social and ethical polyphony see Hall (1997: 93–9).

54 See, for example, Foley (1995); Scodel (2010: 106–19).

55 Note Sourvinou-Inwood's slide (note 52 above) from 'all or most Athenians' to 'Sophocles and his contemporaries'; cf. (1990: 26), where Sophocles' political career is used as evidence against the view that he might have been in any way 'a challenger of the values of polis discourse'.

56 Cf. Hall (1997: 99): 'tragedy cannot be used as a document of the realities of life in Athens. It is essential to acknowledge the processes of artistic mediation.' Holt (1999: 670–90) is an excellent discussion of the ways in which Sophocles' artistic design creates a tension between the orthodoxies of civic life to which the audience might, in the abstract, subscribe and the sympathies that are elicited by the play as we actually have it.

57 Cf. Polyxena's active acceptance of her sacrifice in *Hecuba* 546–65. On virgin sacrifice in Euripides, see Loraux (1987: 43–8, 56–60); for a comparison between Antigone and Euripides' sacrificial heroines, see Belardinelli (2010: 13–18).

58 Cf. Sourvinou-Inwood (1990: 36 n. 16); these differences are rather played down by Belardinelli (2010).

59 See 140–1, 164–7, 187–92, 215–24, 254–60, 307–9, 312–13, 516–18, 605–9, 612–23.

60 Cf. Winnington-Ingram (1980: 123); Holt (1999: 675–6). There is a further ambivalence in their words: though in a sense it is true that Creon has 'the power to use any law he likes concerning the dead and the living', in so far as the treatment of the dead is a legitimate interest of the *polis* and its representatives (Sourvinou-Inwood (1989a: 137–8)), any implication that Creon's power to legislate may extend to the world of the dead is amply refuted by the Chorus's own words in the first stasimon (that man cannot conquer death, 361–2) and Tiresias' observation that it is wrong to attempt 'to kill the dead a second time' (1029–30).

61 So Sourvinou-Inwood (1989a: 148 = 1990: 31–2): 'Kreon was in the wrong, and he was punished. Antigone's cause was right and it was vindicated. Her action was at the same time right and wrong; right, because it reversed the offence against the cosmic order; wrong, because she subverted the order of the polis in fundamental ways. She herself as a character, having set herself up as a source of value in opposition to the established order, was in the wrong, and was punished accordingly. Not just with death, but with a ... "bad death".'

62 See further Cairns (2005b: 306–9).

63 Sourvinou-Inwood (see above, p. 42 and n. 45) would not concede even so much.

64 Brown (1987: 9); cf. Griffith (1999: 32).

65 On the portrayal of the Chorus, cf. Burton (1980: 86–9).

66 Noted by Griffith (1999: 273) in his note on this passage.

67 The possibility that the Chorus keep their feelings about Antigone's conduct to themselves, out of fear of Creon, is raised explicitly by Antigone in the *agôn* at 505, where the form of words used ('were it not that fear keeps their tongues under lock and key') clearly recalls Creon's principle that no statesman should, 'out of fear, keep his tongue under lock and key' (180). Freedom of speech (*parrhêsia*) was a principle of Athenian

democracy, one that Creon (as the scene with Haemon in particular shows) fails to live up to. This may lend some credence to Antigone's observation at 504–5.

68 Haemon's words at 697–8 not only recall the proem of the *Iliad*, with its anticipation of the theme of the mutilation of the corpse (*Iliad* 1. 4–5; see above, p. 38), but also make use of an adjective, 'raw-eating', which is used three times in the *Iliad* in connection with the theme of the mutilation of the corpse (11. 454, 22. 67, 24. 207; and even the fourth Iliadic occurrence at 24. 82 is indirectly related to the theme of the treatment of Hector's body).

69 (1989a: 146); (1990: 15–16).

70 In addition, as Holt wisely observes (1999: 682–3), deceitful reports of offstage action are generally marked as such in Sophocles, while reports that are not so marked are often essential for the plot and generally to be taken at face value.

71 Conceded by Sourvinou-Inwood (1989a: 146).

72 The notion of *hamartia* on Creon's part, both in his treatment of Antigone and in his attitude towards the gods, is first raised explicitly by Haemon at 743–5.

73 See Goldhill (1986: 103–4).

74 'No one is a prophet of what is established for mortals', as the Messenger puts it at 1160, using the same word as Creon used at 1113. For more on the relationship between Creon's edict and 'law', as understood by contemporary Athenians, see Harris (2004).

75 Despite the arguments of Brown (1987: 9) and Sourvinou-Inwood (1989a: 144, 147); cf. Griffith (1999: 32).

76 Heath (1987: 75), cited in n. 9 above.

77 Cf. Goldhill (1986: 175–9); Tyrrell and Bennett (1998: 130).

78 Heath (1987: 80–8).

79 The quotation is from Brown's note on line 569 (1987: 168).

80 See Lattimore (1942: 192–4); Lefkowitz and Fant (1992), nos. 11, 12, 14, 15, 273.

81 See Holt (1999), esp. 685–7.

82 Cf. Burton (1980: 135); Rehm (1993: 67); Segal (1995: 131). On Antigone's grief and Creon's, see further Honig (2013: 95–120).

Chapter 3

1 See especially Euripides' *Suppliant Women* 201–15 and the pseudo-
   Aeschylean *Prometheus Bound* 442–506.

2 For 'man the measure of all things' see Protagoras B 1 DK. In Plato's
   Protagoras 320c–328d the Sophist presents his account of the development
   of civilization first in the form of a (quasi-Hesiodic) myth, and then in that
   of a *logos*, or speech. On the relation between the first stasimon of *Antigone*
   and this current of fifth-century thought, see Utzinger (2003); cf. Guthrie
   (1969: 60–8, 79–84); Goldhill (1986: 202–5); Segal (1986).

3 See Hesiod, *Works and Days* 106–201.

4 Cf. Benardete (1999: 41–5); Susanetti (2012: 228–9).

5 For the ode's ambivalence, cf. Goheen (1951: 53–6); Kirkwood (1958:
   205–6); Linforth (1961: 196–9); G. Müller (1967: 83–9); Coleman (1972:
   10); Gellie (1972: 36–7); Goldhill (1986: 204–5); Nussbaum (1986: 73–5);
   Ditmars (1992: 47–8, 58); Benardete (1999: 40–9); contrast Knox (1979:
   168–72); Brown (1987: 154–5).

6 See further Cairns (2014a).

7 See Friedländer (1969: 191–2). The general relevance of Solon's poem to
   the first stasimon is noted by G. Müller (1967: 87), though he does not
   discuss the detailed correspondences. Cf. his p. 139 on the second
   stasimon, and see also Gagné (2013: 373–6). Solon's poem was clearly well
   known at Athens: see Gagné (2013: 227, 375).

8 Crane (1989: 107) notes the third item, but not the other two.

9 Cf. Linforth (1961: 196); Friedländer (1969: 190–1); Coleman (1972: 10);
   Burton (1980: 96); Staley (1985), esp. 565–8; Crane (1989: 105); Susanetti
   (2012: 224–5).

10 The adjective 'windy' (*anemoeis*) that is applied to *phronêma* at *Ant.* 355
   also appears in *Libation Bearers* 591, of the 'anger of whirlwinds'.

11 Beginning with a reference to their 'passions' (*erôtes*) that accompany
   mortals' *atê* (delusion/disaster), 597–8.

12 So in general G. Müller (1967: 87–8); contrast Staley (1985: 561); Crane
   (1989: 107).

13 Cf. Else (1976: 46); also (at least in general terms), Crane (1989).

14 The manuscript text is emended in two main ways: in the version printed
   in Lloyd-Jones and Wilson (1990b) the reference to wealth is clearer, but

the implication is there even with the alternative emendation printed by Jebb (1900) and by Dawe (1984–5).

15 On *atê* in Homer, see Cairns (2012); in Aeschylus, Sommerstein (2013). For a fuller account of some of the issues raised in what follows, see Cairns (2013). On *atê* in *Antigone*, see also Else (1976: 26–7, 31, 76).

16 Cf. Brown (1987: 176) on 624: 'For a mind there is little difference between *ātē* in the sense "ruin" and in the sense "infatuation", so the two senses are bridged here.' See also G. Müller (1967: 139).

17 Cf. Dawe (1968: 100–1, 108–9); Easterling (1978: 149); Kitzinger (2008: 38–9). Personified Ate and the Erinys are famously associated in Agamemnon's Apology at *Iliad* 19. 87–8.

18 The ambivalence of hope is proverbial: see esp. Hesiod, *Works and Days* 498–501; Semonides fr. 1. 6–10 West (cf. 23); Theognis 637–8; Solon fr. 13. 33–6 West; cf. Easterling (1978: 153).

19 See Cairns (2013: xii–xiii).

20 So Easterling (1978: 152); unnecessarily complicated by Brown (1987: 175–6).

21 *Persians* 93–100, 724–5, 742; cf. Theognis 402–6 and trag. adesp. 455, cited by Jebb (1900: 119–20) on 622ff. and Griffith (1999: 230) on 622–4.

22 Cf. Brown (1987: 170–1): 'The archaic word *ātē* resounds ominously through [the ode] ... Here, though the idea of infatuation is very much present, the word *ātē* itself bears the sense "disaster", as it usually does in tragedy ...'

23 An ominous word, perhaps, especially in the second stasimon, with its focus on the House of Oedipus (600).

24 Cf. the bull at 352.

25 Cf. Susanetti (2012: 229) on 342.

26 The relation between the first and second stasima, and between both and their intertexts, thus exemplifies what Dunn (2012) has identified as the dynamic force of Sophoclean intertextuality.

27 See Solon 13. 25–32 West. For echoes of Solon 13 in the second stasimon, cf. especially the inability to foresee the consequences of one's actions (617–24, with Solon 13. 33–6, 65–70), the image of the storm (586–93; Solon 13. 17–24), the dangers of wealth (614; Solon 13. 9–13, 71–6), the inevitability of fate and the power of the divine (596–7; Solon 13. 29–32, 55–6, 63–4), the power of Zeus (604–14; Solon 13. 17–32, 75–6), and the delusionary nature of hope (615–17; Solon 13. 35–6). In the final case

(hope as a 'deception of light-minded passions, *erôtes*', leading to *atê*), the second stasimon recalls both Solon ('light-minded hope', 13. 36) and Aeschylus' *Libation Bearers* ('the reckless passions, *erôtes*, of women that accompany mortals' ruin, *atai*', 597–8).

28 On the specific debt to *Seven* 653ff., 720–91, 875–1004, see Else (1976: 16–24, 28), esp. 16–18; cf. Bowra (1944: 87); Ditmars (1992: 77–9). Gagné (2013: 373) is more sceptical. The *Seven* is similarly a prominent comparator for *Antigone*'s *parodos* (100–54): see Else (1976: 35–40); Davidson (1983: 41, 43–8); Dunn (2012: 268–70); Rodighiero (2012: 108).

29 Cf. also 'the dust of earth drinks their black-clotted, blood-red blood' (*Seven* 735–6) and 'bloody root' (755) with *Ant.* 599–602, 'for, as it was, a light had been extended over the last root in the House of Oedipus; it in its turn is harvested by the blood-red dust of the nether gods'. See further Cairns (2014b).

30 Cf. Easterling (1978: 156). Her family's woes, of which hers are the worst, are restated in spoken iambic summary at 892–6.

31 For the debate on whether the specific notion of a curse is to be seen as more widely applicable in the play, see Lloyd-Jones (1983: 115–16); M. L. West (1999: 40–1); Sewell-Rutter (2007: 71, 114–20).

32 As in Aeschylus, *Seven against Thebes* 69–70, 655, 695–7, 766–7, 785–7, 832–3, 893, 945–6, 953–5.

33 With line 90's reference to *erôs*, (sexual) passion, cf. the hope that, for many, represents the 'deception of light-minded passions' (*erôtes*) in the second stasimon at 617 (as well as the ironic application to Antigone of the Chorus-leader's statement that no one is so foolish as to be in love (*erôs*) with death, 220; and of course the Hymn to Eros at 781–800).

34 On *hybris*, see Fisher (1992); Cairns (1996). *Hybris* is latent in 473–83, even before it is explicitly enunciated at 480 and 482. The 'too hard *phronêmata*' of 473 activate the ambiguity of *phronêma* that recurs in the play (176, 207, 353, 459). Similarly, the reference to 'high-spirited horses' (477–8) supplies a typical exemplar of *hybris*: Fisher (1992: 119–21, 232–3, 353–4). And finally *phronein mega* ('thinking big') in 479 deploys a familiar periphrasis (used again at 768, of Haemon) to express what is then conveyed by the two uses of *hybris*-words in 480 and 482.

35 On the 'archaic chain' see esp. Solon 4. 34–5 W, with Fisher (1992: 72; cf. 206, 213, 221, 236ff.).

36 Cf. Solon 4. 35 West; Aeschylus, *Persians* 821–2; *Seven against Thebes* 601 (marked as spurious by M. L. West (1998) and Sommerstein (2009), following Musgrave); *Agamemnon* 1655.

37 Antigone takes the Chorus's words not as a reference to Oedipus' guilt, but to the unfortunate destiny (*potmos*, 861) of the Labdacids; but that destiny includes her parents' incest, a horrific transgression – the passage preserves the ambivalence of the second stasimon between inherited suffering and inherited guilt.

38 See Cairns (2012); Sommerstein (2013).

39 Dawe (1968); cf. Bremer (1969: 99–134).

40 Cf. Foley (1993: 111–13) = (2001: 31–3); Garvie (2005: 39).

41 See above, pp. 36–7, 51, 71–2.

42 See e.g. Achilles' prediction that Agamemnon 'will recognize his *atê* in failing to pay honour to the best of the Achaeans' (*Iliad* 1. 412, echoed by Patroclus at 16. 274). This means simply that Agamemnon will regret his action once its consequences have become obvious (as he does: 2. 375–8, 9. 115–20; cf. and contrast 19. 85–144). Definitive recognition of *atê* is retrospective; cf. Cairns (2012: 19–20).

43 Cf. Antigone at 914: 'For Creon, this [my conduct] seemed to be an error (*hamartanein*).'

44 Cf. above, p. 53.

45 On the way that the language of this and the other choral odes implicitly foregrounds the dangers and dubieties of Creon's conduct, see Chapter 2 above and cf. e.g. Jebb (1900: 118) on 615–25; Goheen (1951: 52–74); Kitto (1958: 36–7); Linforth (1961: 198–9, 214–15, 233, 238); G. Müller (1961); Dawe (1968: 112); Coleman (1972: 13–14, 20–1, 24, 26–7); Else (1976: 46, 50, 75–6); Easterling (1978: 157–8); Winnington-Ingram (1980: 91–116, 118, 172); Brown (1987: 172, 187, 202–4); Ditmars (1992: 48–56, 85, 95–7, 139–48, 172); Griffith (1999: 220, 255, 284–5).

46 See Aristotle, *Nicomachean Ethics* 5. 1, 1130a1–2; cf. Bowra (1944: 69); Budelmann and Easterling (2010: 299). Similarly, the metaphor of the touchstone that Creon uses at 177 implies a comparison between the value of gold and that of men that is common in the Theognidea, a corpus of archaic elegiac poetry: see Theognis 119–28, 415–18, 447–52, 963–70, 1105–6, 1164g–h. The language and thought of *Ant.* 175–7 and Theognis 963–70 in particular are close enough for Creon's words to remind an audience of Theognis' warning, that we should not praise a man until we

know his character (964), because many are counterfeit. We shall return below to the play's pervasive confrontation of material with non-material value; on the touchstone metaphor, cf. Seaford (1998: 135–6).

47 See Achilles' verdict on Agamemnon at *Iliad* 1. 343–4 and compare Themistocles at Thucydides 1. 138. 3, Pericles at 2. 62–3, 2. 65. 6 (and in Plutarch's *Comparison of Pericles and Fabius* 2. 3), Phormio at 2. 89. 2, and Nicias at 6. 13. 1. Cf. also Demosthenes 18. 246. For Plato's Socrates, the ability to foresee and forestall future trouble is the mark of a good doctor, lawgiver, and beekeeper (*Republic* 564c).

48 Cf. Cairns (2012: 9–17, esp. 16–17).

49 On *atê*'s relation to results, cf. above (with note 42 on *Iliad* 1. 412). See also Solon 13. 65–70 W (≈ Theognis 585–90).

50 See Sommerstein (2013: 2); cf. Cairns (2012: 1 n. 2). For a clear play on *atê* as both 'loss' (as opposed to profit) and 'disaster', see Theognis 119 (and cf. 133, 205–6).

51 See Goheen (1951: 14–19), and cf. below.

52 The conceit of the sisters as 'two Atai' is repeated, in a different context, at *Oedipus at Colonus* 531.

53 One thinks of the inclusion of medicine among the list of human achievements in the first stasimon (363–4); cf. Goheen (1951: 41–4); Segal (1986: 160).

54 Creon himself was once able to secure the city's safety (*sôtêria*, 1162), but only with Tiresias' help (1058; cf. 995).

55 Similarly, Tiresias' remark that Creon should learn 'to nurture a quieter tongue and a better mind than the one he has now' (1089–90) perhaps evokes 603's 'senselessness of speech and a Fury of the mind'.

56 I follow Lloyd-Jones's and Wilson's Oxford Classical Text (1990b), but translate it slightly differently from Lloyd-Jones himself (1964: 129). For Ate's net see Aeschylus, *Persians* 97–9, *Agamemnon* 355–61; cf. pseudo-Aeschylus, *Prometheus Bound* 1071–9.

57 See Dawe (1968: 113–14 n. 40).

58 For a full defence of this position, see Cairns (2012: 8, 15–16, 22–3, 26–33).

59 Cf. R. M. Torrance (1965: 298–300); Winnington-Ingram (1980: 117, 147).

60 Cf. (once more) Dawe (1968: 113–14 n. 40).

61 An ancient commentator ('scholiast') glosses *hysterophthoroi* as 'those who will later cause harm (*blapsai*)'. If *lôbêtêres* ('agents of ruin') is also being used here to suggest *atê*, then compare the Chorus's apostrophe of Eros at

791–2: 'You seize the minds even of the just and pervert them to injustice, to their ruin (*lôbê*).' Eros is another form of mental aberration that leads, according to the Chorus, to disaster; we shall come back to this below.

62 See Eustathius 2. 777–8 Van der Valk. He has already cited the Sophoclean phrase at 2. 760 on *Iliad* 9. 454.

63 The adjective occurs elsewhere only at Nonnus, *Dionysiaca* 9. 135.

64 See Aeschylus, *Agamemnon* 819: 'the gusts of *atê* are still alive'. Cf. the storm which represents Zeus's punishment, and thus the *atê* which follows *hybris*, in Solon 13. 11–25 West. On the *atê*/*aêmi* etymology, see Francis (1983).

65 Cf. Easterling (1978: 144).

66 Cf. 391, 417–21, 670, 712–17.

67 Cf. 1274, where the divine 'shaking' that Creon suffers echoes both the second stasimon at 584 and the 'shaking' of the ship of state in Creon's opening words at 162–3.

68 Cf. Kitzinger (2008: 35 n. 46).

69 Cf. Cullyer (2005: 15–18).

70 See e.g. Padel (1992: 89–95); Clarke (1999).

71 For the ship of state/seafaring/storm at sea image-complex in general see also 391, 586–92, 1000. Behind the application of this theme to Creon lie passages such as Theognis 671–82, where the ship of state is buffeted in a political storm caused by those who pursue material wealth by illegitimate means. On seafaring as an image of rational control over the forces of nature in the first stasimon and beyond, see Goheen (1951: 44–51); Segal (1986: 159); cf. Oudemans and Lardinois (1987: 125–6, 133–4, 160).

72 See further Segal (1986).

73 See 67–8, 95, 99, 175–6, 179, 207, 220, 281, 310–14 (with the antithesis of *atê* and *sôtêria* in 314), 323, 342–67, 389, 469–70, 473–4, 557, 561–5, 603, 614–25 (hope, delusion, and *atê*), 637–8, 648–9, 681–4, 707–11, 719–27, 754–5, 791–2, 960–1, 1015, 1023–8, 1031–2, 1048–52, 1090, 1098, 1103–4 (the Blabai cut off the imprudent), 1228–9, 1242–3, 1250, 1261–2 ('errors [*hamartêmata*] of a deranged mind', picking up *atê* and *hamartia* in 1259–60), 1265, 1269, 1271, 1339–40, 1347–53, with Goheen (1951: 82–4); Kirkwood (1958: 233–6); Linforth (1961: 257–9); Else (1976: 69 and *passim*); Winnington-Ingram (1980: 121–2); Goldhill (1986: 175–80); Ditmars, (1992: 72–3); Cropp (1997: 143–7); Hall (2012: 312–13).

74 See Winnington-Ingram (1980: 91–116).

75 Cf. Seaford (1990: 87–9; 2012, 331–2), (1993), and (1994: 344–67).
Arguably, Dionysus has been present and at work throughout the play: he
is invoked as chorus-leader not only in the fifth stasimon at 1146–54 but
already in the parodos at 153–4, as 'the god who makes Thebes shake'.
Earlier in the same song, the threat to the city posed by the Seven is
presented in Dionysiac terms – Capaneus 'who, raging (*bakcheuein*) in his
mad onrush, breathed on us with blasts of most hostile winds'; the winds
of madness continue to buffet Thebes throughout the play. On the role of
Dionysus, cf. Winnington-Ingram (1980: 102–16); Segal (1981: 153–4,
165–6, 172–4, 180–3, 199–203); Oudemans and Lardinois (1987: 111–12,
146–8, 154–9, 200–1); Ditmars (1992: 155–63); Benardete (1999: 131–2);
Cullyer (2005). For a more 'optimistic' reading of the fifth stasimon,
emphasizing Eleusinian mystery cult and the hope of immortality for
Antigone, see Henrichs (1990: 265–70); the same phenomena are
interpreted differently by Seaford (1990: 87–9), (1994: 381–2); cf. Scullion
(1998: 119–22). As Scullion shows (1998: 114–22), the 'sickness'
of which the Chorus wish the city to be purified is the mental
impairment that Tiresias identified in Creon at 1015, with its wider
background in the internecine conflicts of the play and the myth
on which it draws.

76 Antigone: esp. 603; Creon: 765 (cf. 755); Haemon: 633 (hypothetically;
cf. 648–9), 754; cf. 790 (of the one who has Eros – clearly Haemon, in
the Chorus's mind, but NB the verb *eran* used of Antigone at 90 and,
indirectly, at 220), 1231; Eurydice: 1254. Cf. Creon of Ismene, 491–2.
Mental disturbance on the human level is also mirrored in the frenzy
(*oistros*) of the birds whose unintelligible cries Tiresias reports at 1001–2.
Cf. also various references to the destructive power of forces such as *orgê*
and *thymos* (718, 766–7, 875, 955–6) and note the ambivalence of both
phronêma and *orgai* at 355–6 in the first stasimon's praise of human
rationality. On this theme, see Else (1976).

77 For 'what is best' in gnomic contexts in archaic poetry, cf. such classic
formulations as Tyrtaeus 12. 13–16 West, Theognis 255–6 (cited by
Aristotle, *Nicomachean Ethics* 1099a27, *Eudemian Ethics* 1214a5), Pindar
Olympian 1. 1, and the drinking song *PMG* 890; for cases in which the
answer is 'not to be born', see Easterling (2013).

78 The *gnômê* is traditional: see e.g. Theognis 1171–6 (where 1172 echoes
Solon 16. 2 West).

79 The juxtaposition of innate capacity and learning as sources of wisdom in 710–11 and 720–3 sounds a Pindaric note: cf. Griffith (1999: 246) on 721. But Haemon's model in 720–3 is an even more canonical passage of archaic poetry, Hesiod, *Works and Days* 293–7:

> That man is best of all who notices everything by himself, devising whatever is better for the immediate future and in its final outcome. But he too is also good who listens to good advice. But one who neither notices by himself nor takes to heart what he hears from another is, for his part, a useless man.

80 Since Creon's words at 1049 highlight the proverbial nature of what Tiresias is about to say, cf. *Ant.* 1050–1 with Theognis 895–6 ('a man has nothing better in him than judgement nor anything more painful than its opposite'); cf. also Theognis 1171–6.

81 The Chorus's closing comments are often regarded as mere cliché, but in fact they recall the opening words of both the first stasimon (πολλῷ τὸ φρονεῖν echoing πολλὰ τὰ δεινά, 332 – i.e. both utterances begin with *poll-* + article + noun) and the second (εὐδαιμονίας πρῶτον ὑπάρχει echoing εὐδαίμονες οἷσι κακῶν ἄγευστος αἰών, 583 – two pronouncements on what constitutes *eudaimonia*). The links between those two odes (and the ethical attitudes that they represent) are central to the meaning of the play, and so rehearsed in its gnomic conclusion.

82 As opposed to Antigone, who at 469–70 observes that she is being accused of foolishness by a fool.

83 Cf. 324–6: 'If you do not reveal the culprits to me, you will declare that base profits (*kerdê*) produce pains'.

84 See Seaford (1998: 132–7) and (2012: 328–31).

85 See Goheen (1951: 14–19). The utterly different notion of *kerdos* put forward by the woman, Antigone, adds point to Creon's observations on the *kerdos* that motivates *andres*, men, at 221–2. There, Creon saw death as the *misthos* for defying his edict and *kerdos* as the inducement that might lead *men* to take the risk; Antigone collapses both *misthos* and *kerdos* into one, in a conception that is wholly different from Creon's.

86 See Theognis 425–8; Bacchylides 5. 160–2; Herodotus 1. 31. 4–5; Sophocles, *Oedipus at Colonus* 1224–7; Easterling (2013). The relevance of the proverb to *Ant.* 460–70 is noted by Benardete (1999: 60).

87 See e.g. Solon 13 West; Theognis 197–208, 227–32. For the distinction
between real prosperity and mere wealth, cf. also Bacchylides 3, esp. 22–3
and 83–4, with Cairns (2010: 70–4). With the *Antigone*'s use of the
language of material wealth (*kerdos, ktêma*, etc.) to emphasize the
superiority of non-material prosperity, cf. passages such as 'we shall not
exchange wealth for virtue' at Solon 15. 2–3 West (roughly = Theognis
316–17), 'you will lay down no better treasure for your children than
respect', Theognis 409–10 (cf. 1161–2); also Solon 24 West/Theognis
719–28. On anxieties over the improper pursuit of wealth in tragedy and
archaic poetry, cf. Seaford (1998), (2004: 149–72), (2012: 170–1, 196–205,
221–2).

88 Cf. esp. the closely similar passage at *Oedipus the King* 1186–96. For 'count
no man happy until he is dead', cf. Simonides 521 *PMG* = 244 Poltera;
Aeschylus, *Agamemnon* 928–9; Euripides, *Children of Heracles* 865–6,
Andromache 100–2, *Trojan Women* 509–10; Herodotus 1. 32. 7; Aristotle,
Nicomachean Ethics 1. 9–10, 1100a4–1101b9.

89 Cf. above all *Iliad* 24. 525–48.

90 For parallels, see *Ajax* 125–6, *Phil.* 946, frr. 13, 659. 6, 945 Radt. Among
earlier examples cf. especially Aeschylus *Agamemnon* 839, frr. 154a.9, 399. 2
Radt, and (above all) Pindar *Pythian* 8. 95–6.

91 Creon's responsibility: 1259–60 (Chorus), 1261–9 (Creon), 1270 (Chorus),
1302–5, 1312–13 (the Messenger, citing Eurydice), 1317–19 (Creon),
1339–40 (Creon); divine intervention: 1272–5 (Creon), 1345–6 (Creon).

92 Cf. 163 (explicitly of the ship of state), 635–6, 675–6, 994 (again, explicitly
of the ship of state). Cf. above, note 71.

93 For the scales as an image of alternation, cf. Theognis 157–8 (and cf.
159–68, 355–60, 441–6, 591–4, 657–66 on the rhythm of alternation in
general). Cf. Seaford (2012: 236–9, 242, 253–4); also his pp. 225–39 on
'form-parallelism' of the sort that we see in *Ant.* 1158–9.

94 Accordingly, when Creon returns, the Messenger ironically addresses him
as a man of wealth (ὡς ἔχων τε καὶ κεκτημένος, 1227), though his
'possessions' now consist in the corpses of his son and his wife; just so,
Haemon is the object of the exchange predicted by Tiresias at 1064–7. For
the use of *ktêmata* etc. of non-material goods, cf. 684, 702, 924, 1050. Cf.
note 87 above, and on the language of exchange in *Ant.* cf. Seaford (2004:
158–60).

95 See Winnington-Ingram (1980: 164) and cf. Reinhardt (1979: 92).

96 In other ways, too, that we shall explore in the next chapter; cf. Griffith (1999: 50); Liapis (2013).

97 See p. 163 n. 22.

98 For Riemer (1991), Creon's 'fate' is the consequence of both his choices and Antigone's, but also a matter of divine punishment that becomes inevitable once Creon has rejected Tiresias' warning. Linforth (1961: 252–5) notes the indications of supernatural influence, but insists that 'Sophocles is interested chiefly in the minds and motives of Antigone and Creon' (p. 255); cf. at greater length Sewell-Rutter (2007: 114–20); indeed so, but these do not exist in a vacuum. For accounts that give supernatural influence its due importance, see Kitto (1958: 36–41); Winnington-Ingram (1980: 91–116, 149, 164–72, 210–11); Scodel (1984: 55–7); cf. also Mogyorodyi (1996).

99 See again 1113–14 with pp. 53, 72 above.

100 For Antigone's 'bad death', see Sourvinou-Inwood (1990: 33).

101 See e.g. Brown (1987: 9).

102 See e.g. Theognis 373–85, 731–52 (esp. 743–6); cf. Hesiod's wish that neither he nor his son be just, unless Zeus can ensure that the just get more *dikê* than the unjust (*Works and Days* 270–3).

103 As we noted above, in the elegiac poem of Solon (13 West) that is one of the *Antigone*'s major intertexts, Zeus is said often to punish children for the crimes of their parents (25–32).

104 Again, despite its main focus on offence and punishment, Solon 13 also comments on the often arbitrary link between desert and outcome (63–70; lines 65–70 = Theognis 585–90).

105 See the fifth stasimon's invocation of Dionysus to come and purify the city (1140–5), a call that comes immediately before the catastrophe. Cf. Chapter 4, p. 113.

Chapter 4

1 See Aristotle, *Nicomachean Ethics* 8. 1, 1155a22–3, 9. 6, 1167a22–b3, and further references in M. W. Blundell (1989: 44). See also Konstan (2010).

2 Konstan (1997) would not accept these formulations in every detail, but the respects in which we differ do not matter for present purposes; for discussion, see Belfiore (2000: 19–20). See also Dover (1974: 273–8); Goldhill (1986: 79–106); M. W. Blundell (1989: 26–59).

3 See *Meno* 71c; *Republic* 332d ff. Cf. Dover (1974: 180–4); Winnington-Ingram (1980: 128–36); M. W. Blundell (1989).

4 See Winnington-Ingram (1980: 128–36); M. W. Blundell (1989); cf. Belfiore (2000).

5 See Winnington-Ingram (1980: 135 n. 55); Griffith (1999: 122–3) on 9–10.

6 Cf. Goldhill (1986: 90).

7 Especially at 551, 'Indeed, if I mock, it is painful for me to mock in your case.' On Antigone's estrangement from Ismene, see Goldhill (2012: 231–48).

8 See Knox (1964: 80–90); Winnington-Ingram (1980: 129–36); Goldhill (1986: 90–106); M. W. Blundell (1989: 106–27, 141–2). On the primacy of the city as the principle that guides Creon's approach to *philia*, and of the family as that which guides Antigone's, see in addition the wider discussion in Knox (1964: 75–116), and cf. Nussbaum (1986: 54–67).

9 See Dover (1974: 301–6).

10 Cf. the Chorus's bestial imagery of the Argive army in the parodos at 117–22 ('with its bloodthirsty spears . . . it went, before it could sate its jaws on our blood').

11 See 144–7, 170–3.

12 See Benardete (1999: 23–6), with further discussion below, pp. 112–13.

13 See Knox (1964: 87). Cf. Ormand (1999: 85–6), noting the connection between 173–4 (Creon's rise to power through kinship) and 192 (the kinship between his principles and his proclamation).

14 Cf. Tyrrell and Bennett (1998: 30–1). On the implications of the play's recurrent use of *auto*-compounds, see Loraux (1986); cf. Rehm (1993: 65–6); Benardete (1999: 2). For the recurrence of these compounds as a feature also of Aeschylus' *Seven*, see Hutchinson (1985: note on lines 734–41); I. M. Torrance (2007: 31–2). *Autadelphos* itself occurs at *Seven* 718, of Eteocles' desire to shed his brother's blood. The adjective also qualifies *haima* (blood) in its only other surviving pre-*Antigone* occurrence at *Eumenides* 89.

15 See below, pp. 104–7, 112.

16 Her claim here that commitment to her *autadelphos* brings her honour (502–4) is echoed by Haemon's use of the same term at 696, in his report of the views of the Theban populace (693–9).

17 Cf. Knox (1964: 79); Segal (1981: 183–7). The prefix *homo-* (same) in
   homosplanchnos ('of the same gut', 511; cf. *homaimos,* 'of the same blood', in
   512 and 513) has a similar force to that of the *auto-*compounds mentioned
   above; cf. Loraux (1986: 172–3 n. 21). Again the feature is taken over from
   Aeschylus' *Seven*: cf. 351, 415, 680, 812, 890, 931–2, 940; see Bruzzese (2010,
   esp. 209–10).

18 On the ways in which Antigone and Creon differ over the meanings of
   terms, cf. Goheen (1951: 17); Kirkwood (1958: 125); Knox (1964: 90).

19 See 511, 922–4, 943 (also Haemon at 745, Creon at 777–80).

20 See 166, 301, 514, 516, 730, 744. The Chorus see the merits of both Creon's
   and Antigone's conceptions of *eusebeia* at 872–5, though their final
   pronouncement is unequivocally condemnatory of Creon's failure to
   respect the gods (1349–50); cf. Kirkwood (1958: 126).

21 So Lloyd-Jones and Wilson (1990a: 126).

22 Critics, e.g. Knox (1964: 105) often point out that Antigone's absolute
   devotion to the rights of all blood-kin to burial is undercut by the priority
   that she accords a brother at 905–12. On these lines, see below. One might
   note, however, that there is no logical incompatibility between recognizing
   a principle of action (that all kin should be buried) and choosing to
   implement that principle, under pain of death, only in the case of
   a brother.

23 On the theme of marriage in *Antigone,* see Goheen (1951: 37–41); Seaford
   (1987:107–8, 113, 120), (1990: 76–9, 86–7); Rehm (1993: 59–71); Tyrrell
   and Bennett (1998: 97–121); Ormand (1999: 79–103).

24 *Odyssey* 6. 180–5.

25 'I give you this woman for the ploughing [not, as a student essay once put
   it, the plumbing] of legitimate children.' The formula is frequent in the
   comedies of Menander, e.g. *Dyskolos* 842–3, *Misoumenos* 974–5,
   Perikeiromene 1013–14, *Samia* 726–7 (line numbers as in Arnott's
   (1979–2000) Loeb edition). On the *Antigone* passage, see Ormand (1999:
   6–7, 20–1, 84).

26 On Haemon's *erôs,* cf. Chapter 2 n. 14. On the wider ramifications of *erôs*
   in the play, see Winnington-Ingram (1980: 92–8).

27 See Jebb (1900: 127) on 650f.; Siewert (1977: 105–7); Sourvinou-Inwood
   (1989a: 144). The oath, its formulas, and the ideals that it embodies clearly
   antedate the formal institution of the *ephebeia* in the fourth century:
   Siewert (1977: 108–9).

28 Not just a civic ideal, as noted by Goldhill (1986: 100), but also a domestic one.

29 See e.g. Bowra (1944: 75); Siewert (1977: 106). The lines are defended as Athenian orthodoxy by Sourvinou-Inwood (1989a: 144 n. 37) and by Liapis (2013: 100), and deleted as an interpolation by Dawe (1984–5), followed by Lloyd-Jones and Wilson (1990b). For discussion, see Lloyd-Jones and Wilson (1990a: 132), (1997: 108).

30 The same opposition between the heat of passion and the coldness of death that we see both in Creon's dismissal of Antigone as 'a cold thing to embrace' at 650 and in the sexualization of Haemon's suicide over the corpse of Antigone (1235–41) appears already in Ismene's observation (in the prologue, line 88) that Antigone has 'a hot heart for cold things', an early indication of the passionate fixation with death and with the dead Polynices that we discuss immediately below.

31 The deletion of lines 905–13 had already been proposed by A. L. W. Jacob in his *Quaestiones Sophocleae* of 1821 when Goethe expressed the wish (in 1827) that a capable philologist might prove the passage inauthentic: see Eckermann (1945: ii. 566); cf. Steiner (1984: 50); Rösler (1993: 90). For recent arguments in favour of the deletion of all of 904–20, see Brown (1987: 199–200); cf. Rösler (1993).

32 See S. West (1999: 129–30).

33 Aristotle, *Rhetoric* 3. 16, 1416a29–33.

34 See Murnaghan (1986); Neuburg (1990); Sourvinou-Inwood (1990: 17–20), (1991b); Cropp (1997); Griffith (1999: 277–9); for an earlier defence, see e.g. Reinhardt (1979: 83–4).

35 Cf. Euripides' *Medea* 13–15; Xenophon, *Oeconomicus* 7. 14, 7. 42–3.

36 Cf. Winnington-Ingram (1980: 130); Seaford (1990: 78), (1994: 349); Johnson (1997); Benardete (1999: 13); Griffith (2010: 114–19).

37 On the uncertainty over which brother is meant here, see Chapter 1, n. 24. Tyrrell and Bennett would add to the uncertainty by making Oedipus a candidate (1998: 32); see also Butler (2000: 77); Honig (2013: 47, 105, 127). But no one in the play makes the observation that the man repeatedly called 'father' of Antigone, Ismene, Eteocles, and Polynices (at 49, 144, 380, 471–2, 859, 865; cf. 2, 168–9, 193, 1018) is also their brother; and where 'father' and 'brother' are separately specified (as here and at 863–71) their identification, in the absence of any explicit encouragement from the text, is very unlikely. It may be significant that the play's kinship terminology

focuses on the normative relationships between family members, not the aberrant ones that derive from Oedipus' incest (for some – not always cogent – ruminations along these lines, see Mader (2005); Chanter (2011: 93–9)). On the other hand, the normative terms may simply operate as the default values, even in such non-normative situations.

38 See Steiner (1984: 263–6).

39 There too, for example, she is a 'living corpse' (Polynices' death destroyed her while she was still alive, 871), but the tone is now one of lamentation.

40 See MacDowell (1978: 86–7), and cf. Seaford (1994: 206–16) for an anthropological analysis of the historical developments here.

41 See Rehm (1993: 63); Seaford (1994: 213–14).

42 See Seaford (1987: 117); Oakley and Sinos (1994), esp. pp. 14–21, with illustrations on pp. 52–3, 59, 62, 64–7, 71–6, 83, 90–1, 95, 97–8, 110, 116–21, 123–7; Stafford (2013).

43 Cf. Sappho fr. 194 in Campbell (1982), Euripides, *Hippolytus* 553; further references and discussion in Seaford (1987: 108, 117).

44 This is suggested not only by the hymeneal content of her lyrics but also by the widespread custom of burying a girl who dies before marriage in her wedding dress. See Chapter 1, n. 64, Chapter 2, n. 80.

45 Cf. 'the god is putting me to bed', 832–3.

46 Cf. 867–8, 876–7.

47 See Jenkins (1983); Sourvinou-Inwood (1987: 139), (1991a: 65–7); Rehm (1993: 36–40); Tyrrell and Bennett (1998: 118); Ormand (1999: 29).

48 See Seaford (1987: 113); Rehm (1993: 63–4); and cf. Chapter 1, p. 21 and n. 64.

49 See Oakley and Sinos (1993: 7, 14, 16–20, 23–8, 30–3, 36, 40, 44–6); Llewellyn-Jones (2003: 219–58); on this motif in *Antigone,* see Seaford (1987: 113); Rehm (1993: 64–5); Tyrrell and Bennett (1998: 142).

50 Albeit a method also used by Antigone's mother (53–4). For hanging as a woman's and especially a virgin's death, see Loraux (1987: 9–10, 52).

51 See King (1983: 113–20), (1998: 78–88); Loraux (1987: 9–10); Johnston (2006: 180–2). For the sexualized nature of Eurydice's suicide, cf. Deianira at *Women of Trachis* 930–1, with Loraux (1987: 14, 54–6).

52 Cf. Johnston (2006: 183–4); for Antigone's remarkable assertiveness and independence of action, see also Riemer (1991), esp. pp. 9–11, comparing her to other tragic heroines and commenting on the assertion of autonomy in the manner of her suicide. Cf. Knox (1964: 116).

53 Cf. Seaford (1987).

54 See Lefkowitz and Fant (1992), text 349, pp. 242–3; also texts 343 and 345, from the Hippocratic *Diseases of Women*. Cf. King (1983: 113–17), (1998: 78–9).

55 See Alexiou (1974: 4, 11–22); on funerary legislation in general, see Engels (1998).

56 As Eurydice observes at 1303–4, with the emended text as printed by Lloyd-Jones and Wilson (1990b) and by Griffith (1999).

57 See Zeitlin (1990); Seaford (1994: 346–55).

58 Cf. above, note 14.

59 Though she killed herself by hanging (cf. note 50 above). For the general point, that Creon's fate comes to exemplify patterns found in the House of Labdacus, cf. Goldhill (1986: 104–5); Loraux (1986: 183–4); Zeitlin (1990: 150–1); Segal (1995: 131); Liapis (2013: 103–7). For Else (1976: 81–96), Sophocles develops this pattern by basing his characterization of Creon in *Antigone* on that of Oedipus in Aeschylus' (lost) *Oedipus*, a phenomenon that explains the similarities in characterization between the Creon of *Antigone* and the Oedipus of *Oedipus Tyrannus*, similarly based on the Aeschylean model. But this is pure speculation.

60 Cf. Winnington-Ingram (1980: 127–8).

61 Recalling Pindar's famous paean for the Thebans, fr. 52k Maehler (on the occasion of an eclipse of the sun), and so suggesting not only the relief of victory, but also further troubles requiring release and healing; cf. Ditmars (1992: 32); Rutherford (1994–5: 126–7). See further Rodighiero (2012: 109–11, 121–8, 134–7).

62 See Else (1976: 26–7, 70–4); Kitzinger (2008: 62–9), (2012: 400–1). See further Seaford (1993) and (1994: 344–67). Perhaps the reference to 'the place where the savage dragon's teeth were sown' at 1124–5 keeps the thought of Creon, a descendant of the Spartoi, in the audience's minds during the fifth stasimon.

Chapter 5

1 Quoted in Mee and Foley (2011: 6).

2 See www.bbc.co.uk/news/magazine-33362642 (accessed 20 August 2015). For more details, see www.apertaproductions.org (accessed 20 August 2015).

3 Delivered on 8 July 2015: http://cadtm.org/Closing-speech-of-PM-Alexis (accessed 15 July 2015).

4 For doubts about the play's ending, see Dawe (2006: 192–203); contrast e.g. Finglass (2009).

5 See Mastronarde (1994: 14); Papadopoulou (2008: 24).

6 Cf. Zimmermann (1993: 141–4); Papadopoulou (2008: 24, 128 n. 31, 131 n. 52). On the issue of interpolation in general, see Mastronarde (1994: 39–49).

7 See Mastronarde (1994: 168–73, 554–5, 591–4) on 88–201, 1480–1581, 1582–1709; cf. Craik (1988: 245) on 1582–1776. Diggle (1994) and Kovacs (2002) are more sceptical.

8 See Lamari (2010: 128, 149–52).

9 See Bremer (1984); Zimmermann (1993: 140); Papadopoulou (2008: 104–9).

10 See Papadopoulou (2008: 110–24) and I. M. Torrance (2007: 118–25) on these and other versions.

11 On the hero-cult at Colonus, see Kelly (2009: 41–5). On the suspicions surrounding the end of *Phoenician Women,* see Mastronarde (1994: 626–7). His view, that the motif is not interpolated from Sophocles' play, is followed by Papadopoulou (2008: 71).

12 On her characterization, see Kelly (2009: 107–10).

13 There is a hint of their later estrangement when Ismene opposes Antigone's request to see Oedipus' grave on the grounds that it is not permitted (1724–33); see Burton (1980: 271); Kelly (2009: 50).

14 See Winnington-Ingram (1980: 261–4, 274–8, 325–6); M. W. Blundell (1989: 226–59); Kelly (2009: 109, 126–7, 130–1).

15 Zimmermann (1993: 198).

16 See Hutchinson (1985: xliii, 209–11); I. M. Torrance (2007: 109). They argue for a date in the late fourth or early third century BC. Zimmermann agrees that the ending is probably influenced by the more or less genuine ending of *Phoenician Women* (1993: 160), but thinks that *Phoenician Women, Oedipus at Colonus,* and the ending of Aeschylus' *Seven against Thebes* all belong to the final years of the fifth century (1993: 189 n. 337).

17 See Taplin (2011: 144).

18 Cropp and Fick (1985: 70, 74, 76) place the play in the period 420–406 BC, with a slight leaning towards the later end of that range; cf. Zimmermann (1993: 139, 189). For an account of the surviving fragments and suggested

reconstructions, see Webster (1967: 181–4); Gantz (1993: 520–1); Zimmermann (1993: 161–88); Collard and Cropp (2008: 156–9, 203).

19 See *Antigone* hypothesis 1. 8–10 (printed, e.g. in Jebb 1900); also the ancient commentator's note (scholion) on *Ant.* 1351.

20 See the inscription printed as Didascaliae A 2a, lines 1–6 in Snell (1986: 26) and translated in Csapo and Slater (1994: 229).

21 On Hyginus, *Fabula* 72, see Zimmermann (1993: 168, 182–3, 216–18, 272–3). Euripides' version has also been referred to two mid-fourth-century South Italian vase-paintings (Ruvo Museo Jatta 423 = *LIMC* 14 and Berlin, Antikensammlungen F 3240 = *LIMC* 15); see Krauskopf in *LIMC* i.1, 826; Taplin (2007: 185–6); Zimmermann (1993: 168, 171–8, 216); Galli (2010: 66–8). For the use of the vases and Hyginus to reconstruct Astydamas' play, see Xanthakis-Karamanos (1980: 48–53); Zimmermann (1993: 216–22); for a potential problem with the dating in this case, see Taplin (2007: 186).

22 See *LIMC* s.v. 'Antigone', i.1, 818–28, i.2, 659–62; Zimmermann (1993: 171–8, 207–17, 297); Galli (2010); Meyer (2010).

23 Taplin (2011: 141).

24 London BM F 175 = *LIMC* 12. In favour of an association with Sophocles' play, see Krauskopf in *LIMC* i.1, 822, 825; Zimmermann (1993: 207–8); Meyer (2010: 260–8); Taplin has reservations at (2007: 94); by (2011: 141–2) he is even more sceptical.

25 On Accius, see Boyle (2006: 109–42); Manuwald (2011: 216–25).

26 See Ribbeck (1875: 483–7); Sconocchia (1972); Holford-Strevens (1999: 224–6). Like Ribbeck (1875: 486–7) and Sconocchia (1972: 282) I see no reason to suspect any influence from Euripides' *Antigone*, despite Dangel (1995: 362).

27 This is more likely than partial preservation of a completed work or deliberate experiment in dramatic form: see Hirschberg (1989: 7–8); Frank (1995: 1, 12–16).

28 See Zimmermann (1993: 240–52); Papadopoulou (2008: 110–12).

29 See Hirschberg (1989: 7).

30 See Hirschberg (1989: 7, 11, 40–1, 90–1); Zimmermann (1993: 251–2); Frank (1995: 103) on 82; Fitch (2002: 276).

31 See Vessey (1973), esp. pp. 69–70, 205–9, 270, 308 on *Phoenician Women* and *Suppliant Women*; Pollmann (2004: 29, 46, 53–7, and commentary, *passim*) and Heslin (2008) argue for a much wider range of Greek tragic

models. On Statius and tragedy more generally, see Marinis (2015) and Criado (2015).

32 Despite Vessey (1973: 69); cf. Holford-Strevens (1999: 237).

33 See Pollmann (2004: 166) on 12. 329–32; Heslin (2008: 116).

34 See Pollmann (2004: 55, 174); Heslin (2008: 116).

35 See Heslin (2008: 116–18).

36 Antigone and Argia are about to be executed, on Creon's order, at 12. 677–82, when Theseus' messenger arrives; Argia, at least, survives (804), and probably (though she is not mentioned again) Antigone too.

37 Cf. the special closeness of Antigone and Polynices at 11. 363–83 (esp. 372, 'sister to you alone').

38 Cf. Vessey (1973: 133); Heslin (2008: 118).

39 For Antigone's *pietas,* cf. her role as Oedipus' guide (8. 249, 11. 706); at 11. 580–633 she leads Oedipus to the battlefield and ultimately, as in Euripides' *Phoenician Women,* prevents his suicide (627–30); at 11. 708–56 she pleads with Creon against her father's exile.

40 Cf. Steiner (1984: 146).

41 Cf. Steiner (1984: 181) on the *Roman de Thèbes,* Bocaccio's *Teseida,* Chaucer's 'Knight's Tale', and Lydgate's 'The Story of Thebes'; see further Battles (2004); Edwards (2015).

42 See Heslin (2015).

43 Steiner (1984: 139–41). Garnier's *Antigone* is the basis of an adaptation by Thomas May, *The Tragedy of Antigone, The Theban Princesse* (London, 1631; Steiner 196). On the humanist background of Garnier's play and other sixteenth- and seventeenth-century versions, see Miola (2014).

44 Steiner (1984: 146, 153, 160–2, 164); cf. I. M. Torrance (2010: 246–8).

45 For a list of operatic versions, see Reid (1993: 105); list and discussion in Piperno (2010). Cf. Steiner (1984: 6, 154–5, 168).

46 On Alfieri, see Jebb (1900: xxxix); Steiner (1984: 144, 146, 153–4, 181, 196).

47 See Steiner (1984: 2–7).

48 See now Billings (2014); cf. Steiner (1984: 7–19, 43–51); Goldhill (2012).

49 Hölderlin (1952: 203–72); English translation in Constantine (2001). For discussion in English, see Harrison (1975), esp. 160–92 on *Antigonä* and *Oedipus der Tyrann.*

50 See Schadewaldt (1960b: 768–9); Pöggeler (2004: 8, 82, 87, 103–4); see also Harrison (1975: 160–1); Steiner (1984: 68, 87).

51 Voß is quoted in Reinhardt (1960: 395); Schadewaldt (1960b: 769); Harrison (1975: 160); Pöggeler (2004: 8). On the extreme literality of Hölderlin's translation see Schadewaldt (1960b: 775); Billings (2014: 197–8).

52 See Reinhardt (1960); Schadewaldt (1960b), esp. 805–14 on the qualities of the translation; Harrison (1975: 177–92); Steiner (1984: 66–103, esp. 67–8); Pöggeler (2004: 79–110); Weber (2015).

53 Translated in Constantine (2001: 113–18), and (with an introduction) in Adler (1983); for discussion see Schadewaldt (1960b: 782–9); Harrison (1975: 169, 173–5); Steiner (1984: 77–84); Pöggeler (2004: 84–102); Billings (2014: 200–21); Weber (2015: 102–14).

54 Notes to *Antigone*, Constantine (2001: 166).

55 Notes to *Antigone*, Constantine (2001: 113); cf. Schadewaldt (1960b: 819); Steiner (1984: 82); Billings (2014: 208).

56 Notes to *Antigone,* Constantine (2001: 118, 115).

57 See Harrison (1975: 161–9, 173–7), Steiner (1984: 73–7), and Billings (2014: 189–221) on the relation between the theory of tragedy expressed in the Notes to *Oedipus* and *Antigone* and Hölderlin's other works. Hölderlin uses the term 'Apollonian' of the irrational and ecstatic qualities that Nietzsche associates with the Dionysian as opposed to the Apollonian. More broadly on Hölderlin's notion of tragedy, see Reinhardt (1960: 381–90); Schadewaldt (1960b: 778–89); Steiner (1984: 72–84).

58 See Reinhardt (1960: 387); cf. Harrison (1975: 160); Steiner (1984: 73); Billings (2014: 200); Weber (2015: 103–4). Further discussion in Dastur (2000); cf. Constantine (2001: 11); Billings (2014: 194, 218); Weber (2015: 103–14).

59 See Reinhardt (1960: 387–90).

60 Notes to *Antigone*, Constantine (2001: 114–15). See further Harrison (1975: 177–80); Billings (2014: 210–15).

61 Notes to *Antigone*, Constantine (2001: 113, 118).

62 Notes to *Antigone*, Constantine (2001: 118). Discussion in Schadewaldt (1960b: 796); Harrison (1975: 192); Steiner (1984: 81); Pöggeler (2004: 100); Billings (2014: 218–20); Weber (2015: 112–13).

63 See Flashar (2009: 138–42, 165, 167–8, 177, 196, 200, 203, 222–4, 240, 245, 267, 275–6, 325–6). Cf. Constantine (2001: 9–10), and in Brecht (2003: 219); cf. Pöggeler (2004: 111–12).

64 On Orff, see Schadewaldt (1960a); Steiner (1984: 169–70, 215); Pöggeler
   (2004: 11, 13, 79, 112–13, 175–9); Flashar (2009: 188–93); Attfield (2010).
   Orff also used Hölderlin's *Oedipus the King* for his 1958 operatic version of
   that play.

65 See Pöggeler (2004: 79, 113–15, 143); cf. Steiner (1984: 68, 89).

66 Steiner (1984: 105).

67 On the overlap between the two, see Schadewaldt (1960b: 804–5); Steiner
   (1984: 82).

68 On Hegel, tragedy, and *Antigone,* see Bradley (1962); Paolucci and Paolucci
   (1962); Hester (1971: 14–17); Steiner (1984: 19–42); Oudemans and
   Lardinois (1987: 110–16); Mills (1998); Pöggeler (2004: 25–78); M. W.
   Roche (2005) and (2006); Thibodeau (2013); Billings (2014). There is also
   an excellent and lucid summary in Stewart (1998: 196–208).

69 See Steiner (1984: 37–8, 41, 295); Goldhill (2012: 199).

70 *Lectures on the Philosophy of Religion* ii. 3. a, in Paolucci and Paolucci
   (1962: 325). For convenience, I cite Hegel, where possible, from this
   one-volume anthology of his major writings on tragedy, indicating, where
   it is not otherwise clear, from which work a given excerpt is drawn.

71 Cf. esp. in the *Aesthetics*: 'the most excellent and satisfying work of art'
   (Paolucci and Paolucci 1962: 73); 'one of the most sublime, and in every
   respect most consummate work of art [*sic*] human effort ever produced'
   (Paolucci and Paolucci 1962: 178); cf. *Lectures on the History of Philosophy*
   in Paolucci and Paolucci (1962: 360): 'the heavenly Antigone, that noblest
   of figures that ever appeared on earth'.

72 Hegel's engagement with *Antigone* spanned his career; for an account of its
   stages, see Steiner (1984: 19–42); Pöggeler (2004: 27–67); Thibodeau (2013:
   17–21).

73 Paolucci and Paolucci (1962: 68, 178).

74 Cf. in particular the *Aesthetics* passages, Paolucci and Paolucci (1962:
   49, 51).

75 On *Eumenides* and *Philoctetes,* see Paolucci and Paolucci (1962: 57, 74–5),
   from *Aesthetics*, and cf. 345 (*Lectures on the History of Religion*); on
   Oedipus at Colonus, see 75–6 (*Aesthetics*), 325–6, 345 (*Lectures on the
   History of Religion*).

76 Paolucci and Paolucci (1962: 71; cf. 49–51, 73, all from *Aesthetics*); see also
   237 (from *Elements of the Philosophy of Right*). On the nature of this
   'reconciliation' see Thibodeau (2013: 169).

77 For a clear and comprehensive account of the role of tragedy in general and *Antigone* in particular in the *Phenomenology*'s account of the development of social and ethical consciousness, see Billings (2014: 161–88).

78 Rosenkranz (1844: 11); cf. Pöggeler (2004: 25, 28–9); Billings (2014: 176–7).

79 Cf. Steiner (1984: 29); Thibodeau (2013: 116).

80 Paolucci and Paolucci (1962: 267–9). On the particularity of Hegel's argument here, see (among others), Steiner (1984: 12–14, 33); Oudemans and Lardinois (1987: 112–13); Butler (2000: 13–14); Thibodeau (2013: 103–5).

81 See Chapter 4, n. 31.

82 Cf. Leonard (2005: 117); Honig (2013: 125); Billings (2014: 170–1).

83 Excerpted in Paolocci and Paolucci (1962: 347–66); see esp. 360–5.

84 Paolocci and Paolucci (1962: 360).

85 Cf. Steiner (1984: 40–1).

86 The influence of Hegel (and German idealism) on later classical scholarship is well traced by Goldhill (2012: 137–263); cf. Billings (2014: 3); Goldhill (2015), esp. 249–50. For a catalogue of later scholars who adopt or modify the 'Hegelian' (*sic*) position, see Hester (1971: 16–17). On the 'philosophization' of *Antigone* cf. Taxidou (2004: 18–20).

87 See Kierkegaard (1987: 138–64). For lucid discussion of the work and its Hegelian inspiration, see Irina (2010). Good introduction in Stewart (1998); see further Stewart (2003). See also Steiner (1984: 51–66); Schweizer (1997: 82–4); Görner (2015: 165–8).

88 See the narrator's statement, Kierkegaard (1987: 153), that 'her thoughts are my thoughts'. Cf. the journal entry for 20 November 1842 in Kierkegaard (1987: 541), where he considers making his Antigone a man who 'forsook his beloved because he could not keep her together with his private agony'; Steiner (1984: 62–3); Irina (2010: 315, 319).

89 For an account of Heidegger's engagement with *Antigone,* Hölderlin, and the Greeks, see Pöggeler (2004: 114–74); cf. Most (2002); Fleming (2015).

90 See Heidegger (2000: 158, 173). Brief discussion: Fleming (2015: 187–90).

91 For discussion, see Pöggeler (2004: 145–56, 160).

92 Heidegger (1996: 63–4, 67, 83–4).

93 Heidegger (1996: 54, 56–7, 69).

94 Cf. Pöggeler (2004: 164). For a brief account of Heidegger's Nazism, see Bernasconi (2013); for the wider debate, see Wolin (1991).

95 See the list in Flashar (2009: 164–8, 395 n. 23); cf. Pöggeler (2004: 112); Fischer-Lichte (2010: 338); Fleming (2015: 179 n. 4).

96 See Fischer-Lichte (2010: 338–45).

97 See e.g. Flashar (2009: 165) for anti-Nazi appropriations of the Antigone theme. For the development of Flashar's reference to Antigone as an inspiration for Sophie Scholl and her circle, see most recently Pattoni (2013) on Marc Rothemund's 2005 film, *Sophie Scholl: Die letzten Tage*, and the 2013 Theater Ulm production of Michael Sommer's play *Antigone/Sophie* (reviewed in *Südwest Presse*, 11 March 2013).

98 For Heidegger's influence on Lacan, see Pöggeler (2004: 171–2).

99 Lacan (1992). See Leonard (2005: 101–30); Miller (2007); Griffith (2010); Buchan (2012). See also Lupton (2005: 96–8); and many of the chapters in Wilmer and Žukauskaitė (2010).

100 Lacan (1992: 247, 249–50, 277–8).

101 Quotations from pp. 262 and 282; for Antigone's 'desire', especially her desire for death, cf. pp. 247, 263, 281, 286.

102 Lacan (1992: 258–9, 267, 277–8, 318, 320).

103 For Creon's *hamartia* in contrast to Antigone's *atê*, see Lacan (1992: 277) – *atê* has nothing to do with *hamartia* and is not 'a mistake or error'; for Creon's *hamartia*, cf. 258; for Antigone's *atê*, cf. 262–4, 269–70, 282–4, 286, 300.

104 Lacan (1992: 278–9).

105 See Lacan's definition of 'heroism' (1992: 319–21).

106 See Lacan (1992: 248, 281).

107 Lacan (1992: 247).

108 Lacan (1992: 267; cf. 299). That Lacan turns Antigone into something like a terrorist becomes commonplace in discussions of his interpretation: see e.g. Žižek (2001: 77); Eagleton (2010: 105).

109 See esp. Leonard (2005). Cf. Griffith (2010).

110 Quotation from Steiner (1984: 29). On *Glas* (Derrida 1986), see esp. Leonard (2005: 135–56); cf. Steiner (1984: 164–5); Oudemans and Lardinois (1987: 123, 235).

111 See esp. Irigaray (1985: 214–26), (1994: 67–70), (2010), with Chanter (1995: 80–126); Leonard (2005: 100–1, 130–5).

112 Butler (2000: 3–4). For discussion, see Žukauskaitė (2010); Honig (2013: 41–50, 54–6).

113 Butler (2000: 17–18, 47, 53).

114 Butler (2000: 22–5, 66–72, 75–9, 82); quotation, p. 72.

115 Hutchings and Pulkkinen (2010); Wilmer and Žukauskaitė (2010). These survey a wider range of feminist, psychoanalytical, queer-theoretical (etc.) Antigones than can be discussed here; cf. also Söderbäck (2010); Honig (2013), Part 1; Chanter and Kirkland (2014).

116 Such as Chanter (2011); Honig (2013).

117 Cf. Pöggeler (2004: 174).

118 For important discussions in English, see Hall and Macintosh (2005: 318–49); Geary (2006); Fischer-Lichte (2010: 329–38); Goldhill (2012: 188–92, 216). In German, see esp. Flashar (2001) and (2009: 63–74); Boetius (2005); cf. Pöggeler (2004: 9–10, 69–75).

119 See Flashar (2009: 52–6); Boetius (2005: 35–48); cf. Pöggeler (2004: 69–70); Hall and Macintosh (2005: 319); Geary (2006: 198).

120 See above, and cf. Pöggeler (2004: 70). For the Donner-Tieck-Mendelssohn version as a decisive break, see above all Boetius (2005).

121 Translation: Boetius (2005: 72–3); Geary (2006: 187, 209, 212); cf. Flashar (2001: 14, 19–22), (2009: 64–5, 69); Fischer-Lichte (2010: 333); Goldhill (2012: 188); music: Geary (2006: 212), with detailed analysis, pp. 201–24; cf. Boetius (2005: 120–38; 149–50, 152–79). Mendelssohn's efforts were much appreciated by his contemporaries, Hermann and Boeckh: see Flashar (2001: 36–7); Boetius (2005: 237–42); Geary (2006: 191). On Mendelssohn's own classical education and learning, see Flashar (2001: 6–11). summarized in (2009: 66); cf. Boetius (2005: 111–12); Geary (2006: 211–12).

122 See Geary (2006: 192, 201–3). Actor's lyric was not sung, but marked as distinct by its musical accompaniment.

123 See Flashar (2001: 14–15), (2009: 68–9); Boetius (2005: 202–34, 253–5); Geary (2006: 187–8); Fischer-Lichte (2010: 331, 334). By the time of the London production in 1845 the chorus had been enlarged to 60: Hall and Macintosh (2005: 322). More briefly on the historicizing impetus of the production, cf. Steiner (1984: 168); Goldhill (2012: 188–90).

124 Boetius (2005: 233–4); Fischer-Lichte (2010: 332).

125 See Flashar (2001: 38–41), (2009: 83, 87, 89–92, 96–8, 108); Boetius (2005: 262–302); cf. Goldhill (2012: 190–2). On the anglophone productions, see Hall and Macintosh (2005: 318–49).

126 *Aesthetics*, Paolucci and Paolucci (1962: 33); see Flashar (2001: 58–61).

127 See Steinberg (1991: 149–51); Flashar (2001: 26); Boetius (2005: 62–6).

128 See Steiner (1984: 142, 146, 170, 218); Pöggeler (2004: 10); Flashar (2009: 127–9).

129 Pöggeler (2004: 10).

130 See Fulcher (2006: 273–6). The published version of the play, complete with Cocteau's stage directions, derives from a 1927 revival.

131 Cocteau (2013), preface; cf. Kirkland (2010).

132 See Pattoni (2010), and her introduction to Sérgio de Sousa (2012); cf. de Fátima Silva (2010).

133 See Spratt (1987: 93–146) and Halbreich (1999: 455–69) for detailed musical analysis; Fulcher (2006) on the political and cultural context.

134 See Steiner (1984: 169); Spratt (1987: 139, 141–2); Halbreich (1999: 451, 457); Fulcher (2006: 261, 281, 289); cf. Honegger (1966: 99).

135 Halbreich (1999: 173–4).

136 See esp. Fulcher (2006).

137 See Fulcher (2006: 278–80, 282–4, 288–91), quotation p. 279.

138 Adapted by the right-wing nationalist Thierry Maulnier, and presented at the Théâtre Charles de Rochefort in May 1944. See Steiner (1984: 143); Witt (2001: 219).

139 Flashar (2009: 172).

140 See Flashar (2009: 169, 396 n. 41).

141 Flashar (2009: 172).

142 See Witt (2001: 220–1, 228); cf. Freeman in Anouilh (2000: xlvix–lviii); Fulcher (2006: 287).

143 For the roots of this interpretation and its debunking, see esp. Flügge (1982); cf. Witt (2001: 228); Fleming (2008: 167–9); Flashar (2009: 168, 171, 173).

144 Claude Roy, *Les Lettres françaises* 14, March 1944, cited by Witt (2001: 228); cf. Fulcher (2006: 287); Fleming (2008: 168). Both Witt and Fleming also cite similar responses in post-liberation criticism.

145 See Witt (2001: 227–8); Fleming (2008: 168, 180–1); cf. Freeman in Anouilh (2000: xlviii). There is an exhaustive collection of contemporary reviews, together with comprehensive analysis of the play's historical contexts and later receptions, in Flügge (1982); for the reviews in particular, see ii. 47–72.

146 See Freeman, in Anouilh (2000: xlviix–lviii); Flashar (2009: 170); cf. and contrast Witt (2001: 218, 221 n. 71, 226); Fleming (2008: 181–2). They

accept this characterization of Creon, but regard Antigone as, in one sense or another, 'fascist'. See also Deppman (2012: 523–4).

147 See the responses cited in Witt (2001: 227–8); Fleming (2008: 181).

148 See esp. Witt (2001: 226; but contrast 229); Fleming (2008: 182).

149 If Lacan's reference to Anouilh's 'little fascist Antigone' (1992: 250) is anything more than a glib sneer, this is perhaps its reference. Lacan's own Antigone, whose beauty lies in her gratuitous prosecution of her desire for death, has much in common with Anouilh's.

150 Anouilh (2000: 55). Page numbers in the text are those of this translation.

151 See esp. Anouilh (2000: 3, 26, 36, 38–9, 40–1).

152 On her 'infantile and irrational rebellion', cf. Ciani (2000: 14).

153 See Steiner (1984: 193–4); cf. and contrast Witt (2001: 218, 226–7).

154 Cf. Deppman (2012: 533–5).

155 See Brecht's journal entry for 16 December 1947 in Brecht (2003: 197); on the rehearsal period, see Flashar (2009: 182). The flurry of German-language productions in the immediate aftermath of World War II included one of Anouilh's play in translation and several of Hölderlin's version, one (in Hamburg in 1946) involving Brecht's 1948 collaborator, Caspar Neher; see Constantine in Brecht (2003: 219); Savage (2008: 151); Flashar (2009: 176–8).

156 See Brecht's journal, 16 December 1947 and 25 December 1947, and his notes on the 1951 adaptation of the play, in Brecht (2003: 197–8, 216).

157 See Savage (2008: 165).

158 See Kuhn and Constantine, in Brecht (2003: 220–2); Flashar (2009: 182–4). In what follows, I quote Constantine's translation (Brecht 2003), which gives the lines of Hölderlin that survive in Brecht's version in the same form as they appear in Constantine (2001); page references in the text are to this version.

159 See Brecht's journal entry for 18 January 1948 and his letter to his son, Stefan, of December 1947, in (2003: 199, 201); cf. the *Antigone-model* (2003: 204), the journal entry for 16 December 1947 (2003: 197), and the notes on the 1951 production (2003: 215–16). For justifiable scepticism regarding Brecht's 'rationalization' of the myth, see Flashar (2009: 182–3, 185); cf. Pöggeler (2004: 179–80); Savage (2008: 165–6).

160 See Taxidou (2008: 245).

161 See esp. the text of the *Antigone-model* in Brecht (2003: 209).

162 This Prelude was omitted when the play was first performed in Germany, in the small town of Greiz in the newly formed German Democratic Republic, in 1951, replaced (after the first performance on 18 November) by a brief verse prologue spoken by the actor playing Tiresias; but this, too, raises the play's relevance to the recent past: 'We beg you / Search in your own hearts and minds for similar deeds / In the recent past or for the absence / Of any such deeds' (Brecht 2003: 218). On the two versions, see Kuhn and Constantine, in Brecht (2003: xiii, 219–20); Flashar (2009: 186); on the interrogative character of the 1948 Prelude, see Savage (2008: 160–4).

163 The expanded role of Megareus in Brecht's version builds on the reference at *Ant.* 1302–5, and is perhaps also indebted to the characterization of Menoeceus in Euripides' *Phoenician Women*, though Brecht's Megareus, unlike Euripides' Menoeceus, never appears onstage.

164 See Brecht's own observation in his draft foreword to the 1948 production (2003: 202): 'Argos becomes a Stalingrad – the parallel is obvious.'

165 Cf. Brecht's journal for 12 January 1948 (2003: 199), the 'bridge verses' which he deployed in rehearsal for the 1948 production, printed as captions in the 1949 *Antigone-model* (2003: 213), and his summary of the fourth chorus in his Notes to the 1951 production (2003: 217).

166 Symbolized in the play, as Berlau's photographs in the *Antigone-model* show, by Antigone's appearing bound to a door from the point at which she is led in, under arrest; see Taxidou (2008: 251–4).

167 On the ambivalence of Antigone's 'example', cf. Savage (2008: 170–1).

168 See *Antigone-model 1948* in Brecht (2003: 204). Cf. Savage (2008: 156); Taxidou (2008: 246).

169 Cf. Kuhn and Constantine in Brecht (2003: 220).

170 See above, pp. 124, 140. Orff's conceptualization and Brecht's are compared by Flashar (2009: 188, 193), who sees 'political' versus 'apolitical' or 'ritualist' adaptations as the two poles of an antithesis of the subsequent performance tradition, with the latter dominating, especially in Germany, until the 1960s.

171 See Lenz (1976).

172 Malina (1990); cf. Guarino (2010). Brecht's version has also been filmed by Jean-Marie Straub and Daniele Huillet: see Michelakis (2004: 211–16).

173 On this juxtaposition, see Elsaesser (2004: 8); Blumenthal-Barby (2007: 159–60); Capeloa Gil (2010: 314–15).

174 On these themes, see Elsaesser (2004), esp. p. 7: 'Although a generation apart, both Schleyer (as a member of the Hitler youth and the SS) and the terrorists (the RAF being referred to as "Hitler's children") are seen as heirs to the "curse" which Nazism had laid upon Germany.' Cf. Honig (2013: 70, 73–4).

175 On the film and its contexts, see esp. Hansen (1981–2); Elsaesser (2004); Blumenthal-Barby (2007); Capeloa Gil (2010). There is also a discussion in Honig (2013: 68–82). The 2004 Art Haus/Kinowelt DVD of the film includes a timeline of events, the press pack that accompanied the original release, and interviews with Volker Schlöndorff and Juliane Lorenz (Rainer Werner Fassbinder's editor and, latterly, partner).

176 See Flashar (2009: 243–6); Fischer-Lichte (2010: 346).

177 See Lenzi (2010); Nelli (2010); Poulson (2012); cf. Fradinger (2011) on this and other Argentinian *Antigones*.

178 Flashar (2009: 277–80); cf. Robinson (2011: 204–5) on 1980s productions in Poland. Flashar notes (2009: 324) that the number of productions of the play declines after German unification; yet it remains the most performed ancient tragedy in German repertory theatre (2009: 324–9).

179 See Nelli (2012) on Bárbara Colio's *Usted está aquí*. In the same volume see also Brunn (2012) on L. R. Sánchez's 1968 *La pasión según Antígona Pérez*.

180 For a sense of the play's reach, see the essays in Mee and Foley (2011), discussing productions/adaptations from the US to Japan and from Indonesia to the Arctic, with an Appendix (415–27) listing further non-US and non-European versions. For a further selection of less well-known versions (mainly in French, Spanish, and Portuguese), see Duroux and Urdician (2010).

181 See esp. Robinson (2011); cf. Flashar (2009: 279–80).

182 See Wetmore (2002, esp. 169–212 on *Antigones*); Budelmann (2004); Raji (2005); Dominik (2007: 118–20); Goff and Simpson (2007); Van Weyenberg (2013).

183 Braithwaite (1967). See Wetmore (2002: 176–81); Budelmann (2004: 7, 13–14); Gibbs (2007: 63–6); Goff and Simpson (2007: 220–38).

184 Bemba (1990). See Wetmore (2002: 203–12); Conteh-Morgan (2004); Goff and Simpson (2011).

185 Kwahulé (1997). See Love (2009).

186 Fugard, Kani, and Ntshona (1986), to which page numbers in the text
  refer. For studies, see Wetmore (2002: 194–203); Raji (2005); Goff and
  Simpson (2007: 271–320); Rehm (2007); Chanter (2011: 74–83).

187 On the play's background, see esp. Fugard (2002).

188 The 1965 New Brighton production is recalled in *The Island* itself (Fugard,
  Kani, and Ntshone 1986: 53–4); see further Fugard (2002) and works cited in
  n. 186 above. For Mandela's portrayal of Creon, see Mandela (1994: 441–2).

189 Osofisan (2007), from which page numbers in the text are taken. For
  studies, see Wetmore (2002: 181–94); Budelmann (2004); Raji (2005);
  Goff (2007); Goff and Simpson (2007: 321–64); Van Weyenberg (2010),
  (2013); Chanter (2011: 87–117).

190 See Raji (2005: 143–5).

191 The play's application to contemporary Nigerian politics is much
  discussed: see Budelmann (2004: 11); Raji (2005: 143–5); Goff (2007:
  41–2); Goff and Simpson (2007: 49, 335–7); Van Weyenberg (2013: 13, 19).

192 A conclusion which they underline with reference to Shelley's
  'Ozymandias': see Wetmore (2002: 192); Raji (2005: 148–9); Goff and
  Simpson (2007: 353–4); Van Weyenberg (2013: 34).

193 For this general reading of the play, see Raji (2005: 146); Chanter (2011:
  108–11); Van Weyenberg (2013: 36); cf. Goff (2007: 52–3). Goff and
  Simpson (2007) are more difficult to pin down.

194 Cf. Chanter (2011: 114–15); Van Weyenberg (2013: 19–20).

195 Tegonni responds in kind: their mutual affection restores an element that has
  not featured prominently in adaptations since Hölderlin, though it is
  prominent in Anouilh, as in the pre-nineteenth-century reception of the play.

196 Paulin (1985), to which all page numbers in the text refer. See Paulin's own
  account (2002); for further discussion, A. Roche (1988: 221–9); Richtarik
  (1994: 216–28); R. Jones (1997: 233–9); Cleary (1999: 524–31); Arkins
  (2002: 208); Deane (2002); McDonald (2002: 53–7); Arkins (2005: 151–2);
  Harkin (2008: 297–300); Arkins (2010: 38–9); Macintosh (2011: 92–7).

197 R. Jones (1997: 233, 235–9); cf. A. Roche (1988: 224–5); Richtarik (1994:
  222–4).

198 Paulin (2002: 167).

199 Harkin (2008: 298). Cf. A. Roche (1988: 224); Arkins (2005: 152);
  Macintosh (2011: 93).

200 Cleary (1999: 530).

201 I.e. Paulin, like the Aldine edition of Sophocles (and some later editions, e.g. Jebb 1900), gives line 572 to Antigone, not Ismene.

202 As Paulin himself later seems to suggest (2002: 169); cf. Deane (2002: 152–3).

203 O'Brien, *The Listener*, 24 October 1968, quoted with additional comments in O'Brien (1972: 156–9).

204 Paulin (1980: 1283).

205 For the background to the play, see A. Roche (1988: 221–4, 226–7); Richtarik (1994: 217–18); R. Jones (1997: 233–5); Cleary (1999: 524); Deane (2002: 151–4); Harkin (2008: 298); Macintosh (2011: 93–4); as well as Paulin's own brief account (2002). See also below on Heaney's *Burial at Thebes*.

206 See A. Roche (1988: 237–47); Arkins (2002: 207–8), (2005: 153–4); McDonald (2005: 126–9); A. Roche (2005: 150–5); Harkin (2008: 295–7); Arkins (2010: 44–5); Macintosh (2011: 97–100). Kennelly's published version (1996, to which all page numbers refer) also contains discussions by Terence Brown, Kathleen McCracken, and Kennelly himself.

207 A. Roche (1988: 238–41) compares Kennelly's Creon in *Antigone* to his Cromwell in his 1983 poem of that name.

208 See Arkins (2002: 208), (2005: 154), (2010: 45); cf. McDonald (2005: 129). As in Paulin, line 572 is attributed to Antigone.

209 Kennelly (2005: 19), alluding to John 1: 1–2.

210 Cf. A. Roche (1988: 237–8, 242–3, 245), (2005: 152).

211 Quoted in A. Roche (1988: 242).

212 Cf. A. Roche (1988: 241–6), (2005: 152–4).

213 Cf. and contrast A. Roche (1988: 246); McCracken in Kennelly (1996: 55).

214 A. Roche (1988: 237).

215 A. Roche (2005: 150); cf. Macintosh (2011: 97).

216 See Younger (2006: 159). On Heaney (cited by page numbers from 2004b), see also Wilmer (2007), (2010); Younger (2007); Harkin (2008: 303–6); Arkins (2010: 40–2); Macintosh (2011: 100–3); Zirzotti (2014: 136–9).

217 Heaney (2004c: 411–13).

218 Heaney (2004c: 416–18).

219 Heaney (2005: 171); cf. (2004a: 76), (2004c: 421). Heaney also notes the Middle Eastern setting of Conall Morrison's version of the play, which was already on tour when he was approached to produce his own adaptation: (2004a: 75), (2005: 170).

220 See esp. Wilmer (2007); Younger (2007).

221 For Heaney's thoughts on the 'too brutal simplicity' of Margaret Thatcher's insistence that 'Crime is crime, is crime. It is not political,' see (2004c: 412); also (2004c: 421–2) on the similarity between these attitudes and the treatment of those imprisoned at Guantanamo Bay, and cf. Harkin (2008: 305); Wilmer (2007: 236), (2010: 389).

222 Cf. Heaney (2004a: 76), (2005: 170).

223 See Wilmer (2007: 237), (2010: 386).

224 Agamben (2005); cf. Wilmer (2007: 235), (2010: 386, 389–91).

225 Heaney (2004c: 421–2).

226 Heaney (2004a: 76).

227 Heaney (2004c: 422).

228 Heaney (2004c: 426).

229 The importance of this model is emphasized by Heaney in all three of his published accounts of the genesis of his version: see (2004a: 76–8), (2004c: 423–6), (2005: 171–3). For the importance of the tradition of Irish lament in Kennelly's *Antigone*, cf. Macintosh (2011: 110).

230 Antigone herself alludes to Irish ritual when she laments that she will have 'No wake. No keen.' Creon observes that 'If people had the chance to keen themselves / Before they died, they'd weep and wail forever' (p. 39). Earlier he had decreed 'no keening' for Polynices (p. 11); eventually there is keening in his own house, as heard by Eurydice (p. 50).

231 Cf. Wilmer (2007: 231–4).

232 See esp. Harkin (2008: 304–5).

233 To judge from Wilmer's description, (2007: 239–40).

234 See Macintosh (2011: 102).

235 In that respect, the Gothic Line Project (reported by Treu 2011), which performed *Antigone* in a World War II German cemetery in northern Italy in 2006, is remarkable for the extent to which it raises thought-provoking (and very Hellenic) questions about the boundaries that separate friend and foe, us and them.

236 Cf. Mee and Foley (2011: 3, 5–6); Chanter (2011: 58).

Guide to Further Reading

I have tried to give useful references for each major topic at the point at which it is first discussed in the text. The following guide is therefore brief, confined to accessible works in English, and focused at the more general and introductory end of the spectrum. For detailed discussion of specific issues see the notes and the references cited there.

There are several good general reference works on tragedy that will shed useful light on the *Antigone*, its contexts, and the issues it raises. Most useful are Justina Gregory's *Blackwell Companion to Greek Tragedy* (Malden MA: Wiley-Blackwell, 2005) and Hanna Roisman's *Encyclopedia of Greek Tragedy* (Malden MA: Wiley-Blackwell, 2014). Of the various short introductions to tragedy on the market, Ruth Scodel's *Introduction to Greek Tragedy* (Scodel 2010) is both accurate and stimulating. As thorough and thought-provoking introductions to the whole enterprise of interpreting Greek tragedy, the contrasting approaches of Goldhill (1986) and Heath (1987) remain very valuable.

Ruth Scodel has also produced a very useful one-volume study of Sophocles (Scodel 1984), though my own favourite in this category is still the classic work of Winnington-Ingram (1980). Garvie (2005) is very accessible and covers a great deal of ground for such a short book. Goldhill (2012) combines analysis of the plays with an illuminating account of some of the forces that have shaped their modern interpretation. There are two recent companions to Sophocles: *Brill's Companion to Sophocles* (Leiden: Brill, 2012), edited by A. Markantonatos, and *A Companion to Sophocles* (Malden MA: Wiley-Blackwell, 2012), by K. Ormand. Each has a short chapter on *Antigone*.

For the interpretation of the play itself, I'd start – after reading the play at least once – with the stimulating article by Sourvinou-Inwood (1989a). Once you have begun to formulate arguments against Sourvinou-Inwood's vigorous and apparently plausible polemic, you're well on the way to understanding Sophocles' drama. Holt (1999) will provide useful ammunition.

For those reading the play in Greek, the commentaries by Jebb (1900), Brown (1987), and Griffith (1999) are indispensable. Brown's volume is fully accessible to those who know no Greek, as are the introduction and many of the notes in Griffith. Brown also provides a reliable and close translation. Similarly accurate is the translation of Hugh Lloyd-Jones in *Sophocles: Antigone, The Women of Trachis, Philoctetes, Oedipus at Colonus* (Loeb Classical Library 21, Cambridge MA: Harvard University Press, 1994). Of the many more literary (and so often less literal) translations on the market, Robert Fagles's *Sophocles: The Three Theban Plays* (Harmondsworth: Penguin, 1984), is probably the most popular. There are more recent versions by Reginald Gibbons and Charles Segal (Oxford: Oxford University Press, 2003) and by David Franklin and John Harrison (Cambridge: Cambridge University Press, 2003). Elizabeth Wyckoff's translation was one of the least successful in the Chicago series of Complete Greek Tragedies, but it has recently been revised by Mark Griffith and Glenn Most (*Sophocles* i, Chicago: University of Chicago Press, 2013). Still useful are the versions of E. F. Watling in *Sophocles: The Theban Plays* (Harmondsworth: Penguin, 1947) and H. D. F. Kitto in *Sophocles: Three Tragedies* (Oxford: Oxford University Press, 1962, revised 1994).

For a discussion of modern translations of the play, see D. H. Roberts, 'Reading *Antigone* in Translation: Text, Paratext, Intertext', in Wilmer and Žukauskaitė (2010: 283–312). That volume is one of many recent contributions to the study of the play's modern reception; many more are cited in the notes to Chapter 5. The best place to start is still Steiner (1984), supplemented especially by the recent volume edited by Mee and Foley (2011). See the notes to Chapter 5 for more specific studies, and for work in other languages.

Bibliography

Adams, S. M. (1931), 'The Burial of Polyneices', *Classical Review* 45: 110–11.

Adler, J. (1983), 'Friedrich Hölderlin on Tragedy: "Notes on the Oedipus" and "Notes on the Antigone"', in *Comparative Criticism* 5: 205–44.

Agamben, G. (2005), *State of Exception,* trans. K. Attell, Chicago: University of Chicago Press. Italian original, 2003.

Alexiou, M. (1974), *The Ritual Lament in Greek Tradition*, Oxford: Oxford University Press.

Allen, D. (2000), *The World of Prometheus: The Politics of Punishing in Classical Athens*, Princeton: Princeton University Press.

Anouilh, J. (2000), *Antigone*, trans. B. Bray, with commentary and notes by T. Freeman, London: Methuen.

Arkins, B. (2002), 'Women in Irish Appropriations of Greek Tragedy', in M. McDonald and J. M. Walton (eds), *Amid our Troubles: Irish Versions of Greek Tragedy,* 198–212, London: Methuen.

Arkins, B. (2005), *Hellenising Ireland: Greek and Roman Themes in Modern Irish Literature*, Newbridge: The Goldsmith Press.

Arkins, B. (2010), *Irish Appropriation of Greek Tragedy*, Dublin: Carysfort Press.

Arnott, W. G., ed. (1979–2000), *Menander*, three volumes, Cambridge MA: Harvard University Press; Loeb Classical Library 132, 459, 460.

Attfield, N. (2010), 'Restaging the *Welttheater*: A Critical View of Carl Orff's *Antigonae* and *Oedipus der Tyrann*', in P. Brown and S. Ograjenšek (eds), *Ancient Drama in Music for the Modern Stage*, 340–68, Oxford: Oxford University Press.

Bain, D. (1981), *Masters, Servants, and Orders in Greek Tragedy*, Manchester: Manchester University Press.

Baldry, H. C. (1956), 'The Dramatization of the Theban Legend', *Greece & Rome* 3: 24–37.

Battles, D. (2004), *The Medieval Tradition of Thebes: History and Narrative in the Roman de Thèbes, Boccaccio, Chaucer, and Lydgate*, New York: Routledge.

Belardinelli, A. M. (2010), 'Introduzione: Antigone e il dono di sé', in A. M. Belardinelli and G. Greco (eds), *Antigone e le Antigoni: Storia forme fortune di un mito*, 1–23, Florence: Le Monnier Università.

Belardinelli, A. M. and G. Greco, eds (2010), *Antigone e le Antigoni: Storia forme fortune di un mito*, Florence: Le Monnier Università.

Belfiore, E. (2000), *Murder among Friends: Violation of Philia in Greek Tragedy*, New York: Oxford University Press.

Bemba, S. (1990), *Black Wedding Candles for Blessed Antigone*, in *Theatre and Politics: An International Anthology*, 1–62, New York: Ubu Repertory Theater Productions.

Benardete, S. (1999), 'A Reading of Sophocles' *Antigone*', in *Sacred Transgressions: A Reading of Sophocles' Antigone*, 1–143, South Bend IN: St Augustine's Press. Originally published in three parts in *Interpretation* 4.3 (1975), 148–96; 5.1 (1975), 1–55; and 5.2 (1975), 148–84.

✳ Bennett, L. and W. B. Tyrrell (1990), 'Sophocles' *Antigone* and Funeral Oratory', *American Journal of Philology* 111: 441–56.

Bernasconi, R. (2013), 'Heidegger, Nietzsche, National Socialism: The Place of Metaphysics in the Political Debate of the 1930s', in F. Raffoul and E. S. Nelson (eds), *The Blackwell Companion to Heidegger*, 47–54, Malden MA: Wiley-Blackwell.

Bethe, E. (1891), *Thebanische Heldenlieder: Untersuchungen über die Epen des thebanisch-argivischen Sagenkreises*, Leipzig: Hirzel.

Billings, J. (2014), *Genealogy of the Tragic: Greek Tragedy and German Philosophy*, Princeton: Princeton University Press.

Blumenthal-Barby, M. (2007), '*Germany in Autumn*: Return of the Human', *Discourse* 29: 140–68.

Blundell, M. W. (1989), *Helping Friends and Harming Enemies: A Study in Sophocles and Greek Ethics*, Cambridge: Cambridge University Press.

Blundell, S. (1995), *Women in Ancient Greece*, Cambridge MA: Harvard University Press.

Boetius, S. (2005), *Die Wiedergeburt der griechischen Tragödie auf der Bühne des 19. Jahrhunderts,* Tübingen: Niemeyer.

Bowra, C. M. (1944), *Sophoclean Tragedy*. Oxford: Oxford University Press.

Boyle, A. J. (2006), *An Introduction to Roman Tragedy*, London: Routledge.

Bradley, A. C. (1962), 'Hegel's Theory of Tragedy', in A. and H. Paolucci, *Hegel on Tragedy,* 367–88, Garden City NY: Anchor Books. Reprinted from *Oxford Lectures on Poetry*, London: Macmillan, 1950, 69–95. First published 1909.

Bradshaw, A. T. von S. (1962), 'The Watchman Scenes in the *Antigone*', *Classical Quarterly* 12: 200–11.

Braithwaite, E. K. (1967), *Odale's Choice*, Ibadan: Evans Brothers.

Brecht, B. (2003), *Collected Plays: Eight (The Antigone of Sophocles, The Days of the Commune, Turandot or The Whitewashers' Congress)*, edited and introduced by T. Kuhn and D. Constantine, London: Methuen.

Bremer, J. M. (1969), *Hamartia: Tragic Error in the Poetics of Aristotle and in Greek Tragedy*, Amsterdam: A. M. Hakkert.

Bremer, J. M. (1984), 'The Popularity of Euripides' *Phoenissae* in Late Antiquity', in J. Harmatta (ed.), *Proceedings of the VIIth Congress of the International Federation of the Societies of Classical Studies*, 281–8, Budapest: Akadémiai Kiadó.

Brown, A. L., ed. (1987), *Sophocles: Antigone*, Warminster: Aris and Phillips.

Brunn, V. (2012), 'Revolutionizing Antigone: A Puerto Rican Adaptation of Sophocles' Tragedy', *Romance Quarterly* 59: 36–47.

Bruzzese, L. (2010), 'Dai *Sette contro Tebe* di Eschilo all' *Antigone* di Sofocle: la dualità nel mito dei Labdacidi', in A. M. Belardinelli and G. Greco, *Antigone e le Antigoni: Storia forme fortune di un mito,* 190–215, Florence: Le Monnier Università.

Buchan, M. (2012), 'Sophocles with Lacan', in K. Ormand (ed.), *A Companion to Sophocles*, 492–504, Malden MA: Wiley-Blackwell.

Budelmann, F. (2004), 'Greek Tragedies in West African Adaptations', *Proceedings of the Cambridge Philological Society* 50: 1–28.

Budelmann, F. and P. E. Easterling (2010), 'Reading Minds in Greek Tragedy', *Greece & Rome* 57: 289–303.

Burton, R. W. B. (1980), *The Chorus in Sophocles' Tragedies*, Oxford: Oxford University Press.

Bushnell, R., ed. (2005), *A Companion to Tragedy*, Oxford: Blackwell.

Butler, J. (2000), *Antigone's Claim: Kinship between Life and Death*, New York: Columbia University Press.

Cairns, D. L. (1996), 'Hybris, Dishonour, and Thinking Big', *Journal of Hellenic Studies* 116: 1–32.

Cairns, D. L. (2005a), 'Bullish Looks and Sidelong Glances: Social Interaction and the Eyes in Ancient Greek Culture', in D. L. Cairns (ed.), *Body Language in the Greek and Roman Worlds*, 123–55, Swansea: Classical Press of Wales.

Cairns, D. L. (2005b), 'Values', in J. Gregory (ed.), *The Blackwell Companion to Greek Tragedy*, 305–20, Malden MA: Wiley-Blackwell.

Cairns, D. L. (2010), *Bacchylides: Five Epinician Odes (3, 5, 9, 11, 13)*, Cambridge: Francis Cairns.

Cairns, D. L. (2012), '*Atê* in the Homeric Poems', *Papers of the Langford Latin Seminar* 15: 1–52.

Cairns, D. L. (2013), 'Introduction: Archaic Thought and Tragic Interpretation', in D. L. Cairns (ed.), *Tragedy and Archaic Greek Thought*, ix–liv, Swansea: Classical Press of Wales.

Cairns, D. L. (2014a), 'From Solon to Sophocles: Intertextuality and Interpretation in Sophocles' *Antigone*', *Japan Studies in Classical Antiquity* 2: 3–30.

Cairns, D. L. (2014b), 'The Bloody Dust of the Nether Gods: Sophocles, *Antigone* 599–603', in E. K. Emilsson, A. Maravela, and M. Skoie (eds), *Paradeigmata: Studies in Honour of Øivind Andersen*, 39–51, Athens: Norwegian Institute at Athens.

Calder, W. M. (1968), 'Sophokles' Political Tragedy: *Antigone*', *Greek, Roman, and Byzantine Studies* 9: 389–407.

Campbell, D. A., ed. (1982), *Greek Lyric* i, Loeb Classical Library 142, Cambridge MA: Harvard University Press.

Campbell, D. A., ed. (1991), *Greek Lyric* iii, Loeb Classical Library 476, Cambridge MA: Harvard University Press.

Capeloa Gil, I. (2010), 'L'Automne d'Antigone: Le Mythe grec et le *deutscher Herbst* (1977)', in R. Duroux and S. Urdician (eds), *Les Antigones contemporaines (de 1945 à nos jours),* 308–19, Clermont-Ferrand: Presses Universitaires Blaise Pascal.

Carter, D. M. (2012), '*Antigone*', in A. Markantonatos (ed.), *Brill's Companion to Sophocles,* 111–28, Leiden: Brill.

Cerri, G. (1979), *Legislazione orale e tragedia greca: studi sull' Antigone di Sofocle e sulle Supplici di Euripide.* Naples: Liguori.

Chanter, T. (1995), *Ethics of Eros: Irigaray's Rewriting of the Philosophers*, New York: Routledge.

Chanter, T. (2011), *Whose Antigone? The Tragic Marginalization of Slavery*, Albany NY: SUNY Press.

Chanter, T. and S. D. Kirkland, eds (2014), *The Returns of Antigone*, Albany NY: SUNY Press.

Ciani, M. G., ed. (2000), *Sofocle, Anouilh, Brecht: Antigone. Variazioni sul mito*, Venice: Marsilio.

Cingano, E. (2003), 'Figure eroiche nell'*Antigone* di Sofocle e nella tradizione mitografica arcaica', in G. Avezzù (ed.), *Il dramma sofocleo: testo, lingua, interpretazione,* 69–84, Stuttgart: Metzler.

Clarke, M. (1999), *Flesh and Spirit in the Songs of Homer: A Study of Words and Myths*, Oxford: Oxford University Press.

Cleary, J. (1999), 'Domestic Troubles: Tragedy and the Northern Ireland Conflict', *South Atlantic Quarterly* 98: 501–37.

Cocteau, J. (2013), *Antigone*, Paris: Gallimard. First published 1927.

Coleman, R. (1972), 'The Role of the Chorus in Sophocles' *Antigone*', *Proceedings of the Cambridge Philological Society* 18: 4–27.

Collard, C. and M. J. Cropp, eds (2008), *Euripides: Fragments – Aegeus-Meleager*, Loeb Classical Library 504, Cambridge MA: Harvard University Press.

Collard, C., M. J. Cropp, and J. Gibert, eds (2004), *Euripides: Selected Fragmentary Plays* ii, Warminster: Aris and Philips.

Constantine, D., trans. (2001), *Hölderlin's Sophocles: Oedipus and Antigone*, Newcastle upon Tyne: Bloodaxe.

Conteh-Morgan, J. (2004), 'Antigone in the "Land of the Incorruptible"': Sylvain Bemba's *Noces Posthumes de Santigone* (*Black Wedding Candles for Blessed Antigone*)', in J. Conteh-Morgan and T. Olaniyan (eds), *African Drama and Performance*, 78–87, Bloomington IN: Indiana University Press.

Craik, E. M., ed. (1988), *Euripides: Phoenician Women*, Warminster: Aris and Phillips.

Crane, G. (1989), 'Creon and the "Ode to Man" in Sophocles' *Antigone*', *Harvard Studies in Classical Philology* 92: 103–16.

Criado, C. (2015), 'The Constitutional Status of Euripidean and Statian Theseus: Some Aspects of the Criticism of Absolute Power in the *Thebaid*', in W. J. Dominik, C. F. Newlands, and K. Gervais (eds), *Brill's Companion to Statius*, 291–306, Leiden: Brill.

Cropp, M. J. (1997), 'Antigone's Final Speech (Sophocles, *Antigone* 891–928)', *Greece & Rome* 44: 137–60.

Cropp, M. J. and G. Fick (1985), *Resolutions and Chronology in Euripides: The Fragmentary Tragedies*, London: *Bulletin of the Institute of Classical Studies* Supplement 43.

Csapo, E. and W. J. Slater (1994), *The Context of Ancient Drama*, Ann Arbor MI: University of Michigan Press.

Cullyer, H. (2005), 'A Wind that Blows from Thrace: Dionysus in the Fifth Stasimon of Sophocles' *Antigone*', *Classical World* 99: 3–20.

Dangel, J., ed. (1995), *Accius: Oeuvres (fragments)*, Paris: Les Belles Lettres.

Dastur, F. (2000), 'Holderlin and the Orientalisation of Greece', *Pli: The Warwick Journal of Philosophy* 10: 156–73.

Davidson, J. F. (1983), 'The Parodos of the *Antigone*: A Poetic Study', *Bulletin of the Institute of Classical Studies* 30: 41–51.

Dawe, R. D. (1967), 'The End of the *Seven against Thebes*', *Classical Quarterly* 17: 16–28.

Dawe, R. D. (1968), 'Some Reflections on *Atê* and *Hamartia*', *HSCP* 72: 89–123.

Dawe, R. D., ed. (1984–5), *Sophoclis tragoediae*, second edition, Leipzig: Teubner.

Dawe, R. D., ed. (2006), *Sophocles: Oedipus Rex*, second edition, Cambridge: Cambridge University Press.

Deane, S. (2002), 'Field Day's Greeks (and Russians)', in M. McDonald and J. M. Walton (eds), *Amid our Troubles: Irish Versions of Greek Tragedy*, 148–64, London: Methuen.

de Fátima Silva, M. (2010), 'Le Mythe d'Antigone sur la scène portugaise du xxe siècle', in R. Duroux and S. Urdician (eds), *Les Antigones contemporaines (de 1945 à nos jours)*, 287–94, Clermont-Ferrand, Presses Universitaires Blaise Pascal.

Deppman, J. (2012), 'Jean Anouilh's *Antigone*', in K. Ormand (ed.), *A Companion to Sophocles*, 523–37, Malden MA: Wiley-Blackwell.

Derrida, J. (1986), *Glas*, trans. J. P. Leavey and R. Rand, Lincoln NE: University of Nebraska Press. French original 1974.

Develin, R. (1989), *Athenian Officials, 684–321 BC*, Cambridge: Cambridge University Press.

Diggle, J., ed. (1994), *Euripidis fabulae* iii, Oxford: Oxford University Press.

Diller, H. (1956), 'Über das Selbstbewußtsein der sophokleischen Personen', *Wiener Studien* 69: 70–85.

Dillon, J. and S. E. Wilmer, eds (2005), *Rebel Women: Staging Ancient Greek Drama Today*, London: Methuen.

Ditmars, E. van N. (1992), *Sophocles' Antigone: Lyric Shape and Meaning*, Pisa: Giardini.

Dominik, W. J. (2007), 'Africa', in C. Kallendorf (ed.), *A Companion to the Classical Tradition*, 117–31, Malden MA: Wiley-Blackwell.

Dover, K. J. (1974), *Greek Popular Morality in the Time of Plato and Aristotle*, Oxford: Blackwell.

Drachmann, A. B. (1908), 'Zur Composition der sophokleischen *Antigone*', *Hermes* 43: 67–76.

Dué, C. (2012), 'Lament as Speech Act in Sophocles', in K. Ormand (ed.), *A Companion to Sophocles*, 236–50, Malden MA: Wiley-Blackwell.

Dunn, F. M. (2012), 'Dynamic Allusion in Sophocles', in A. Markantonatos, *Brill's Companion to Sophocles*, 263–79, Leiden: Brill.

Duroux, R. and S. Urdician, eds (2010), *Les Antigones contemporaines (de 1945 à nos jours)*, Clermont-Ferrand, Presses Universitaires Blaise Pascal.

Easterling, P. E. (1978), 'The Second Stasimon of *Antigone*', in R. D. Dawe, J. Diggle, and P. E. Easterling (eds), *Dionysiaca: Nine Studies in Greek Poetry by Former Pupils Presented to Sir Denys Page on his Seventieth Birthday*, 141–58, Cambridge: Faculty of Classics.

Easterling, P. E. (2013), 'Sophocles and the Wisdom of Silenus: A Reading of *Oedipus at Colonus* 1211–48', in D. L. Cairns (ed.), *Tragedy and Archaic Greek Thought*, 193–204, Swansea: Classical Press of Wales.

Eckermann, J. P. (1945), *Gespräche mit Goethe in den letzen Jahren seines Lebens*, two volumes, Basel: Birkhäuser.

Edwards, R. R. (2015), 'Medieval Statius: Belatedness and Authority', in W. J. Dominik, C. F. Newlands, and K. Gervais (eds), *Brill's Companion to Statius*, 497–511, Leiden: Brill.

Eagleton, T. (2010), 'Lacan's Antigone' in S. Wilmer and A. Žukauskaitė, *Interrogating Antigone in Postmodern Philosophy and Criticism*, 101–9, Oxford: Oxford University Press.

Elsaesser, T. (2004), 'Antigone Agonistes: Urban Guerrilla or Guerrilla Urbanism? The Red Army Fraction, *Germany in Autumn* and *Death Game*', *Rouge* 4, www.rouge.com.au/4/antigone.html, accessed 1 June 2015.

Else, G. F. (1976), *The Madness of Antigone*, Abhandlungen der Heidelberger Akademie der Wissenschaften, Philosophisch-historische Klasse 1976. 1; Heidelberg, Carl Winter Universitätsverlag.

Engels, J. (1998), *Funerum sepulchrorumque magnificentia: Begräbnis- und Grabluxusgesetze in der griechisch-römischen Welt mit einigen Ausblicken auf Einschränkungen des funeralen und sepulkralen Luxus im Mittelalter und in der Neuzeit*, *Hermes* Einzelschrift 78, Stuttgart: Steiner.

Ferrario, S. (2006), 'Replaying Antigone: Changing Patterns of Public and Private Commemoration at Athens c. 440–350', in C. B. Patterson (ed.), *Antigone's Answer: Essays on Death and Burial, Family and State in Classical Athens*, 79–117, *Helios* Supplement 33, Lubbock TX: Texas Tech University Press.

Finglass, P. J. (2009), 'The Ending of Sophocles' *Oedipus Rex*', *Philologus* 153: 42–62.

Finglass, P. J., ed. (2011), *Sophocles: Ajax*, Cambridge: Cambridge University Press.

Fischer-Lichte, E. (2010), 'Politicizing *Antigone*', in S. Wilmer and A. Žukauskaitė, *Interrogating Antigone in Postmodern Philosophy and Criticism*, 329–52, Oxford: Oxford University Press.

Fisher, N. R. E. (1992), *Hybris: A Study in the Values of Honour and Shame in Ancient Greece*, Warminster: Aris and Phillips.

Fitch, J. G., ed. (2002), *Seneca: Hercules; Trojan Women; Phoenician Women; Phaedra*, Loeb Classical Library 62; Cambridge MA: Harvard University Press.

Flashar, H. (2001), *Felix Mendelssohn-Bartholdy und die griechische Tragödie*, Abhandlungen der Sächsischen Akademie der Wissenschaften zu Leipzig. Philologisch-historische Klasse 78. 1.

Flashar, H. (2009), *Inszenierung der Antike: Das griechische Drama auf der Bühne der Neuzeit 1585–1990*, second edition, Munich: Beck. First edition 1991.

Fleming, K. (2008), 'Fascism on Stage: Jean Anouilh's *Antigone*', in V. Zajko and M. Leonard (eds), *Laughing with Medusa: Classical Myth and Feminist Thought*, 163–86, Oxford: Oxford University Press.

Fleming, K. (2015), 'Heidegger's *Antigone*', in J. Billings and M. Leonard (eds), *Tragedy and the Idea of Modernity*, 178–93, Oxford: Oxford University Press.

Flügge, M. (1982), *Verweigerung oder Neue Ordnung: Jean Anouilhs Antigone im politischen und ideologischen Kontext der Besatzungszeit 1940–1944*, Rheinfelden: Schäuble.

Foley, H. P. (1993), 'The Politics of Tragic Lamentation', in A. H. Sommerstein, S. Halliwell, J. Henderson, and B. Zimmermann (eds), *Tragedy, Comedy, and the Polis*, 101–43, Bari: Levante, 1993. Reprinted in *Female Acts in Greek Tragedy*, Princeton: Princeton University Press, 2001, 19–56.

Foley, H. P. (1995), 'Tragedy and Democratic Ideology: The Case of Sophocles' *Antigone*', in B. Goff (ed.), *History, Tragedy, Theory: Dialogues on Athenian Drama*, 131–50, Austin TX: University of Texas Press.

Foley, H. P. (2001), *Female Acts in Greek Tragedy*, Princeton: Princeton University Press.

Fowler, B. H. (1967), 'Plot and Prosody in Sophocles' *Antigone*', *Classica et Mediaevalia* 28: 143–71.

Fowler, R. L. (2000), *Early Greek Mythography* volume 1: *Texts*, Oxford: Oxford University Press.

Fowler, R. L. (2013), *Early Greek Mythography* volume 2: *Commentary*, Oxford: Oxford University Press.

Fradinger, M. (2011), 'An Argentine Tradition', in E. B. Mee and H. P. Foley (eds), *Antigone on the Contemporary World Stage*, 67–89, Oxford: Oxford University Press.

Fraenkel, E. (1964), 'Zum Schluß der *Sieben gegen Theben*', *Museum Helveticum* 21: 58–64.

Francis, E. D. (1983), 'Virtue, Folly, and Greek Etymology', in C. A. Rubino and C. W. Shelmerdine (eds), *Approaches to Homer*, 74–121, Austin TX: University of Texas Press.

Frank, M. (1995), *Seneca's Phoenissae: Introduction and Commentary*, Leiden: Brill.

Friedländer, P. (1969), 'πολλὰ τὰ δεινά (Sophokles, *Antigone* 332–375)', in *Studien zur antiken Literatur und Kunst*, 183–92, Berlin: De Gruyter. First published in *Hermes* 69 (1934): 56–63.

Von Fritz, K. (1962), 'Haimons Liebe zu Antigone', in *Antike und moderne Tragödie*, Berlin: Weidmann. First published in *Philologus* 89 (1934), 19–34.

Fugard, A. (2002), '*Antigone* in Africa', in M. McDonald and J. M. Walton (eds), *Amid our Troubles: Irish Versions of Greek Tragedy*, 128–47, London: Methuen.

Fugard, A., J. Kani, and W. Ntshona (1986), *Statements*, New York: Theatre Communications Group. First published 1974.

Fulcher, J. F. (2006), 'French Identity in Flux: Vichy's Collaboration, and Antigone's Operatic Triumph', *Proceedings of the American Philosophical Society* 150: 261–95.

Gagné, R. (2013), *Ancestral Fault in Ancient Greece*, Cambridge: Cambridge University Press.

Galli, M. (2010), 'Le immagini di Antigone: per un'archeologia delle emozioni', in A. M. Belardinelli and G. Greco (eds), *Antigone e le Antigoni: Storia forme fortune di un mito*, 59–70, Florence: Le Monnier Università.

Gantz, T. (1980), 'The Aeschylean Tetralogy', *American Journal of Philology* 101: 133–64.

Gantz, T. (1993), *Early Greek Myth*, Baltimore: Johns Hopkins University Press.

Garland, R. (1985), *The Greek Way of Death*. London: Duckworth.

Garvie, A. F. (2005), *The Plays of Sophocles*, London: Bristol Classical Press.

Gatrell, V. A. C. (1994), *The Hanging Tree: Execution and the English People 1770–1868*, Oxford: Oxford University Press.

Geary, J. (2006), 'Reinventing the Past: Mendelssohn's *Antigone* and the Creation of an Ancient Greek Musical Language', *The Journal of Musicology* 23: 187–226.

Gellie, G. H. (1972), *Sophocles: A Reading*, Melbourne: Melbourne University Press.

Gibbs, J. (2007), 'Antigone and her African Sisters: West African Versions of a Greek Original', in L. Hardwick and C. Gillespie (eds), *Classics in Post-Colonial Worlds*, 54–71, Oxford: Oxford University Press.

Gibert, J. (1995), *Change of Mind in Greek Tragedy*, Göttingen: Vandenhoeck and Ruprecht.

Görner, R. (2015), 'The (Operatic) Tragedy of Culture: Notes on a Theme in Kierkegaard, Hebbel, and Wagner', in J. Billings and M. Leonard (eds), *Tragedy and the Idea of Modernity*, 159–77, Oxford: Oxford University Press.

Goff, B. (2007), 'Antigone's Boat: The Colonial and the Postcolonial in *Tegonni: An African Antigone* by Femi Osofisan', in L. Hardwick and C. Gillespie (eds), *Classics in Post-Colonial Worlds*, 40–53, Oxford: Oxford University Press.

Goff, B. and M. Simpson (2007), *Crossroads in the Black Aegean: Oedipus, Antigone, and Dramas of the African Diaspora*, Oxford: Oxford University Press.

Goff, B. and M. Simpson (2011), 'Voice from the Black Box: Sylvain Bemba's *Black Wedding Candles for Blessed Antigone*', in E. B. Mee and H. P. Foley (eds), *Antigone on the Contemporary World Stage*, 324–39, Oxford: Oxford University Press.

Goheen, R. F. (1951), *The Imagery of Sophocles' Antigone: A Study of Poetic Language and Structure*, Princeton: Princeton University Press.

Goldhill, S. D. (1986), *Reading Greek Tragedy*, Cambridge: Cambridge University Press.

Goldhill, S. D. (2012), *Sophocles and the Language of Tragedy*, Oxford: Oxford University Press.

Goldhill, S. D. (2015), 'The Ends of Tragedy: Schelling, Hegel, and Oedipus', in J. Billings and M. Leonard (eds), *Tragedy and the Idea of Modernity*, 231–50, Oxford: Oxford University Press.

Gould, J. (1980), 'Law, Custom, and Myth: Aspects of the Social Position of Women in Classical Athens', *Journal of Hellenic Studies* 100: 38–59.

Griffith, M., ed. (1999), *Sophocles: Antigone*, Cambridge: Cambridge University Press.

Griffith, M. (2010), 'Psychoanalysing *Antigone*', in S. E. Wilmer and A. Žukauskaitė (eds), *Interrogating Antigone in Postmodern Philosophy and Criticism*, 110–34, Oxford: Oxford University Press.

Guarino, R. (2010), 'Antigone e una svolta del Novecento: da Brecht (1947–1948) al Living Theatre (1967)', in A. M. Belardinelli and G. Greco (eds), *Antigone e le Antigoni: Storia forme fortune di un mito*, 37–49, Florence: Le Monnier Università.

Guthrie, W. K. C. (1969), *A History of Greek Philosophy* iii: *The Fifth-Century Enlightenment*, Cambridge: Cambridge University Press.

Halbreich, H. (1999), *Arthur Honegger*, trans. R. Nichols, Portland OR: Amadeus Press. French original 1992.

Hall, E. (1997), 'The Sociology of Athenian Tragedy', in P. E. Easterling (ed.), *The Cambridge Companion to Greek Tragedy*, 93–126, Cambridge: Cambridge University Press.

Hall, E. (2011), '*Antigone* and the Internationalization of Theatre in Antiquity', in E. B. Mee and H. P. Foley (eds), *Antigone on the Contemporary World Stage*, 51–63, Oxford: Oxford University Press.

Hall, E. (2012), 'The Necessity and Limits of Deliberation in Sophocles' Theban Plays', in K. Ormand (ed.), *A Companion to Sophocles*, 301–15, Malden MA: Wiley-Blackwell.

Hall, E. and F. Macintosh (2005), *Greek Tragedy and the British Theatre 1660–1914*, Oxford: Oxford University Press.

Hame, K. J. (2008), 'Female Control of Funeral Rites in Greek Tragedy: Klytaimestra, Medea, and Antigone', *Classical Philology* 103: 1–15.

Hansen, M. (1981–2), 'Co-operative Auteur Cinema and Oppositional Public Sphere: Alexander Kluge's Contribution to Germany in Autumn', *New German Critique* 24–5: 36–56.

Harkin, H. (2008), 'Irish Antigones: Towards Tragedy Without Borders?' *Irish University Review* 38: 292–309.

Harris, E. M. (2004), 'Antigone the Lawyer, or the Ambiguities of *Nomos*', in E. M. Harris and L. Rubinstein (eds), *The Law and the Courts in Ancient Greece*, 19–56, London: Duckworth.

Harrison, R. B. (1975), *Hölderlin and Greek Literature*, Oxford: Oxford University Press.

Hasenclever, W. (1919), *Antigone: Tragödie in 5 Akten*, eighth edition, Berlin: P. Cassirer.

Heaney, S. (2004a), 'A Note on *The Burial at Thebes*', in S. Heaney, *The Burial at Thebes*, 75–9, New York: Farrar, Strauss and Giroux.

Heaney, S. (2004b), *The Burial at Thebes*, London: Faber and Faber.

Heaney, S. (2004c), 'Title Deeds: Translating a Classic', *Proceedings of the American Philosophical Society* 148: 411–26.

Heaney, S. (2005), '"Me" as in "Metre": On Translating *Antigone*', in J. Dillon and S. Wilmer (eds), *Rebel Women: Staging Ancient Greek Drama Today*, 169–73, London: Methuen.

Heath, M. (1987), *The Poetics of Greek Tragedy*, London: Duckworth.

Heidegger, M. (1996), *Hölderlin's Hymn, 'The Ister'*, trans. W. McNeill and J. Davis, Bloomington IN: Indiana University Press. German original 1984.

Heidegger, M. (2000), *Introduction to Metaphysics*, trans. G. Fried and R. Polt, New Haven: Yale University Press, from *Einführung in die Metaphysik*, *Gesamtausgabe* 40, Frankfurt: Klostermann, 1983. First published 1953.

Henrichs, A. (1990), 'Between City and Country: Cultic Dimensions of Dionysus in Athens and Attica', in M. Griffith and D. J. Mastronarde (eds), *Cabinet of the Muses: Essays on Classical and Comparative Literature in Honor of Thomas G. Rosenmeyer*, 257–77, Chico CA: Scholars' Press.

Heslin, P. J. (2008), 'Statius and the Greek Tragedians on Athens, Thebes, and Rome', in J. J. L. Smolenaars, H.-J. van Dam, and R. R. Nauta (eds), *The Poetry of Statius*, 111–28, *Mnemosyne* Supplement 306, Leiden: Brill.

Heslin, P. J. (2015), 'Statius in Dante's *Commedia*', in W. J. Dominik, C. F. Newlands, and K. Gervais (eds), *Brill's Companion to Statius*, 512–26, Leiden: Brill.

Hester, D. A. (1971), 'Sophocles the Unphilosophical: A Study in the *Antigone*', *Mnemosyne* 24: 11–59.

Hirschberg, T. (1989), *Senecas Phoenissen: Einleitung und Kommentar*, Berlin: De Gruyter.

Hölderlin, F. (1952), *Sämtliche Werke* v: *Übersetzungen*, ed. F. Beissner, Stuttgart: W. Kohlhammer.

Holford-Strevens, L. (1999), 'Sophocles at Rome', in J. Griffin (ed.), *Sophocles Revisited: Essays Presented to Sir Hugh Lloyd-Jones*, 219–59, Oxford: Oxford University Press.

Holt, P. (1999), '*Polis* and Tragedy in the *Antigone*', *Mnemosyne* 52: 658–90.

Honegger, A. (1966), *I am a Composer*, trans. W. O. Clough and A. A. Willman, London: Faber and Faber. French original 1951.

Honig, B. (2013), *Antigone, Interrupted*, Cambridge: Cambridge University Press.

Hutchings, K. and T. Pulkkinen, eds (2010), *Hegel's Philosophy and Feminist Thought: Beyond Antigone?* New York: Palgrave-Macmillan.

Hutchinson, G. O., ed. (1985), *Aeschylus: Septem contra Thebas*, Oxford: Oxford University Press.

Huxley, G. (1973), 'The Date of Pherecydes of Athens', *Greek, Roman, and Byzantine Studies* 14: 137–43.

Irigaray, L. (1985), *Speculum of the Other Woman*, trans. G. C. Gill, Ithaca NY: Cornell University Press. First published as *Speculum de l'autre femme*, Paris: Éditions de Minuit, 1974.

Irigaray, L. (1994), *Thinking the Difference: For a Peaceful Revolution*, trans. K. Montin, London: Athlone Press. First published as *Le Temps de la différence: pour une révolution pacifique*, Paris: Librairie Générale Française, 1989.

Irigaray, L. (2010), 'Between Myth and History: The Tragedy of Antigone', in S. E. Wilmer and A. Žukauskaitė (eds), *Interrogating Antigone in Postmodern Philosophy and Criticism*, 197–211, Oxford: Oxford University Press.

Irina, N. (2010), 'Sophocles: The Tragic of Kierkegaard's Modern *Antigone*', in J. Stewart and K. Nun (eds), *Kierkegaard and the Greek World* ii. *Aristotle and Other Greek Authors,* 313–26, Farnham: Ashgate.

Jacoby, F. (1947), 'The First Athenian Prose Writer', *Mnemosyne* 13: 13–64.

Jebb, R. C., ed. (1900), *Sophocles: The Plays and Fragments*. Part iii, *The Antigone*, third edition. Cambridge: Cambridge University Press.

Jenkins, I. (1983), 'Is There Life After Marriage? A Study of the Abduction Motif in Vase Paintings of the Athenian Wedding Ceremony', *Bulletin of the Institute of Classical Studies* 30: 137–45.

Johnson, P. J. (1997), 'Women's Third Face: A Psycho/Social Reconsideration of Sophocles' *Antigone*', *Arethusa* 30: 369–98.

Johnston, S. I. (2006), 'Antigone's Other Choice', in C. B. Patterson (ed.), *Antigone's Answer: Essays on Death and Burial, Family and State in Classical Athens*, 179–86, *Helios* Supplement 33, Lubbock TX: Texas Tech University Press.

Jones, J. (1962), *On Aristotle and Greek Tragedy*, London: Methuen.

Jones, R. (1997), 'Talking amongst Ourselves: Language, Politics, and Sophocles on the Field Day Stage', *International Journal of the Classical Tradition* 4: 232–46.

Jouanna, J. (2007), *Sophocle*, Paris: Fayard.

Just, R. (1989), *Women in Athenian Law and Life*, London: Routledge.

Kamerbeek, J. C. (1978), *The Plays of Sophocles* iii, *Antigone*, Leiden: Brill.

Kelly, A. (2009), *Sophocles: Oedipus at Colonus*, London: Duckworth.

Kennelly, B. (1996), *Sophocles' Antigone*, Newcastle upon Tyne: Bloodaxe.

Kennelly, B. (2005), 'The Good', in J. Scally (ed.), *An Easter People: Essays in Honour of Sr Stanislaus Kennedy,* 19–21, Dublin: Veritas.

Kierkegaard, S. (1987), *Either/Or: Part I*, edited and translated by H. V. Hong and E. H. Hong, Princeton: Princeton University Press. Danish original 1843.

King, H. C. (1983), 'Bound to Bleed: Artemis and Greek Women', in A. Cameron and A. Kuhrt (eds), *Images of Women in Antiquity*, 109–27, London: Croom Helm.

King, H. C. (1998), *Hippocrates' Woman*, London: Routledge.

Kirkland, S. D. (2010), 'Speed and Tragedy in Cocteau and Sophocles', in S. Wilmer and A. Žukauskaitė, *Interrogating Antigone in Postmodern Philosophy and Criticism*, 313–28, Oxford: Oxford University Press.

Kirkwood, G. M. (1958), *A Study of Sophoclean Drama*, Ithaca NY: Cornell University Press.

Kitto, H. D. F. (1956), *Form and Meaning in Drama: A Study of Six Greek Plays and of Hamlet*, London: Methuen.

Kitto, H. D. F. (1958), *Sophocles: Dramatist and Philosopher*, London: Oxford University Press.

Kitzinger, R. (2008), *The Choruses of Sophokles' Antigone and Philoktetes: A Dance of Words*, Leiden: Brill.

Kitzinger, R. (2012), 'Sophoclean Choruses', in A. Markantonatos (ed.), *Brill's Companion to Sophocles*, 385–407, Leiden: Brill.

Knox, B. M. W. (1964), *The Heroic Temper: Studies in Sophoclean Tragedy*, Berkeley and Los Angeles: University of California Press.

Knox, B. M. W. (1979), *Word and Action: Essays on the Ancient Theatre*, Baltimore: Johns Hopkins University Press.

Konstan, D. (1997), *Friendship in the Classical World*, Cambridge: Cambridge University Press.

Konstan, D. (2010), 'Are Fellow Citizens Friends? Aristotle versus Cicero on *Philia, Amicitia*, and Social Solidarity', in R. M. Rosen and I. Sluiter (eds), *Valuing Others in Classical Antiquity*, 233–48, Leiden: Brill.

Kovacs, P. D., ed. (2002), *Euripides: Helen, Phoenician Women, Orestes*, Cambridge MA: Harvard University Press (LCL 11).

Kwahulé, K. (1997), *Bintou*, Carnières-Morlanwelz: éditions Lansman.

Lacan, J. (1992), *The Ethics of Psychoanalysis, 1959–1960: The Seminar of Jacques Lacan*, trans. D. Porter, New York: Norton. French original 1986.

Lamari, A. A. (2010), *Narrative, Intertext, and Space in Euripides' Phoenissae*, Berlin: De Gruyter.

Lattimore, R. (1942), *Themes in Greek and Latin Epitaphs,* Urbana IL: University of Illinois Press.

Lefkowitz, M. and M. B. Fant (1992), *Women's Life in Greece and Rome: A Sourcebook in Translation*, second edition, London: Duckworth.

Lenz, L. (1976), 'Eine moderne Antigone. Zu Hochhuths tragischer Novelle', *Antike und Abendland* 22: 156–74.

Lenzi, M. B. (2010), '*Antígona furiosa* de Griselda Gambaro ou de la mémoire', in R. Duroux and S. Urdician (eds), *Les Antigones contemporaines (de 1945 à nos jours)*, 357–71, Clermont-Ferrand, Presses Universitaires Blaise Pascal.

Leonard, M. (2005), *Athens in Paris: Ancient Greece and the Political in Post-War French Thought*, Oxford: Oxford University Press.

Lewis, R. G. (1988), 'An Alternative Date for Sophocles' *Antigone*', *Greek, Roman, and Byzantine Studies* 29: 35–50.

Liapis, V. (2013), 'Creon the Labdacid: Political Confrontation and the Doomed *Oikos* in Sophocles' *Antigone*', in D. L. Cairns (ed.), *Tragedy and Archaic Greek Thought*, 81–118, Swansea: Classical Press of Wales.

Linforth, I. M. (1961), 'Antigone and Creon', *University of California Publications in Classical Philology* 15: 183–260.

Llewellyn-Jones, L. (2003), *Aphrodite's Tortoise: The Veiled Woman of Ancient Greece*, Swansea: Classical Press of Wales.

Lloyd-Jones, H. (1959), 'The End of the *Seven against Thebes*', *Classical Quarterly* 9: 80–115.

Lloyd-Jones, H. (1964), 'Sophocles, *Antigone* 1096–7 (and *Philoctetes* 324)', *Classical Review* 14: 129–30. Reprinted in *Greek Epic, Lyric, and Tragedy: Academic Papers* (Oxford: Oxford University Press, 1990), 388–9.

Lloyd-Jones, H. (1983), *The Justice of Zeus*, second edition, Berkeley and Los Angeles: University of California Press.

Lloyd-Jones, H. (2002), 'Curses and Divine Anger in Early Greek Epic: The Pisander Scholion', *Classical Quarterly* 52: 1–14.

Lloyd-Jones, H. and N. G. Wilson (1990a), *Sophoclea: Studies on the Text of Sophocles*, Oxford: Oxford University Press.

Lloyd-Jones, H. and N. G. Wilson, eds (1990b), *Sophoclis fabulae*, Oxford: Oxford University Press.

Lloyd-Jones, H. and N. G. Wilson (1997), *Sophocles: Second Thoughts*, Hypomnemata 100, Göttingen: Vandenhoeck and Ruprecht.

Loraux, N. (1986), 'La Main d'Antigone', *Mètis* 1: 165–96.

Loraux, N. (1987), *Tragic Ways of Killing a Woman*, trans. A. Forster, Cambridge MA: Harvard University Press. French original 1985.

Love, C. (2009), 'Koffi Kwahulé's *Bintou* and Sophocles' *Antigone*: The Silent Form of Adaptation', *New Voices in Classical Reception Studies* 4, www2. open.ac.uk/newvoices, accessed 14 July 2009.

Lupton, J. R. (2005), 'Tragedy and Psychoanalysis: Freud and Lacan', in Bushnell, *A Companion to Tragedy,* 88–105, Oxford: Blackwell.

MacDowell, D. M. (1978), *The Law in Classical Athens*, London: Thames and Hudson.

MacDowell, D. M., ed. (2000), *Demosthenes on the False Embassy (Oration 19)*, Oxford: Oxford University Press.

Macintosh, F. (2011), 'Irish *Antigone* and Burying the Dead', in E. B. Mee and H. P. Foley (eds), *Antigone on the Contemporary World Stage*, 90–103, Oxford: Oxford University Press.

Mader, M. B. (2005), 'Antigone's Line', *Bulletin de la societé Américaine de philosophie de la langue Française* 14.2: 18–40.

Malina, J. (1990), *Antigone in a Version by Bertolt Brecht*, trans. Judith Malina, New York: Applause.

Mandela, N. (1994), *Long Walk to Freedom*, London: Little, Brown, and Company.

Manuwald, G. (2011), *Roman Republican Theatre,* Cambridge: Cambridge University Press.

March, J. R. (1987), *The Creative Poet: Studies on the Treatment of Myths in Greek Poetry*, *BICS* Supplement 49, London: Institute of Classical Studies.

Marinis, A. (2015), 'Statius' *Thebaid* and Greek Tragedy: The Legacy of Thebes', in W. J. Dominik, C. F. Newlands, and K. Gervais (eds), *Brill's Companion to Statius*, 343–61, Leiden: Brill.

Mastronarde, D. M., ed. (1994), *Euripides: Phoenissae*, Cambridge: Cambridge University Press.

McCall, M. (1972), 'Divine and Human Action in Sophocles: The Two Burials of the *Antigone*', *Yale Classical Studies* 22: 103–17.

McDonald, M. (2002), 'The Irish and Greek Tragedy', in M. McDonald and J. M. Walton (eds), *Amid our Troubles: Irish Versions of Greek Tragedy,* 37–86, London: Methuen.

McDonald, M. (2005), 'Rebel Women: Brendan Kennelly's Versions of Irish Tragedy', *New Hibernia Review* 9: 123–136.

McDonald, M. and J. M. Walton, eds (2002), *Amid our Troubles: Irish Versions of Greek Tragedy*, London: Methuen.

Mee, E. B. and H. P. Foley, eds (2011), *Antigone on the Contemporary World Stage*, Oxford: Oxford University Press.

Meyer, M. (2010), 'Reclaiming Femininity: Antigone's "Choice" in Art and Art History', in S. Wilmer and A. Žukauskaitė, *Interrogating Antigone in Postmodern Philosophy and Criticism*, 254–79, Oxford: Oxford University Press.

Michelakis, P. (2004), 'Greek Tragedy in Cinema', in E. Hall, F. Macintosh, and A. Wrigley (eds), *Dionysus since 69: Greek Tragedy and the Dawn of the Third Millennium*, 199–217, Oxford: Oxford University Press.

Miller, P. A. (2007), 'Lacan's Antigone: The Sublime Object and the Ethics of Interpretation', *Phoenix* 61: 1–14.

Mills, P. J. (1998), 'Hegel's *Antigone*', in J. Stewart (ed.), *The Phenomenology of Spirit Reader: Critical and Intepretative Essays*, 243–7, Albany NY: SUNY Press.

Miola, R. S. (2014), 'Early Modern Antigones: Receptions, Refractions, Replays', *Classical Receptions Journal* 6: 221–44.

Mogyorodyi, E. (1996), 'Tragic Freedom and Fate in Sophocles' *Antigone*: Notes on the Role of the "Ancient Evils" in "the Tragic"', in M. S. Silk (ed.), *Tragedy and the Tragic: Greek Theatre and Beyond*, 358–76, Oxford: Oxford University Press.

Morwood, J., ed. (2007), *Euripides: Suppliant Women*, Warminster: Aris and Phillips.

Most, G. W. (2002), 'Heidegger's Greeks', *Arion* 10: 59–88.

Most, G. W., ed. (2007), *Hesiod: The Shield, Catalogue of Women, and Other Fragments*, Loeb Classical Library 503, Cambridge MA: Harvard University Press.

Müller, C. W. (1984), *Zur Datierung des sophokleischen Ödipus*, Wiesbaden: Steiner.

Müller, G. (1961), 'Überlegungen zum Chor der *Antigone*', *Hermes* 89 (1961), 398–422.

Müller, G., ed. (1967), *Sophokles: Antigone,* Heidelberg: Winter.

Mueller, M. (2011), 'The Politics of Gesture in Sophocles' *Antigone*', *Classical Quarterly* 61: 412–25.

Murnaghan, S. (1986), '*Antigone* 904–920 and the Institution of Marriage', *American Journal of Philology* 107: 192–207.

Nelli, M. F. (2010), 'From Ancient Greek Drama to Argentina's "Dirty War"; *Antígona Furiosa*: On Bodies and the State', in S. Wilmer and A. Žukauskaitė, *Interrogating Antigone in Postmodern Philosophy and Criticism*, 353–65, Oxford: Oxford University Press.

Nelli, M. F. (2012), '*Usted está aquí*: Antigone against the Standardization of Violence in Contemporary Mexico', *Romance Quarterly* 59: 55–65.

Neuburg, M. (1990), 'How Like a Woman: Antigone's "Inconsistency"', *Classical Quarterly* 40: 54–76.

Nicolai, R. (2010), 'Antigone allo specchio', in A. M. Belardinelli and G. Greco (eds), *Antigone e le Antigoni: Storia forme fortune di un mito*, 182–9, Florence: Le Monnier Università.

Nussbaum, M. C. (1986), *The Fragility of Goodness*, Cambridge: Cambridge University Press.

Oakley, J. H. and R. H. Sinos (1993), *The Wedding in Ancient Athens*, Madison WI: University of Wisconsin Press.

O'Brien, C. C. (1972), *States of Ireland*, London: Hutchinson.

Ormand, K. (1999), *Exchange and the Maiden: Marriage in Sophoclean Tragedy*, Austin TX: University of Texas Press.

Osofisan, F. (2007), *Tegonni: An African Antigone,* Lagos: Concept Publications. First published 1999.

Oudemans, T. C. W. and A. P. M. H. Lardinois (1987), *Tragic Ambiguity: Anthropology, Philosophy, and Sophocles' Antigone*, Leiden: Brill.

Padel, R. (1992), *In and Out of the Mind: Greek Images of the Tragic Self*, Princeton: Princeton University Press.

Paolucci, A. and H. (1962), *Hegel on Tragedy*, Garden City NY: Anchor Books.

Papadopoulou, T. (2008), *Euripides: Phoenician Women,* London: Duckworth.

Parker, R. C. T. (1983), *Miasma: Pollution and Purification in Early Greek Religion*, Oxford: Oxford University Press.

Patterson, C. B. (1991), 'Marriage and the Married Woman in Athenian Law', in S. B. Pomeroy (ed.), *Women's History and Ancient History*, 48–72, Chapel Hill NC: University of North Carolina Press.

Patterson, C. B., ed. (2006a), *Antigone's Answer: Essays on Death and Burial, Family and State in Classical Athens*, *Helios* Supplement 33, Lubbock TX: Texas Tech University Press.

Patterson, C. B. (2006b), 'The Place and Practice of Burial in Sophocles' Athens', in C. B. Patterson (ed.), *Antigone's Answer: Essays on Death and Burial, Family and State in Classical Athens*, 9–48, *Helios* Supplement 33, Lubbock TX: Texas Tech University Press.

Pattoni, M. P. (2010), 'Riusi sofoclei e allegorie politiche nell'*Antígona* di António Sérgio de Sousa', in A. M. Belardinelli and G. Greco (eds), *Antigone e le Antigoni: Storia forme fortune di un mito*, 123–58, Florence: Le Monnier Università.

Pattoni, M. P. (2013), 'Una moderna Antigone al cinema: Sophie Scholl secondo Marc Rothemund', *Dioniso* 3 (2013), 319–38.

Paulin, T. (1980), 'The Making of a Loyalist', *The Times Literary Supplement*, 14 November 1980, 1283–5. Reprinted in *Ireland and the English Crisis*, Newcastle upon Tyne: Bloodaxe, 1984, 23–38.

Paulin, T. (1985), *The Riot Act: A Version of Sophocles' Antigone*, London: Faber and Faber.

Paulin, T. (2002), '*Antigone*', in M. McDonald, J. M. Walton (eds), *Amid our Troubles: Irish Versions of Greek Tragedy*, 165–70, London: Methuen.

Petersmann, H. (1978), 'Mythos und Gestaltung in Sophokles' *Antigone*', *Wiener Studien* n.s. 12: 67–96.

Pickard-Cambridge, A. W. (1988), *The Dramatic Festivals of Athens*, second edition, revised with a supplement and corrections, Oxford: Oxford University Press.

Piperno, F. (2010), 'Su alcune *Antigoni* operistiche del Settecento', in A. M. Belardinelli and G. Greco (eds), *Antigone e le Antigoni: Storia forme fortune di un mito*, 71–108, Florence: Le Monnier Università.

Pöggeler, O. (2004), *Schicksal und Geschichte: Antigone im Spiegel der Deutungen und Gestaltungen seit Hegel und Hölderlin*, Munich: Fink.

Pollmann, K. F. L., ed. (2004), *Statius, Thebaid 12*, Paderborn: Schöningh.

Poulson, N. K. (2012), 'In Defense of the Dead: *Antígona furiosa*, by Griselda Gambaro', *Romance Quarterly* 59: 48–54.

Radt, S. L., ed. (1985), *Tragicorum Graecorum Fragmenta* iii: *Aeschylus*, Göttingen: Vandenhoeck and Ruprecht.

Radt, S. L. (1988), *The Importance of the Context*. Koninklijke Nederlandse Akademie van Wetenschappen, Mededelingen van de Afdeling Letterkunde n.s. 51.9, Amsterdam.

Raji, W. (2005), 'Africanizing *Antigone*: Postcolonial Discourse and Strategies of Indigenizing a Western Classic', *Research in African Literatures* 36. 4: 135–54.

Redfield, J. M. (2001), 'The Proem of the *Iliad*: Homer's Art', in D. L. Cairns (ed.), *Oxford Readings in Homer's Iliad*, 456–77, Oxford: Oxford University Press. First published in *Classical Philology* 74 (1979), 94–110.

Rehm, R. (1993), *Marriage to Death: The Conflation of Wedding and Funeral Ritual in Greek Tragedy*, Princeton: Princeton University Press.

Rehm, R. (2007), '"If you are a woman": Theatrical Womanizing in Sophocles' *Antigone* and Fugard, Kani, and Ntshona's *The Island*', in L. Hardwick and C. Gillespie (eds), *Classics in Post-Colonial Worlds*, 211–27.

Reid, J. D. (1993), *The Oxford Guide to Classical Mythology in the Arts, 1300–1990s*, Oxford: Oxford University Press.

Reinhardt, K. (1960), 'Hölderlin und Sophokles', *Tradition und Geist: Gesammelte Essays zur Dichtung*, 381–97, Göttingen: Vandenhoeck and Ruprecht.

Reinhardt, K. (1979), *Sophocles*, trans. H. and D. Harvey, Oxford: Blackwell. First published 1933, second edition, 1943.

Ribbeck, O. (1875), *Die römische Tragödie*, Leipzig: Teubner.

Richtarik, M. J. (1994), *Acting between the Lines: The Field Day Theatre Company and Irish Cultural Politics, 1980–1984*, Oxford: Oxford University Press.

Riemer, P. (1991), *Sophokles, Antigone – Götterwille und menschliche Freiheit*, Stuttgart: Steiner.

Robert, C. (1915), *Oidipus: Geschichte eines poetischen Stoffes im griechischen Altertum*, Berlin: Weidmann.

Robinson, M. (2011), 'Declaring and Rethinking Solidarity: *Antigone* in Cracow', in E. B. Mee and H. P. Foley (eds), *Antigone on the Contemporary World Stage*, 201–18, Oxford: Oxford University Press.

Roche, A. (1988), 'Ireland's *Antigones*: Tragedy North and South', in M. Kenneally (ed.), *Cultural Contexts and Literary Idioms in Contemporary Irish Literature*, 221–50, Gerrards Cross: Colin Smythe.

Roche, A. (2005), 'Kennelly's Rebel Women', in J. Dillon and S. E. Wilmer (eds), *Rebel Women: Staging Ancient Greek Drama Today*, 149–68, London: Methuen.

Roche, M. W. (2005), 'The Greatness and Limits of Hegel's Theory of Tragedy', in R. Bushnell (ed.), *A Companion to Tragedy*, 51–67, Oxford: Blackwell.

Roche, M. W. (2006), 'Introduction to Hegel's Theory of Tragedy', *PhaenEx* 1. 2: 11–20.

Rodighiero, A. (2012), *Generi lirico-corali nella produzione drammatica di Sofocle*, Tübingen: Narr.

Rösler, W. (1993), 'Die Frage der Echtheit von Sophokles, *Antigone* 904–20 und die politische Funktion der attischen Tragödie', in A. H. Sommerstein, S. Halliwell, J. Henderson, and B. Zimmermann (eds), *Tragedy, Comedy, and the Polis*, 81–99, Bari: Levante.

Rosenkranz, K. (1844), *G. W. F. Hegels Leben*, Berlin: Duncker and Humblot.

Rosivach, V. J. (1983), 'On Creon, *Antigone* and Not Burying the Dead', *Rheinisches Museum* 126: 193–211.

Rouse, W. H. D. (1911), 'The Two Burials in *Antigone*', *Classical Review* 25: 40–2.

Rutherford, I. (1994–5), 'Apollo in Ivy: The Tragic Paean', *Arion* 3. 3. 1: 112–35.

Savage, R. I. (2008), *Hölderlin after the Catastrophe: Heidegger, Adorno, Brecht*, Rochester NY: Camden House.

Schadewaldt, W. (1960a), 'Einleitung zur "Antigone" des Sophokles von Hölderlin in der Vertonung von Carl Orff', *Hellas und Hesperien: Gesammelte Schriften zur Antike und zur neueren Literatur*, 247–77, Zurich: Artemis.

Schadewaldt, W. (1960b), 'Hölderlins Übersetzung des Sophokles', *Hellas und Hesperien: Gesammelte Schriften zur Antike und zur neueren Literatur*, 767–824, Zurich: Artemis.

Schweizer, H. (1997), *Suffering and the Remedy of Art*, Albany NY: SUNY Press.

Scodel, R. (1984), *Sophocles*, Boston: Twayne Publishers.

Scodel, R. (2010), *An Introduction to Greek Tragedy*, Cambridge: Cambridge University Press.

Sconocchia, S. (1972), 'L'*Antigona* di Accio e l'*Antigone* di Sofocle', *Rivista di Filologia e di Istruzione Classica* 100: 273–83.

Scullion, S. (1998), 'Dionysos and *Katharsis* in *Antigone*', *Classical Antiquity* 17: 96–122.

Scullion, S. (2002), 'Tragic Dates', *Classical Quarterly* 52: 81–101.

Seaford, R. (1984), 'The Last Bath of Agamemnon', *Classical Quarterly* 34: 247–54.

Seaford, R. (1987), 'The Tragic Wedding', *Journal of Hellenic Studies* 107: 106–30.

Seaford, R. (1990), 'The Imprisonment of Women in Greek Tragedy', *Journal of Hellenic Studies* 110: 76–90.

Seaford, R. (1993), 'Dionysus as Destroyer of the Household: Homer, Tragedy, and the Polis', in T. H. Carpenter and C. A. Faraone (eds), *Masks of Dionysus*, 115–46, Ithaca NY: Cornell University Press.

Seaford, R. (1994), *Reciprocity and Ritual: Homer and Tragedy in the Developing City-State*, Oxford: Oxford University Press.

Seaford, R. (1998), 'Tragic Money', *Journal of Hellenic Studies* 118: 119–39.

Seaford, R. (2004), *Money and the Early Greek Mind*, Cambridge: Cambridge University Press.

Seaford, R. (2012), *Cosmology and the Polis: The Social Construction of Space and Time in the Tragedies of Aeschylus*, Cambridge: Cambridge University Press.

Seale, D. (1982), *Vision and Stagecraft in Sophocles*, London: Croom Helm.

Segal, C. P. (1971), *The Theme of the Mutilation of the Corpse in the Iliad*, Leiden: Brill.

Segal, C. P. (1981), *Tragedy and Civilization: An Interpretation of Sophocles*, Cambridge MA: Harvard University Press.

Segal, C. P. (1986), 'Sophocles' Praise of Man and the Conflicts of the *Antigone*', in *Interpreting Greek Tragedy*, 137–61, Ithaca NY: Cornell University Press. Revised and expanded from *Arion* 3 (1964), 46–66.

Segal, C. P. (1995), *Sophocles' Tragic World: Divinity, Nature, Society*, Cambridge MA: Harvard University Press.

Sérgio de Sousa, A. (2012), *Antigone*, Italian translation and notes by C. Cuccoro, introductory essay by M. P. Pattoni, Milan: Università Cattolica del Sacro Cuore.

Sewell-Rutter, N. J. (2007), *Guilt by Descent: Moral Inheritance and Decision Making in Greek Tragedy*, Oxford: Oxford University Press.

Shapiro, H. A. (2006), 'The Wrath of Creon: Withholding Burial in Homer and Sophocles', in C. B. Patterson (ed.), *Antigone's Answer: Essays on Death and Burial, Family and State in Classical Athens*, 119–34, *Helios* Supplement 33, Lubbock TX: Texas Tech University Press.

Siewert, P. (1977), 'The Ephebic Oath in Fifth-Century Athens', *Journal of Hellenic Studies* 97: 102–11.

Snell, B., ed. (1986), *Tragicorum Graecorum Fragmenta* i, revised R. Kannicht, Göttingen: Vandenhoeck and Ruprecht.

Söderbäck, F., ed. (2010), *Feminist Readings of Antigone*, Buffalo: SUNY Press.

Sommerstein, A. H., ed. (2009), *Aeschylus,* three volumes, Loeb Classical Library 145, 146, 505; Cambridge MA: Harvard University Press.

Sommerstein, A. H. (2012), 'Fragments and Lost Tragedies', in A. Markantonatos (ed.), *Brill's Companion to Sophocles*, 191–209, Leiden: Brill.

Sommerstein, A. H. (2013), '*Atê* in Aeschylus', in D. L. Cairns (ed.), *Tragedy and Archaic Greek Thought*, 1–15, Swansea: Classical Press of Wales.

Sourvinou-Inwood, C. (1987), 'A Series of Erotic Pursuits: Images and Meanings', *Journal of Hellenic Studies* 107: 131–53.

Sourvinou-Inwood, C. (1989a), 'Assumptions and the Creation of Meaning: Reading Sophocles' *Antigone*', *Journal of Hellenic Studies* 109: 131–48.

Sourvinou-Inwood, C. (1989b), 'The Fourth Stasimon of Sophocles' *Antigone*', *Bulletin of the Institute of Classical Studies* 36: 141–65.

Sourvinou-Inwood, C. (1990), 'Sophocles' Antigone as a "Bad Woman"', in F. Dieteren and E. Kloek (eds), *Writing Women into History*, 11–38, Amsterdam: Historisch Seminarium van de Universiteit van Amsterdam.

Sourvinou-Inwood, C. (1991a), *'Reading' Greek Culture*, Oxford: Oxford University Press.

Sourvinou-Inwood, C. (1991b), 'Sophocles, *Antigone* 904–20: A Reading', *Annali del istituto universitario orientale di Napoli* 9–10, 1987–8: 19–35.

Spratt, G. K. (1987), *The Music of Arthur Honegger*, Cork: Cork University Press.

Stafford, E. J. (2013), 'From the Gymnasium to the Wedding: Eros in Athenian Art and Cult', in E. Sanders, C. Thumiger, C. Carey, and N. J. Lowe (eds), *Erôs in Ancient Greece*, 175–208, Oxford: Oxford University Press.

Staley, G. A. (1985), 'The Literary Ancestry of Sophocles' "Ode to Man"', *Classical World* 78: 561–70.

Steinberg, M. P. (1991), 'The Incidental Politics to Mendelssohn's *Antigone*', in R. L. Todd (ed.), *Mendelssohn and his World*, 137–57, Princeton: Princeton University Press.

Steiner, G. (1984), *Antigones: How the Antigone Legend Has Endured in Western Literature, Art, and Thought*, Oxford: Oxford University Press.

Stewart, J. (1998), 'Hegel's Influence on Kierkegaard's Interpretation of *Antigone*', *Persona y derecho* 39: 195–216.

Stewart, J. (2003), *Kierkegaard's Relations to Hegel Reconsidered*, New York: Cambridge University Press.

Susanetti, D., ed. (2012), *Sofocle: Antigone*, Rome: Carocci editori.

Suter, A. (2008), 'Male Lament in Greek Tragedy', in A. Suter (ed.), *Lament: Studies in the Ancient Mediterranean and Beyond*, 156–80, Oxford: Oxford University Press.

Taplin, O. (1978), *Greek Tragedy in Action*, London: Methuen.

Taplin, O. (2007), *Pots and Plays: Interactions between Greek Tragedy and the Vase-Painting of the Fourth Century BC*, Los Angeles: Getty Publications.

Taplin, O. (2011), 'Antiphanes, Antigone, and the Malleability of Tragic Myth', *Japan Studies in Classical Antiquity* 1: 136–51. Italian version in A. M. Belardinelli and G. Greco (eds), *Antigone e le Antigoni: Storia forme fortune di un mito*, 27–36, Florence: Le Monnier Università.

Taxidou, O. (2004), *Tragedy, Modernity, and Mourning*, Edinburgh: Edinburgh University Press.

Taxidou, O. (2008), 'Machines and Models for Modern Tragedy: The Brecht/ Berlau *Antigone-Model 1948*', in R. Felski (ed.), *Rethinking Tragedy*, 241–62, Baltimore: Johns Hopkins University Press.

Thibodeau, M. (2013), *Hegel and Greek Tragedy*, Lanham MD: Lexington Books.

Todd, S. C. (2000), 'How to Execute People in Fourth-Century Athens', in V. Hunter and J. Edmondson (eds), *Law and Social Status in Classical Athens*, 31–51, Oxford: Oxford University Press.

Torrance, I. M. (2007), *Aeschylus: Seven against Thebes*, London: Bloomsbury.

Torrance, I. M. (2010), 'Antigone and her Brother: What Sort of Special Relationship', in S. Wilmer and A. Žukauskaitė (eds), *Interrogating Antigone in Postmodern Philosophy and Criticism*, 240–53, Oxford: Oxford University Press.

Torrance, R. M. (1965), 'Sophocles: Some Bearings', *Harvard Studies in Classical Philology* 69: 269–327.

Treu, M. (2011), 'Never Too Late: *Antigone* in a German Second World War Cemetery on [*sic*] the Italian Appenines', in E. B. Mee and H. P. Foley (eds), *Antigone on the Contemporary World Stage*, 307–23, Oxford: Oxford University Press.

Tyrrell, W. B. and L. J. Bennett (1998), *Recapturing Sophocles' Antigone*, Lanham MD: Rowman and Littlefield.

Utzinger, C. (2003), *Periphrades Aner: Untersuchungen zum ersten Stasimon der Sophokleischen Antigone und zu den antiken Kulturentstehungstheorien*, Göttingen: Vandenhoeck and Ruprecht.

Van Weyenberg, A. (2010), 'Revolutionary Muse: Femi Osofisan's *Tegonni: An African Antigone*', in S. E. Wilmer and A. Žukauskaitė (eds), *Interrogating Antigone in Postmodern Philosophy and Criticism*, 366–78, Oxford: Oxford University Press.

Van Weyenberg, A. (2013), *The Politics of Adaptation: Contemporary African Drama and Greek Tragedy*, Amsterdam: Rodopi.

Vernant, J.-P. (1991), 'A "Beautiful Death" and the Disfigured Corpse in Homeric Epic', in *Mortals and Immortals: Collected Essays*, 50–74, Princeton: Princeton University Press.

Vessey, D. (1973), *Statius and the Thebaid*, Cambridge: Cambridge University Press.

Waldock, A. J. A. (1951), *Sophocles the Dramatist*, Cambridge: Cambridge University Press.

Weber, S. (2015), 'Tragedy and *Trauerspiel*: Too Alike?', in J. Billings and M. Leonard (eds), *Tragedy and the Idea of Modernity*, 88–114, Oxford: Oxford University Press.

Webster, T. B. L. (1936), *An Introduction to Sophocles*, Oxford: Oxford University Press.

Webster, T. B. L. (1967), *The Tragedies of Euripides*, London: Methuen.

West, M. L., ed. (1998), *Aeschyli tragoediae cum incerti poetae Prometheo*, Leipzig: Teubner.

West, M. L. (1999), 'Ancestral Curses', in J. Griffin (ed.), *Sophocles Revisited: Essays Presented to Sir Hugh Lloyd-Jones*, 31–45, Oxford: Oxford University Press.

West, M. L., ed. (2003), *Greek Epic Fragments*, Loeb Classical Library 497, Cambridge MA: Harvard University Press.

West, S. (1999), 'Sophocles' *Antigone* and Herodotus Book Three', in J. Griffin (ed.), *Sophocles Revisited: Essays Presented to Sir Hugh Lloyd-Jones*, 109–36, Oxford: Oxford University Press.

Wetmore, K. (2002), *The Athenian Sun in an African Sky*, Jefferson NC: McFarland & Company.

Whitehorne, J. E. G. (1983), 'The Background to Polyneices' Disinterment and Reburial', *Greece & Rome* 30: 129–42.

Whitman, C. H. (1951), *Sophocles: A Study of Heroic Humanism,* Cambridge MA: Harvard University Press.

Wilmer, S. E. (2007), 'Finding a Post-Colonial Voice for Antigone: Seamus Heaney's *Burial at Thebes*', in L. Hardwick and C. Gillespie (eds), *Classics in Post-Colonial Worlds*, 228–44, Oxford: Oxford University Press.

Wilmer, S. E. (2010), 'Performing *Antigone* in the Twenty-First Century', in S. E. Wilmer and A. Žukauskaitė (eds), *Interrogating Antigone in Postmodern Philosophy and Criticism*, 379–92, Oxford: Oxford University Press.

Wilmer, S. E. and A. Žukauskaitė, eds (2010), *Interrogating Antigone in Postmodern Philosophy and Criticism*, Oxford: Oxford University Press.

Winnington-Ingram, R. P. (1980), *Sophocles: An Interpretation*, Cambridge: Cambridge University Press.

Witt, M. A. F. (2001), *The Search for Modern Tragedy: Aesthetic Fascism in Italy and France*, Ithaca NY: Cornell University Press.

Wolin, R. (1991), *The Heidegger Controversy: A Critical Reader*, Cambridge MA: MIT Press.

Woodbury, L. (1970), 'Sophocles among the Generals', *Phoenix* 24, 209–24.

Xanthakis-Karamanos, G. (1980), *Studies in Fourth-Century Tragedy*, Athens: Academy of Athens.

Younger, K. (2006), 'Irish Antigones: Burying the Colonial Symptom', *COLLOQUY text theory critique* 11: 148–62.

Younger, K. (2007), 'Antigone and Terrorism: Seamus Heaney Sends a Letter to George W. Bush', in S. E. Constantinidis (ed.), *Text & Presentation 2007*, 205–12, Jefferson NC: McFarland & Company.

Zeitlin, F. I. (1990), 'Thebes: Theater of Self and Society in Athenian Drama', in J. J. Winkler and F. I. Zeitlin (eds), *Nothing to do with Dionysus? Athenian Drama in its Social Context*, 130–67, Princeton: Princeton University

Press. First published (1986), in J. P. Euben (ed.), *Greek Tragedy and Political Theory,* 101–41, Berkeley and Los Angeles: University of California Press.

Zimmermann, C. (1993), *Der Antigone-Mythos in der antiken Literatur und Kunst,* Tübingen: Narr.

Zirzotti, E. (2014), 'Translating Tragedy: Seamus Heaney's Sophoclean Plays', *Studi irlandesi* 4: 129–43.

Žižek, S. (2001), *Enjoy Your Symptom! Jacques Lacan in Hollywood and Out,* second edition, New York: Routledge. First published 1992.

Žukauskaitė, A. (2010), 'Biopolitics: Antigone's Claim', in S. Wilmer and A. Žukauskaitė (eds), *Interrogating Antigone in Postmodern Philosophy and Criticism,* 67–81, Oxford: Oxford University Press.

Glossary

agôn contest

amor love

anêr (**pl.** *andres*) man (as opposed to woman)

anoia senselessness

anthrôpos human being

antistrophe second stanza of a choral triad

apatê deception

atê ruin, delusion

autonomos self-ruled

autos self

blabê harm

deinos awesome, terrible, formidable

dysboulia bad judgement

dyssebeia lack of respect, impiety

echthros enemy, hostile

eikein to yield

ekkyklêma wheeled theatrical device for revealing interior tableaux

elpis hope, expectation

epeisodion in Aristotle's terminology, a sequence of dialogue preceded and
    followed by a choral song

epode third and final stanza of a choral triad

Erinys (pl. Erinyes) Fury, the Furies

erôs sexual desire, sexual love

euboulia good judgement

eudaimonia happiness, flourishing

eusebeia reverence, piety

exodos final scene of a tragedy

gynê (**pl.** *gynaikes*) woman

haima blood

hamartia error

hybris arrogant over-confidence amounting to contempt for others

hyperbasia transgression

kerdos profit

kommos lament sung by chorus and actor

koros satiety

kyrios (legal) guardian

Litai (personified) Prayers, as in Phoenix's allegory in *Iliad* 9

logos speech, reason

miasma stain, pollution

nomos law, custom

oikos household

olbos prosperity

orgê anger

parodos entrance song of the Chorus

philein to love, to like

philia friendship, relationship among *philoi*

philos friend, dear one, relative

phrenes wits

phronêma thought, purpose, (negative) pride

pietas sense of obligation

polis city-state

sebein to respect, to revere

sôtêria safety

stasimon a term for all choral songs in a tragedy except the parodos or
    entrance song

strophe first stanza of a choral triad

technê skill, art

theomachia fighting the god(s)

theos god

thymos anger, spirit

tychê chance, fortune

Index